Finding and Losing Faith
Studies in Conversion

Studies in Religion and Culture Series

Fundamentalisms
  edited by Christopher Partridge

Mysticisms East and West: Studies in Mystical Experience
  edited by Christopher Partridge and Theodore Gabriel

Cinema and Sentiment
  Clive Marsh

Mission Implausible: Restoring Credibility to the Church
  Duncan MacLaren

Finding and Losing Faith
Studies in Conversion

Edited by
Christopher Partridge and Helen Reid

PATERNOSTER

Copyright © 2006 The Editors and Contributors

First published in 2006 by Paternoster Press

11 10 09 08 07 06 7 6 5 4 3 2 1

Paternoster Press is an imprint of Authentic Media,
9 Holdom Avenue, Bletchley, Milton Keynes MK1 1QR, UK
and
P.O. Box 1047, Waynesboro, GA 30830-2047, USA

www.authenticmedia.co.uk

The right of The Editors and Contributors to be identified as the Author of
this Work has been asserted by them in accordance with the Copyright,
Designs and Patents Act 1988.

British Library Cataloguing in Publication Data
A catalogue record for this book is available from the British Library

ISBN 1-84227-410-4

Typeset by WestKey Ltd, Falmouth, Cornwall
Print Management by Adare Carwin
Printed and Bound in Great Britain by J. H. Haynes & Co. Ltd., Sparkford

Contents

Studies in Religion and Culture
Series Preface

Perhaps more than ever before, there is a need for Christians to understand the shifting sands of religion and culture. Unfortunately, it is with some justification that the church has been criticized, by both insiders and outsiders, for failing to understand the deep social, religious and cultural changes taking place. This major series invites scholars to provide sensitive, emphatic, reliable and accessible studies that will advance thinking about important subjects such as fundamentalism, mysticism, globalisation, postmodernism, secularisation, the religious significance of contemporary film, art, music, literature, information technologies, youth culture, religious pluralism, the changes taking place in contemporary world religions, and the emergence of new, influential and alternative forms of spirituality. Whilst the majority of the contributors will be Christian thinkers writing with the needs of Christian community in mind, the series will be of interest to all those concerned with contemporary religion and culture.

Christopher Partridge

List of Contributors

Stephen J. Chester is Lecturer in New Testament Studies and MTh in Biblical Interpretation Programme Leader at International Christian College, Glasgow. He gained his PhD from the University of Glasgow and is a minister of the Church of Scotland.

Peter Cotterell is Associate Senior Lecturer at the Centre for Islamic Studies, London School of Theology (formerly London Bible College), England.

Theodore Gabriel is Honorary Research Fellow, University of Gloucestershire, England.

Elizabeth Harris is Secretary for Interfaith Relations, The Methodist Church, UK.

Graham Harvey is Lecturer in Religious Studies, The Open University, UK.

Michael Ipgrave is Archdeacon of Southwark, formerly Inter-Faith Advisor to the Archbishops' Council and Secretary to the Churches' Commission on Inter Faith Relations.

William Kay is Senior Lecturer in Theology and Education, King's College London, University of London, England, and Director of the Centre for Pentecostal and Charismatic Studies, University of Wales, Bangor.

Philip Lewis is Inter-Faith Adviser to the Anglican Bishop of Bradford and Lecturer in the Department of Peace Studies, University of Bradford, England.

Gordon Lynch is Lecturer in Practical Theology at the University of Birmingham, England.

Jonathon Romain MBE is a writer and broadcaster and serves as minister of the Maidenhead Synagogue in Berkshire.

Brian Stanley is Director of the Henry Martyn Centre for the Study of Mission and World Christianity and a Fellow of St Edmund's College, University of Cambridge, England.

Robin Thomson is Director of Satya Bhavan, UK.

Derek Tidball is Principal of the London School of Theology, England.

Editors
Christopher Partridge is Professor of Contemporary Religion at the University of Chester, England.

Helen Reid is Director of Faith to Faith, UK.

Introduction

Christopher Partridge and Helen Reid

Conversion, committing oneself to a faith or ideology, has played a significant role in the history of religions. For example, the conversions of kings and communities through contact with Roman and Celtic Christians – from a relatively early period in Christian history – had a fundamental impact on the shaping of British history and society. More recently, the influence of nineteenth-century revivalist movements and the work of missionaries throughout the then British Empire have, through numerous conversions, changed the course of history. However, perhaps surprisingly, the concept of 'conversion' per se is rarely discussed. Hence, a meeting of scholars interested in the area was organised and met in Cambridge, England, in July 2002. Several of the chapters in this volume were read as papers at that gathering. Since then, several more were commissioned to further explore the area.

Gradually, over the last few decades, Christian understandings of mission and conversion have been refined and defined by the Anglican Church's 'Decade of Evangelism', post-colonial theologies have emerged throughout the world, and there has been increased dialogue between faith communities, which often live side by side in the modern world's religiously plural societies. Also, whereas, certainly in the West, the stream of conversions tended to flow primarily in the direction of Christian faith and culture, since the 1960s it has slowed to almost a trickle, and the flow of those converting to alternative forms of spirituality and other world faiths has increased significantly. Indeed, as Gordon

Lynch's article indicates, there has been a significant flow of people away from traditional, conservative Christian beliefs towards other, more liberal forms of faith and, indeed, to broadly secular worldviews. Hence, bearing in mind that the concept of 'conversion' in the West has been shaped largely by Christian culture, and certainly by monotheistic cultures, these developments are forcing scholars to consider broader understandings of what conversion might be.

In order to maintain some cohesion, this volume has intentionally focused on conversion to and from Christianity or within culturally Christian contexts. Moreover, this is done principally through the filter of the British context, including the legacy of British colonialism. Having said that, it is very clearly not a book solely about Christianity and the British. It is primarily a religio-cultural exploration of conversion per se, which, overall, raises key issues relating to conversion and life in religiously plural societies.

One such key issue concerns the very nature of 'conversion' itself. In the context of multi-faith communities, religious conversion is usually understood to be the changing of affiliation from one faith to another. Taken as a whole, however, this collection of studies re-examines the assumption that conversion *only* takes place between different faith communities and considers whether a conversion experience might also happen between different traditions within a single faith or, indeed, whether individuals can be described as converting out of faith – in effect, 'de-converting'.

This whole question of what constitutes 'conversion' is very helpfully analysed in Stephen Chester's chapter, which discusses, amongst other issues, whether or not Paul was a convert. His rebuttal of Krister Stendahl's argument that Paul was 'called' but not 'converted' is illuminating and introduces the reader to some of the core issues in conversion studies. How much *change*, for example, is necessary for the term 'conversion' to become applicable? Again, should scholars seek a definition that is universally applicable? Or should one focus on understandings of conversion that are culturally and historically specific? This, of course, is an issue raised implicitly or explicitly in several chapters in this volume. In the final analysis, studies of conversion (including some contributions to this volume) indicate, as Chester points out, not only that there are 'common elements in conversion across space and time', but also that 'such elements may be combined in very different ways within conversion according to historical and cultural context'. Again, he usefully draws attention to the 'complex web of relationships between conversion experiences, conversion accounts and the interpretations of conversion authorised by particular communities as part of their social identity'. Overall, with reference to important studies such as A.D. Knock's classic 1933 work *Conversion* and more recent treatments, such as those by Lewis Rambo and Karl Morrison,[1] Chester argues that conversion cannot be understood as a single universal phenomenon, but must rather be understood as 'a cluster of related phenomena'.

From a different perspective, similar issues are addressed in Gordon Lynch's chapter. For example, he critiques current understandings of conversion that reduce the experience to a psychological process, overlooking its social and cultural construction. Having thus identified the key characteristics of conversion from one faith to another, he argues that a similar process can happen within a faith community and describes this process as religious transition. He applies this thesis to people who have moved from one Christian tradition, namely, evangelicalism, into other forms of Christianity, and describes the profound implications of this transition in terms of their understanding of the world, the church, the self, and participation in community life. This analysis is then used to practical effect when he identifies ways in which faith communities can respond supportively to people undergoing religious transition and invites religious communities to develop more sophisticated understandings of the construction and deconstruction of belief and identity.

The focus on evangelicalism is apposite, in that the Christian experience of 'conversion' is especially significant for those within this particular Christian tradition. Indeed, along with 'activism (the expression of the Christian message in physical effort), 'biblicism' (a particular regard for the authority of the Bible), and

---

[1] A.D. Nock, *Conversion: The Old and the New in Religion from Alexander the Great to Augustine of Hippo* (Oxford: Oxford University Press, 1933); L. Rambo, *Understanding Religious Conversion* (New Haven: Yale University Press, 1993); K.F. Morrison, *Understanding Conversion* (Charlotesville: University of Virginia Press, 1992).

'crucicentrism' (a stress on the absoluteness of the salvific significance of Christ's death on the cross), the leading historian of evangelicalism, David Bebbington, lists 'conversionism' as a central pillar, or 'special mark', of evangelical belief.[2] Arguably typifying post-Enlightenment individualism, evangelicalism has often focused on the decision of the individual self, the choice that an autonomous, rational individual makes about his or her future. Without treading the well-worn theological path debating the tension between human responsibility and divine predestination, the emphasis in the modern period has tended towards the individual's responsibility for their own conversion and, thus, salvation. The evangelist makes the offer to a rational mind and that mind must make a choice.

That this is so, is, to some extent, confirmed by Derek Tidball's thought-provoking research into evangelical experiences of conversion. Presenting an analysis of data on 'evangelical conversion' gathered from students applying to the London School of Theology, an evangelical theological college, Tidball identifies distinctive trends in descriptions of coming to faith: as personal, rational choice; as encounter with God; as relationship with God; and, to a lesser extent, as theological rhetoric. A particularly interesting feature of Tidball's analysis is his critical use of Rational Choice theory, the general orientation of which, he argues, has much to commend it. Indeed, with reference to his data, he argues that it provides a true insight into the way people make religious choices and the significance of the religious economy. The 'dominant paradigm of conversion', he says, 'is not of encountering God or of his initiative in people's lives, or of conviction of sin, as once would have been considered the "evangelical" view of conversion, but one of making a life-choice. It is the *human* element that is uppermost.' That said, in his analysis of the six conversion 'motifs' provided by John Lofland and Norman Skonovd (i.e. intellectual, mystical, experimental, affectional, revivalist, coercive), he concludes that the dominant motif is 'affectional' – so much so that it could be considered the 'evangelical motif'. In other words, conversion takes place over time, and is the result of attachments a

---

[2] See D.W. Bebbington, *Evangelicalism in Modern Britain* (London: Unwin Hyman, 1989), p. 3.

convert has. Both social pressure and affective arousal are moderate, the key characteristic being that belonging precedes believing – affective experience is supported by long-term socialisation processes.

Approaching the analysis of evangelical conversion from a different and particularly fruitful perspective, William Kay discusses understandings of conversion within Pentecostalism. The chapter makes several important contributions to the volume. First, it provides interesting historical analysis of Pentecostalism which facilitates an understanding of contemporary perspectives on conversion both within the tradition and also, more generally, within charismatic theologies. Secondly, it discusses Pentecostal theorising concerning the 'stages of conversion' with reference to biblical material. Finally, it provides thoughtful analysis of a large-scale survey of Pentecostal ministers in Britain, which shows that while ministers without a churchgoing backgrounds often had a dramatic conversion to the faith, those with churchgoing backgrounds had a more gradual conversion experience. More significantly, the former are far more likely to be enthusiastic preachers who expect similar conversion experiences in their ministry. Consequently, as Kay comments, 'what this implies is that ministers who have undergone a sudden conversion experience are an important point of growth within Pentecostalism. It is they who, in general terms, are most likely to press a conversionist gospel upon the next generation.' Indeed, bearing in mind that he also argues that, for the vast majority of churchgoers, experience rather than doctrine is paramount and that, in turn, great importance is attached to conversion experiences being conveyed through personal testimony or public narrative, it is very likely that the importance of dramatic conversion accounts will continue within the tradition.

Reflection on evangelical conversion, however, is, in common with other religious communities, often shaped by a dualistic interpretative framework, in which the convert is encouraged to think in terms of passing from one state to another: *from* death *to* life; *from* darkness *to* light; *from* life governed by the flesh *to* life governed by the spirit; *from* religion *to* personal faith; *from* the morally broad, permissive road *to* the ethically narrow, disciplined path. Although dualism is clearly not a modern way of thinking about the world, being particularly evident in, for example, Jewish apocalyptic literature, it has led to an insistence on the convert's complete separation with their previous life, including prior faith commitments. This raises basic questions for those whose conversion leads them to what is, in effect, a dual identity – which may, of course, be understood as a fuller, more mature identity. Elizabeth Harris and, to a lesser extent, Graham Harvey and Jonathon Romain examine the possibilities of such identities. What does it mean to be a Christian Buddhist, or a Jewish Buddhist, or a Jewish Pagan? This, again, leads to questions about the definition of conversion. For example, the following definition by the sociologist Rodney Stark, which assumes a dualistic mindset, is difficult to apply to such converts: 'to *convert* is *to newly form an exclusive commitment to a God.*'[3] But, is exclusivity always the result of conversion? Apparently not. To some extent, Stark recognises this, noting that in polytheistic settings, the inclusion of a new deity into one's pantheon 'does not require that one abandon one's old Gods any more than enjoying a new soda requires one to cease drinking others'.[4] However, this, he argues, cannot be described as 'conversion'. The problem is that, on the one hand, those with what Harris describes as 'dual belonging' are not involved in a process of the easy absorption of other deities, as described (indeed, caricatured) by Stark, and, on the other hand, neither can they be described as 'exclusivists'.

Through analysing individual narratives of Buddhist and Christian faith journeys, Elizabeth Harris explores a variety of triggers to conversion. Given this variety, she then identifies two main trends: conversion as a process of finding faith; and conversion as a process of first losing (a) faith and then finding (a new) faith. More particularly, she provides, as indicated above, an illuminating discussion of people who have developed a 'dual belonging' as 'Buddhist Christians' and those who draw deeply on the 'other' faith while remaining firmly within their own faith. The point is that, through their experiences, these people are questioning the assumption that Buddhism and Christianity necessarily

---

[3] R. Stark, *One True God: Historical Consequences of Monotheism* (Princeton, NJ: Princeton University Press, 2001), p. 50.
[4] Stark, *One True God*, p. 50.

demand individuals make a direct choice in their faith journey between different faiths and communities. Hence, the experiences outlined and analysed in this chapter highlight a range of dialogue and conversion possibilities between Christianity and Buddhism.

Working from a different angle, the need for revising understandings of conversion is evident in Harvey's account of his own faith journey from Christianity to Paganism. Indeed, both this and the chapter by Lynch are particularly valuable in this respect, in that they help us to understand the inversion of the process of conversion to Christian faith. That said, to describe Harvey's chapter as an analysis of the inversion of Christian conversion is slightly misleading, in that the chapter provides an account of a process that is different in many respects from that commonly described in Christian conversion narratives. In other words, he describes it, not in a Christian way, but in an authentically Pagan way, which focuses on stories about the essence of being Pagan. He also asks us to think differently about the whole process of travelling from one faith to another and, in an illuminating way, helps the reader to understand the challenge many 'converts' experience when seeking to maintain continuity in their life and relationships. Conversion includes the demands of seeking reconciliation between the past, the present, and the future in the journey of faith.

Having said that, there are also strong continuities between understandings of conversion. For example, while Romain notes the distinctiveness of conversion to Judaism, especially compared to Christianity, he also highlights some continuities between Jewish and Christian approaches to conversion. Similarly, drawing on historical and present-day understandings of conversion among Hindus in India and the diaspora, Robin Thomson – who has been closely involved in Christian–Hindu dialogue in Britain – while describing different, and sometimes oppositional, understandings of conversion, also identifies common themes. These common themes, he argues, suggest the potential for a shared approach to issues surrounding conversion and their impact on community relations. The chapter closes with reflection on how this could positively affect Christian involvement in mission and Christian–Hindu relations in India and Britain.

Thomson's discussion, like Harvey's, also indicates discontinuities and some of the problems that converts can experience and cause. Indeed, as the volume as a whole argues, these problems can be far-reaching. In particular, while conversion is largely experienced as a joyous, spiritual event by an individual, in practice it has, for many converts, social implications and, by its very nature, is disruptive of established communities. Hence, it is unsurprising that all the chapters, in one way or another, address both the spiritual and socio-political aspects of conversion. They examine, for example, both how communities respond to the 'concept' of a convert (i.e. the theological implications) and the reality of a convert (i.e. their familial and societal status as persons). Certainly, in practical terms, when a person converts from one faith tradition to another there are issues, first, of integration into the new community and, secondly, of the accepting of an individual's right to leave a community.

As well as issues relating to families and the religious communities to which they belong, there are also broader social and ethnic issues. Romain, for example, not only acknowledges developments in the Jewish interpretation of scripture and tradition, but explores the impact of social and political factors throughout Jewish history and particularly within the current British context. He describes and analyses both the trigger for conversion and the process of becoming a Jew, as experienced by the individual, how this is interpreted by the community, and, particularly, how conversion challenges the links between faith, community and ethnic identity.

More specifically political issues surrounding conversion are explored by Peter Cotterell, who begins his chapter on conversion from Islam to Christianity by arguing that what is addressed by Christians as 'conversion' is addressed within Islam as 'apostasy'. Moreover, he argues, given that Islam does not distinguish between 'religion' and 'state', treatment of the apostate in Islam is a matter of importance for the faith community and the Islamic nation-state. To do this, he reviews teaching and interpretation from the Qur'an, Tradition and Law Schools on the matter of Islamic responses to apostasy. He also gives examples of how this is applied, in particular, in Islamic nation-states today, and how it might challenge the United Nations' assumptions of universal assent to human rights as currently defined with particular reference to freedom of religion.

At the time of finalising this book for publication, a public debate on the matter of conversion from Islam was taking place in Britain. At the invitation of the editors, Philip Lewis kindly agreed to write a short chapter outlining the views of key speakers in this debate. Hence, following on from Cotterrell's discussion, this is an important and helpful overview of the issues facing those who have sought to relate their Islamic tradition to their life as authentic British citizens.

A common type of criticism that some communities have levelled against those converting to Christianity has focused on the motivation of the convert. In particular, it is argued that poor communities have been targeted by missionaries because the poor are more likely to be impressed by the Western wealth within which they perceive the Christian message to be packaged. This is one of the central issues explored in Theodore Gabriel's discussion of Christian conversion in India. Indeed, he notes that much legislation in India – and other developing countries – is designed to combat conversion inspired by material gain and, more generally, Westernisation.

This, of course, touches upon another issue raised elsewhere in this volume. To what extent is conversion more cultural than spiritual? To what extent is Christianisation a part of the process of Westernisation and, more broadly, globalisation? Whether this is always the case or not – and it is difficult to argue that it has not been the case – it is certainly how the Christian faith is perceived. As Gabriel argues, for many Indians, the terms 'Christian' and 'Western' are almost synonymous.

Working from an explicitly missiological perspective, but examining related issues, Brian Stanley provides a rigorous critique of the assumption that conversion is tantamount to a colonisation of the mind. He argues that the process of conversion to Christianity was less tightly controlled by the missionary than its critics claimed, or, indeed, than some Christian evangelists desired. From the earliest days of Christian expansion, 'evangelisation conducted by indigenous agents in a vernacular medium defies control by those who initiate the mission process in any particular region'. In other words, a principal point he makes is that the Christian message and biblical narratives have been consistently contextualised by converts. Hence, the missionary encounter has tended to be creatively open-ended and conversion unpredictable. The process of conversion is thus one of deconstruction, in which the missionary's faith is translated into a new context, history and way of thinking. It should be borne in mind, of course, that this is, as is now commonly acknowledged, always the case. However, Stanley argues, while this can be understood as an enriching of the Christian faith – or, indeed, of any faith that is replanted in new soil – there are also dangers, in that the principal theological influence might become that of the reception culture, which *may* then distort the new faith by moulding it in its own image. Hence, he is keen to distinguish between *conversion to Christ* and merely *conversion to Christianity*. This brings us back to the issue concerning the motivation to convert discussed by Gabriel and others. As Stanley comments, the problem is how Christians might make theological sense of the unavoidable reality that 'conversion to Christ' is, to some extent (arguably a large extent), contingent upon social, cultural and economic contexts.

More broadly, but with concerns that overlap those expressed in all the chapters, Michael Ipgrave looks at multi-faith Britain and at the issues conversion raises for the interaction of its faith communities. He looks at the impact of conversion on community, family, interfaith dialogue and identity. As well as insightfully describing the implications of conversion, he seeks to develop an understanding that will be helpful to people of all faiths, an understanding that will encourage support for individuals who convert, and an understanding of 'conversion' in which affirmation and respect are central. Indeed, if this volume achieves nothing else, the editors hope that it will contribute to the understandings that this opening chapter by Ipgrave encourages.

Part One

Understanding Conversion in Multi-faith and Post-Christian Contexts

1

Conversion, Dialogue and Identity

Reflections on the British Context

Michael Ipgrave

Introduction

How does conversion from one religion to another affect interfaith relationships between individuals, families and communities? More particularly, what impact do conversions have on the
practice of interfaith dialogue? This paper offers some reflections
on these questions from the personal perspective of a Christian
committed to the task of building relationships of trust and understanding with people of different faiths.[1] It draws on my experiences in the British context, where interfaith issues are of high if
comparatively recent profile, and where inter-religious conversions are also attracting growing attention.[2]

The question of conversion has generally been marginalised in
the theory and practice of interfaith work in Britain. In what
follows, I shall argue that this marginalisation of conversion can
be seen as a consequence of the problematic which it poses on

---

[1] This paper is developed from ideas in an address given to the annual
European meeting of 'Societas Oecumenica' at Sarum College, Salisbury
in 2002 – published in Dagmar Heller (ed.), *Bekehrung und Identität*
(Frankfurt: Otto Lembeck, 2003).

[2] According to Jonathan Romain, 'a thousand people in Britain convert
to a different faith each day' – *Your God Shall Be My God: Religious
Conversion in Britain Today* (London: SCM, 2000), p. 2. Romain's text
does not provide a basis for this figure, which seems surprisingly high.

various levels for interfaith relations. I shall then look at some of
the ways in which those committed to interfaith work have
responded to these challenges, and conclude by identifying some
areas where new thinking is needed to address the issue of conversion in relation to the sense of religious identity in interfaith
settings.

The Problematic of Conversion in Interfaith Contexts

The extent of the problematic for interfaith relations can be
mapped out over four areas: the socio-political implications of
conversions from one religion to another; the impact they have on
families; their place within the theory and practice of interfaith
dialogue; and the questions they raise for religious identity.

Socio-political implications

There are several interfaith encounters in Britain where conversion is a particularly contentious issue because of its wider perceived connotations, which could be described as 'political' in the
broad sense of the term as relating to the self-understanding of a
community or society and the claims it has over individuals. Some
of these arise specifically in the British context; others show the
impact on Britain of situations overseas. I shall give four examples.

Christian-Jewish relations in Britain today remain deeply
affected by the forceful attempts that have repeatedly been made
throughout history to turn Jewish people into Christians. Some of
these have been the result of missionary attempts to bring a
message of salvation to the Jews. Others have been the alternative
to expulsion presented by coercive governments wishing to bring
religious uniformity to their people. In either case, though, they
have been experienced by the Jewish community as deliberate
attempts to destroy Jewish peoplehood.[3] As a result, contemporary Jewish-Christian encounters are always alert to what are

---

[3] Contemporary Messianic believers strongly deny that there is any
incompatibility between being disciples of Jesus and being authentically
Jewish, but for the mainstream Jewish community their conversions too
are seen, against the background of this history of aggression, as a continuing attempt to destroy Israel.

variously seen as the opportunities or the dangers of conversion. The Council of Christians and Jews has explicitly disallowed 'aggressive proselytism' among its membership;[4] Archbishop George Carey had already endorsed this position when he declined an invitation to become patron of the Church's Ministry among Jewish People.[5] Both of these events received a high level of media coverage, demonstrating the continuing sensitivity of the issue of conversions in the context of Jewish-Christian relations.

Secondly, relations between Muslims and other communities in Britain can be affected by the treatment, or perceived treatment, of those who convert from Islam to another religion. In most traditional Islamic jurisprudence, this is equated with the crime of apostasy, *ridda*. A saying attributed to the Prophet states, 'Kill the one who changes his religion', and on this basis some have argued that apostasy – and therefore conversion – is a capital offence in Islam, a ruling which is encoded in the legal systems of some Muslim countries. Other Muslim scholars, by contrast, insist that the reference of the saying is not to apostasy (*ridda*) as such, but to high treason (*hirāba*), i.e. it applies only to situations where 'apostasy is accompanied by hostility and rebellion against the community and its legitimate leadership'. Such situations, they argue, rarely apply in the case of converts today, and therefore an authentically Islamic response should treat apostasy/conversion as a matter between the individual and God.[6] In the British context, it is, of course, not possible in any case to enact any Islamic strictures against converts, though they may experience rejection or ostracism from their families and communities. However, the question of religious freedom for ex-Muslims in other countries is a concern

---

[4] CCJ's 1996 'Code of Practice for Members' states: 'Aggressive proselytism is always wrong and if this or any unsuitable behaviour is reported to CCJ, appropriate action will be taken.'

[5] CMJ, formerly the Church's Mission to the Jews. Dr. Carey's letter in 1992 explained that his desire to build up the trust of the Jewish community would not be helped by close association with an organisation 'entirely directed towards another faith community' – Michael Ipgrave (ed.), *Sharing One Hope? The Church of England and Christian-Jewish Relations* (London: Church House Publishing, 2001), p. 35.

[6] Mohammad Hashim Kamali, *Freedom of Expression in Islam* (Cambridge: Islamic Texts Society, 1997), pp. 93–98.

raised with increasing frequency and force in interfaith encounter, particularly by British Christians.[7]

A third example of the political resonances of conversions can be found in current debates between Hindus and Christians in Britain about the missionary and social work of the churches in India. While Christians tend to see the issues in terms of minority freedom and repression in a society where traditional religion is used to support an unequal and unjust social order, the proponents of *Hindutva* resurgence have represented Christianity as engaged in an assault on the Hindu culture which they see as constituting the essence of Indian nationhood. The very idea of 'conversion' naturally becomes a focus of contest in such arguments: is it to be seen as a legitimate exercise of self-determination or as an instance of the coercion or manipulation of some people by others? There are few issues which create more distrust between Christians and Hindus than this, and consequently few more urgently requiring to be addressed in Christian-Hindu dialogue.[8]

Fourthly, the majority community in Britain can be affected in its attitudes to other faiths, particularly towards Islam, by perceptions of the magnitude and significance of the phenomenon of conversion. The publicity afforded to some British people who have converted to Islam from a Christian or a secular background has fed among many anxieties about the growth of the Muslim community which bear little proportion to reality.[9] Such anxieties in turn can then be profoundly inhibiting of the trust which is needed for positive inter faith relations.

---

[7] In 2004, the British-based Barnabas Fund presented to the UN High Commissioner for Human Rights a major international petition signed by 90,000 people calling for 'Muslims who choose to convert to another faith' to be 'free to do so without having to face a lifetime of fear as a result' – text available on www.barnabasfund.org.

[8] The informal Hindu Christian Forum for the UK, after several meetings and intensive discussion, in 2003 produced an agreed 'goodwill statement' concerning the issue of conversion, seeking to identify what was appropriate and what was inadmissible in this area.

[9] My friend and colleague Andrew Wingate reports that, when he asks church groups in Leicestershire to estimate the number of Muslims in Britain, they regularly suggest 10 or even 20 million – as compared to the 2001 UK census total of just under 1.6 million.

Family impacts

Conversions can also be seen as a direct threat to the unity and continuity of the family in its role as medium and guarantor of religious observance. This threat is seen to be focused at a number of key points. Perhaps the most controversial is that of interfaith marriages. Many individual conversions occur when one marriage partner adopts the faith of the other; even when both partners attempt to maintain their own faith, there can be a notable degree of distancing from either or both of the original communities and families, and faith practice may be weakened as a result. The issue of 'marrying out' has been a particularly fraught one in modern Judaism. Whereas Orthodox rabbis have tended to maintain a strict prohibition on the practice, those in more liberal traditions have in recent years responded more often in terms of offering support for those involved – including a positive welcome for those who decide to convert to Judaism in the context of a marriage.[10] Parallel issues occur in general for leaders in other faiths, too, who have to balance a concern to maintain the continuity and integrity of their traditions with a realistic acceptance of individuals' aspirations.

The nurture of children and young people forms another area where anxieties about conversion can be marked. This will clearly be an issue in the case of children born in an interfaith marriage or other relationship, but educational institutions also provide an arena where parents and faith community leaders feel strongly about the importance of maintaining an environment which supports the inherited religious practice and culture of young people. The primary motivation here is to prevent the loss of faith, rather than the replacement of one faith by another. However, the result can be a suspicion of any attempts to introduce students to the beliefs and practices of religions other than their own – the claim being made that this would be 'confusing' to them at this stage in their life.

A (literally) final point at which the possibility of conversion may be seen as profoundly threatening is in relation to death and funerary customs. The death of one who has converted 'out of' a

---

[10] Lawrence J. Epstein (ed.), *Readings in Conversion to Judaism* (Northvale, NJ: Jason Aronson Inc, 1995).

particular religious tradition can be a particularly painful time for the bereaved relatives, who see their family member's departure marked by alien rites – it is interesting in this regard to note the custom in some Hindu families of holding a symbolic funeral service during the lifetime of a relative who has converted to another faith. Equally, there may also be the anxiety that converts will not maintain the traditional religious observances to honour and pray for their deceased ancestors. The depth of the psychological issues involved here can generate strong opposition to any possibility of conversion.[11]

Conversion and dialogue

Situations of inter faith dialogue – that is to say, situations where people of different faiths engage in conversation with the aims of understanding one another better and seeking the truth together – are always more or less fragile and highly sensitive to nuances in mutual perception. In a dialogue, the personal presence of converts from one faith to another can prove profoundly unsettling for many participants. At a thematic level, even their mere conceptual presence as a subject of discussion can also be difficult to handle. There are, in particular, two different types of approach to dialogue which are severely challenged by the phenomenon of conversion.

One is the attitude which in its popular mode relies on such analogies as 'many paths all leading to the summit of the same mountain', and which in its sophisticated theological expression issues in the pluralism of John Hick or Alan Race.[12] The fundamental datum of this approach is the idea of 'rough

---

[11] This can be illustrated by the famous story of the group of Japanese who told St Francis Xavier that, though they were deeply impressed by the prospect of heaven which he gave them in his preaching, they would choose rather to go to hell since they could not bear to be parted from their unbaptised (and therefore, as Xavier had assured them, unsaved) ancestors – cf. letter of Xavier from Cochin dated 29 January 1552, cited in Kosuke Koyama, *Mount Fuji and Mount Sinai: A Pilgrimage in Theology* (London: SCM, 1984), p. 169.

[12] E.g. John Hick, *An Interpretation of Religion: Human Responses to the Transcendent* (London: Macmillan, 1989); Alan Race, *Christians and Religious Pluralism* (2nd edn.; London: SCM, 1994).

parity':[13] that truth is more or less equally, if differently, apprehended; and that 'salvation' is more or less equally, if differently, apprehended in the various world faiths. My purpose
here is not to argue for or against such a view, but simply to note
that the phenomenon of inter-religious conversion poses quite a
challenge to it.[14] Directly contrary to the supposition of rough
parity, the convert presents him- or herself as one who has
found in their own life that the disparity in the apprehension of
truth, or in the mediation of salvation, is such that they have
taken radical action to re-orient their life. Of course, the actual
reasons for somebody's conversion may be far more circum-
stantial than a change in theological conviction. Nevertheless,
the convert must appear to a liberal pluralist understanding as a
threat to the very presuppositions of dialogue. For what room
in the 'many paths up the mountain' model can there be for
somebody who scrambles across the scree from one path to
another? What sense does it make in the 'Copernican system'
for somebody to hop impertinently from one planet to another?
The claim to have moved from a religion with less or even no
truth to tell, less or even no salvation to mediate, to one that is
truer, more effective, is frustrating for those committed to
liberal pluralism, as from their standpoint such journeys are
ultimately pointless.[15]

It is not only liberal pluralism which is challenged by the insis-
tent questions about truth that the convert poses. In situations
where issues about the fulfilment of one faith by another are at

---

[13] The phrase was coined by Langdon Gilkey – 'Plurality and Its Theo-
logical Implications', in John Hick and Paul Knitter (eds.), *The Myth of
Christian Uniqueness: Toward a Pluralistic Theology of Religions*
(Maryknoll, NY: Orbis, 1987), p. 37.

[14] Among the many refutations of the liberal pluralist thesis, one of the
most trenchant recently has been Gavin D'Costa, *The Meeting of Religions and the Trinity* (Maryknoll, NY: Orbis, 2000).

[15] Arun Shourie, *Missionaries in India* (New Delhi: Harper Collins,
1998), writing from a *Hindutva* perspective, exemplifies a Hindu version
of the pluralist argument against conversion. He begins by affirming
Hinduism as the most tolerant of all religions, because it offers so many
ways to God. He then moves quickly from that to the corollary that there
is no convincing reason why anybody should feel a need to find a path
outside Hinduism.

stake also, converts play an unsettling role. Jewish people who are accustomed to resisting evangelical Gentile Christian claims that their religion is completed through the coming of Jesus as Messiah may be profoundly disconcerted to hear the same claim being made by a Messianic believer, who has been brought up in a Jewish home and looks and behaves like a Jew.[16] Christians accustomed to seeing their faith as the fulfilment and authentic meaning of Judaism may be startled to receive an invitation from an Islamic 'revert' away from Christianity who asks them to recognise that the gospel, rightly understood, points to the coming of Muhammad, and that genuine, uncorrupted Christian discipleship is found through living according to the precepts of Islam.[17] The confusion can be all the greater when the conversion movement is in the opposite direction – when a Christian becomes a Jew, say, or a Muslim becomes a Christian, since this directly reverses the later faith's understanding of itself as an improvement on the former. In short, converts are a *skandalon* in dialogue, challenging equally and variously the different religions' claims to finality, to self-sufficiency and to replacement of the other.

Questioning religious identity

At a still deeper level, the sense of frustration, puzzlement or even indignation which the presence of the convert introduces can reach beyond the immediate context of interfaith dialogue to place a question mark against the religious identity of everybody in a multi-faith situation. Identity, a notoriously elusive concept, is perhaps most clearly recognised when it is most felt to be under threat, and most explicitly relied upon in times of rapid social adjustment. Britain – like other Western European countries – is in just such a time, as society has moved in less than a generation

---

[16] In 2004, the Board of Deputies of British Jews led community complaints to the Advertising Standards Agency over newspaper adverts by the zealously missionising group 'Jews for Jesus'. The Board claimed that the adverts were offensive to Jewish people, but the complaint was not upheld by the ASA – cf. www.asa.org.uk.

[17] The publications of the late controversialist Ahmed Deedat have been particularly prolific in such endeavours, generating in turn a range of Christian apologetic responses such as those on the website www.answering-islam.org.uk.

from relative homogeneity to a startling diversity, at least in urban areas. Over the last thirty years, the language and concepts which have been used to express individual and corporate identities in this rapidly changing situation have themselves changed – immigrant status, colour, race or ethnicity, and culture have successively been the focus of attention.

To this complex scene the last few years have added a growing recognition of the importance of religion as a constitutive element of identity. A defining moment in this process was the controversy over Salman Rushdie's *Satanic Verses*, which saw British Muslims emerge as a high profile community in society, but the effects have been felt by other communities also, notably Hindus and the black Christian community. In terms of legislation, there is now for the first time in Great Britain a measure of protection against discrimination specifically on the grounds of religion or belief.[18] In a parallel process, a debate continues about the possibility of legislation to outlaw incitement to religious hatred.[19]

This developing recognition of the importance of religion as a key element of identity is in many ways timely, or even overdue. However, because the social policy discussion of the question has grown out of an earlier community relations discourse of ethnicity, there is a certain danger that a monolithic and inflexible understanding of religious identity will be assumed. That is to say, just as people can be described in terms of ethnicity depending on their family background, so too they will be categorised as 'Muslim', 'Christian', and so on according to their upbringing and community membership. However, the 'givenness' and invariance of ethnicity cannot simply be transferred to religion. While family background will often play the dominant part in forming a person's faith involvement, there remains in principle an element of choice, and converts are those who serve as living reminders that the principle of choice is put into practice by some people.[20] This

---

[18] The legislation, prepared to comply with a European Union directive, is restricted to discrimination in the area of employment or occupation.

[19] Proposals to include clauses outlawing incitement to religious hatred were included in anti-terrorist legislation, but lost after protracted parliamentary debate in 2001.

[20] See Michael Ipgrave (ed.), *Religious Discrimination: A Christian Response* (London: Churches Together in Britain and Ireland, 2001), p. 15.

exercise of choice, placing as it does a question mark over the fixity of religious identity, can be unsettling to interfaith relations.

Responses from the Interfaith Context to the Issue of Conversion

I have argued that the phenomenon of conversion poses some sharp challenges to the way that interfaith relations are conceptualised and practiced in Britain, on the socio-political, familial and dialogical levels, and with respect to underlying questions of religious identity. I turn now to outline some of the responses which have been made from within the British interfaith world to the first three of these challenges, before suggesting some points for further exploration in relation to identity.

Responses to socio-political issues

Allegations that conversions represent an attack on the integrity of other faiths with political repercussions have generated some discussion in interfaith circles. There is a communications problem here, in that those interfaith circles rarely include either converts or those most vigorously seeking the conversion of others. Where discussions have taken place, an important principle has been to try to establish a distinction between two senses of the word 'convert': on the one hand, self-referentially, 'to change one's own religious affiliation'; on the other hand, with reference to another, 'to seek to induce a change in their religious affiliation'.[21] This distinction of two senses of conversion is easy to grasp in principle, but it can be more difficult to define in practical situations. The line between actively commending faith and manipulating the other to change faith is not always clear. Considerable effort has been focused here on distinguishing between the propagation of a faith, on one hand, and proselytisation, on the other. The former is deemed acceptable, the latter illegitimate. The availability of two

---

[21] The latter usage is a Christian shorthand that is unfortunate in the resonances it creates both among Christians and others. For a missionary to say, 'I have converted so many hundred people' is bad for the missionary's spiritual pride, and it is threatening to the unconverted neighbours of those hundreds.

words, one 'good' and the other 'bad', is very useful strategically, since everybody can readily agree that they are in favour of freedom to propagate faith but against license to proselytise. Genuine conversions, it is then explained, are in response to propagation rather than to proselytisation.

When it comes to actually establishing the respective boundaries of conversion and proselytisation, though, there is no consensus even about the kind of criteria which count. For some, the key issue is that of missionary motivation: conversions are the more or less unlooked for consequence of a sharing of one person's faith with others, whereas proselytisation involves the use of deliberate strategies to change people's allegiances. For others, the identity of the person's changing faith is crucial: converts are responsible adults who have made free decisions, whereas proselytes are vulnerable, disadvantaged, or otherwise constrained individuals or groups who have been singled out for targeting. A third way of interpreting the conversion/proselytisation distinction is based on the degree of respect accorded to the culture associated with the previous faith, and the extent to which elements of continuity are permitted across the conversion experience.[22] Finally, the distinction may be made in a practical way through trying to regulate the methods and etiquette used in encounters between people of different faiths. One of the most useful and influential examples of this kind is a code of conduct established by the Inter Faith Network for the UK, which states, *inter alia*, that 'Some people will also want to persuade others to join their faith. In a multi-faith society where this is permitted, the attempt should always be characterised by self-restraint and a concern for the other's freedom and dignity', and goes on to specify five parameters which give concrete reality to this.[23]

---

[22] Andrew Walls, for example, claims that authentic Christianity is committed to a 'conversion' rather than a 'proselytisation' model, as shown by its insistence on the need to 'translate' the gospel into every culture – *The Missionary Movement in Christian History: Studies in Transmission of Faith* (Maryknoll, NY: Orbis, 1996), p. 47.

[23] 'Building Good Relations with People of Different Faiths and Beliefs', on www.interfaith.co.uk – the sections on commending faith to others for part of a wider set of recommendations about encounter between people of different faiths.

Such an attempt to develop a shared 'ethic of conversion' is a very important and a very complex task, with much depending on the dynamics of the particular interfaith situation. Much can depend on the shades of meaning given to particular words, as is clear from my outline of the variety of ways in which 'conversion' and 'proselytisation' can be distinguished. At times, the process of establishing an agreed pattern of conduct can feel more like negotiation than dialogue, but that is perhaps inevitable given its wider socio-political ramifications.

Responses to familial issues

Less attention has been paid from an interfaith perspective to the implications of individual conversions for relations between communities and families, though this will surely have to change as conversions multiply in modern plural societies.[24] There is, though, a growing recognition of the need to develop interfaith responses to conversions associated with the marriage of somebody from one faith to somebody of another. Interfaith marriages themselves – that is to say, marriages in which each partner retains their original faith identity – are highly controversial for many faith communities, but there have begun to grow up some informal networks of support and dialogue for such situations.[25] These networks are found among the couples themselves and also, to some extent, among religious leaders in the communities concerned. When one partner converts, however, it can seem that the marriage no longer bears any relation to one of the two faith communities, and so there is no impetus towards any interfaith consideration of it. This is unfortunate, since the convert is likely still to have family and friends belonging to the original faith community, and in any case will still carry in his or her own self deep elements of personal identity drawn from that faith and culture. For the converted marriage partners themselves, there are questions of the

----

[24] Jonathan Romain's *Your God Shall Be My God* (London: SCM Press, 2000) provides a masterly survey of the complex range of reactions to conversions from families, friends, and religious colleagues in both old and new faiths, and I could not attempt to summarise what he says there.
[25] E.g. the resource material for interfaith couples on www.interfaithmarriage.org.uk, or the support group for Muslim-Christian marriages on www.mocmarriage.org.uk.

extent to which conversion can be adequately described as a 'clean break', to which I shall return later. For the wider circles of those associated with the married couple, there may be a need to find ways of enabling dialogue between the two faith communities. It may be that the slowly growing interfaith relationships supporting interfaith marriages can be further developed to reach into these situations also.

Responses to dialogical issues

I outlined above some of the ways in which converts can seem to threaten the very basis of dialogue between people of different faiths, as they call into radical question many of the assumptions on which dialogues may be built. On the other hand, the motif of 'conversion' is clearly too important a theme, particularly for Christians, to be entirely ignored in an interfaith context. Three approaches in particular have been influential in the British context.

The first proceeds by emphasising an understanding of conversion as a turning towards God. It proposes that this happens in interfaith dialogue primarily through a renewal and deepening of one's own faith commitment. In other words, conversion means in the first place Christians becoming better Christians, Hindus becoming better Hindus and so on, as all are led closer to God through dialogue.[26] There is much of value in this approach, and it expresses an important dynamic within the interfaith context. Dialogue can indeed be a real opportunity for a renewal of such an intense nature that it can be fairly described as a conversion. However, it is not obvious that all 'conversions' can be adequately defined in these terms. Jonathan Romain proposes a fourfold classification of the phenomena: 'Acquiring Faith' (a person with no previous religious allegiance discovers faith), 'Born Again' (someone sees their nominal faith in a new light), 'Denominational' (conversion from one group

---

[26] It may even be the case that in some sense one could say that the person of another faith is the agent for the conversion of their dialogue partner. For example, if I meet in my Hindu neighbour evidences of hospitality, generosity, and love which should also be core values in my own Christian discipleship, and I am challenged by that experience to a deeper realisation of my own faith, then I could say that I have been 'converted' to a renewed Christianity through the evangelism of that Hindu.

to another within the same faith), and 'Transference' (conversion from one faith to another).[27] The sense of conversion as a mutual turning to God falls most readily into his second category.[28] Yet it is 'Transference', i.e. full-blooded conversion in the inter-religious sense, that raises the most acute problems, and these will not simply go away through redefining the meaning of 'conversion'. It cannot be assumed that transference will not happen in the interfaith context. Indeed, there is a possibility that transference will be one result of the very process of engaging in dialogue.

The second approach builds on this possibility and defines one of the pre-conditions of genuine dialogue as being a mutual openness to the possibility of conversion from one's own position to the position of the other. In other words, a radical orientation of oneself to 'convertibility' is the measure of commitment to a spirit of dialogue. At the same time, in this account, activity specifically designed to bring about conversion of the other is not appropriate within dialogue. The dialogical spirit is characterised by a receptivity to seeking the truth together, even at the cost of radical personal change, rather than by efforts to persuade the other of one's already held convictions. Here, inter-religious conversion has indeed been given a central place in dialogue, but at the same time it has been redefined by being given a primarily reflexive reference, pointed back to the self rather than projected towards the other – it is one's own readiness to change that is at stake. This is certainly an interesting way of addressing the issue of conversion within dialogue, but it is not wholly convincing to insist that a readiness to be converted should in fact be explicitly required of those engaged in dialogue. Such a commitment would be much more exacting for some than for others – for example, in cases where conversion away from a faith is seen as culpable apostasy rather than as a rational decision to opt for another path, or where it would lead to the breaking of family and social ties. Moreover, this approach does not address the situation in dialogue of those who have already been converted.

---

[27] Romain, *Your God Shall Be My God*, p. 225.
[28] I have to admit, though, that I have never heard anybody describe themselves as becoming a 'born again Christian' through their experience of interfaith dialogue – more often, being born again seems to exclude the possibility of dialogue.

A third approach builds on the second by adding a theological dimension to the focus on human attitudes. Of course, such a theological dimension will be expressed differently in different faiths. In Christian terms, it amounts to an emphasis on the inviolability of the space of human autonomy as the place where the freedom of the Spirit alone is privileged to operate, in leading the individual to the possibility of conversion. In fact, even this inner realm of decision-making is itself best characterised as a dialogue, of the human being with God, in which the Spirit does not compel but 'bears witness with (*symmarturei*) our spirit'.[29] This is an extremely important insight from a Christian perspective. It draws a theological line between witness as a human responsibility and conversion as a divine responsibility, and so it constantly recalls the importance of avoiding any form of coercion or manipulation. It locates the core reality of conversion in the *forum internum* of the human soul, recognised as the inalienable domain of a free conscience.[30] It is also not difficult to see how parallel distinctions could be made in other faith traditions also. There are Qur'anic passages, for example, which make a very similar point in insisting that the Prophet's responsibility is fulfilled in the faithful discharge of his witness: 'If they embrace Islam, they are rightly-guided, but if they turn their backs on it, then your only duty is to convey the message.'[31] Distinctions of this kind between what pertains to humans and what pertains to God can provide a theological framework within which issues of conversion can be addressed in an inter faith context. On the human side of the demarcation, though, there are tangled questions of religious identity which are highlighted by the phenomena of conversion.

---

[29] Rom. 8:16.

[30] The idea of the *forum internum* is central to modern human rights jurisprudence in relation to religious freedom, yet its boundaries have proved difficult to define – cf. Carolyn Evans, *Freedom of Religion Under The European Convention on Human Rights* (Oxford: Oxford University Press, 2001), pp. 72ff.

[31] Qur'an 3:20. Kamali, *Freedom of Expression*, p. 103, also cites the following Qur'anic verses as implying the same distinction: Qur'an 5:92, 99; Qur'an 88:21, 22.

Interfaith Conversion and Religious Identity: Four Questions

Conversion and conflict

In the 'classic' situation of inter-communal conversion, two defin-able groups are in contact with one another, each possessed of a differing pattern of identity where faith and culture are bound up together, and often also ethnicity and language are interwoven. In such a setting, it has proved easy to conceptualise conversion, par-ticularly large-scale movements of conversion, in terms of conflict, whether that is understood as new forces of spiritual liberation being opposed by old forces of religious repression or as new forces of alien aggression being resisted by old forces of cultural integrity. Conflict is not easy for dialogue to handle, and so con-version itself has proved to be a difficult issue to address in inter-faith contexts when seen in these terms. *Are there non-conflictual models of conversion available, or at least models which do justice to the complexity of the factors involved in conflict?*

A fascinating exploration of the complexity of issues involved in the tensions between two identity systems is found in Gauri Viswanathan's analysis of nineteenth-century conversions as involving resistance to attempts at cultural colonisation, rather than the assimilation they are generally assumed to imply.[32] Viswanathan points to the subversive effect of the convert's sepa-ration of religious faith from the cultural nexus of identity. On a more straightforward level, the almost forgotten patristic image of initiation, culminating in baptism, as 'illumination' (*photismos*) might provide a non-conflictual model of conversion in the Chris-tian tradition.[33] There is indeed an implication that the previous existence was characterised by darkness, but this is not really the emphasis of *photismos*. It points rather to the invitation to enter into a situation which casts new light on the identity both of God and of self. These, in any case, are only two possible examples; what other ways are open to speak convincingly of transference between faiths without categorising this in oppositional terms?

---

[32] Gauri Viswanathan, *Outside the Fold: Conversion, Modernity and Belief* (Princeton, NJ: Princeton University Press, 1998).
[33] E.g. Justin Martyr, *I Apol.* 61.

Conversion and fluidity

It is important also to think of inter-religious conversion in situations other than the traditional instances of two communities in juxtaposition. This is a point forcibly made by Jonathan Romain, when he points to a growing dissociation of religious adherence from family background or community membership: 'It has become much more a matter of personal choice than of inherited tradition. People do not automatically follow the faith of their family.'[34] This makes possible a much more individual-centred and fluid sense of conversion. Some conversions involve entering spiritual paths where the very concept of community is exiguous, being replaced by a much looser form of networking.[35] Romain suggests that what we are seeing here is less the classic inter-community problem, and more something like shopping at a spiritual supermarket. I think that he may be underplaying the extent to which more conservative patterns of continuity in religious affiliation still apply. With reference to England, for example, his analysis perhaps fits the interfaith situation in Home Counties better than it does in the North and Midlands. Still, the phenomena he describes are important and raise the question: *How do we understand interfaith conversion in the absence of any significant community dimension?*

This is a difficult question for traditional religious communities to address, precisely because the corporate dimension is so important in their understanding of faith. There is a certain tendency among Christians to regard conversions of this kind (for example to Buddhism or to forms of alternative spirituality) as not quite real, as more akin to taking up a hobby than to taking on a religious commitment. But this can be unfair to the seriousness with which people take such decisive steps in their lives, and it also ignores the fact that converts towards Christianity itself in modern Western societies may also see their faith in terms of personal quest rather than conscious intention to participate in a community of faith.

---

[34] Romain, *Your God Shall Be My God*, p. 7.
[35] E.g. some varieties of New Age or some of the groups focused on centres such as Glastonbury.

Conversion and liminality

There is a need to take more seriously the developing experiences of converts within the new faith they have joined. Much has been written about the reception or rejection of new adherents by their fellow believers. However, there is another dynamic which needs attention alongside this: namely, the convert's own relationship to their previous faith. It would be unrealistic to expect this suddenly to terminate completely, especially if involvement in the previous faith was active rather than merely nominal. For some converts, an internal relationship of retrospection, questioning and partial affirmation directed towards the previous faith continues to such an extent that they embody a virtual interfaith dialogue within their own persons. The question then arises: *How can the liminal experience of continued relationship to an old faith from the perspective of a new faith be appreciated?*

In some cases, this may prove difficult or impossible – for example, when the process of conversion has involved painful experiences of rejection, or even persecution, converts may well try to obliterate all traces of their former faith from their consciousness. In other cases, however, there may develop a growing respect for, and in some sense a re-appropriation of, elements of the religious tradition from which the convert has come. In a longer generational frame, this reappraisal may be made not by the original converts but by their children or grandchildren, as they become aware of the depths of the religious heritage out of which their forebears came. The Pentecostal theologian, Amos Yong, reviewing a collection of autobiographical reflections by Asian-American Christians, goes so far as to describe this process as being in itself a conversion: 'Without ever leaving either Christian faith or the church', he points out, 'all of the contributors at various points in their lives were "converted" back to Asia even as they reconnected with their Asian roots and heritages. In that process, they discovered valuable resources by which to understand their Christian identities and to articulate Asian-American Christian theologies.'[36] Yong describes this freshly articulated

---

[36] Peter Phan and Jung Young Lee (eds.), *Journeys at the Margin: Toward an Autobiographical Theology in Asian-American Perspective* (Collegeville, MN: Liturgical Press, 1999), reviewed by Amos Yong in *Asian Journal of Pentecostal Studies* 3.2 (July 2000), pp. 327–31.

identity as being in some sense 'betwixt and between' – a position which can open up fresh perspectives on the complexities of religious identity.

Conversion and belonging

Even more explicitly 'betwixt and between' are those people who, while remaining rooted in one faith tradition, have an intimate participation in another faith to such an extent that they can be described as having a 'dual belonging'.[37] It has for some time been not uncommon in an ecumenical age for people to have dual membership of different Christian traditions. Despite the vastly greater complications that arise, it is natural to expect similar patterns to grow between the faiths also. The degree of joint participation in some cases may even be such as to enable us to speak of a 'partial conversion'. However, this should not be taken to suggest a 'halfway' position between two faiths, but rather a parallel life in a second faith while remaining in the first. *How can the experience of people with a dual religious identity enhance an understanding of conversion?*

Such situations may arise in various ways. Within an interfaith marriage, for example, one or both partners may join more or less regularly in the life of the other's faith community; or their children may grow up with some sense of belonging to both. A different scenario is the committed member of one faith who develops a deep interest in and knowledge of the lived reality of another, to such an extent that they have an empathy bordering on identification with the other. In this connection, it is intriguing to reflect on the way in which the Christian missionary movement has produced some of the most impressive and sympathetic scholarship relating to other religions. An analytic model often suggested in this connection is that of 'translation'. This may be proposed as an analogy, in the recasting of insights from one faith in terms accessibility to people of the other, but it may also apply in a more literal sense, given the centrality of inter-linguistic communication for so much missiology and religious studies. 'Bilingualism' might be a useful metaphor for the sense of dual religious belonging,[38] and

---

[37] Jacques Scheuer and Dennis Gira (ed.), *Vivre de Plusieurs Religions: Promesse ou Illusion* (Paris: Les Éditions de l'Atelier, 2000).
[38] David Lochhead, *The Dialogical Imperative: A Christian Reflection on Interfaith Encounter* (London: SCM, 1988), p. 69.

this could then illuminate our understanding of the dynamics of conversion as a consummation of inter-religious communication.

In these and other ways, conversions between religions in Britain today are raising intriguing questions about the inner depths and the outer boundaries of religious identity. Such challenges in the short term can certainly be unsettling to interfaith relations, but in the longer term to take them seriously will lead to a more honest, more engaged, and a more open interfaith *praxis*.

2

Beyond Conversion

Exploring the Process of Moving Away from Evangelical Christianity

Gordon Lynch

I

The relationship between the academic discipline of the study of religion and the phenomena it claims to describe and analyse is a complex one. At first glance, it may appear that the academic study of religion offers a neutral set of terms and concepts for making sense of religious institutions, behaviour, belief and experience. From this viewpoint, academic concepts are merely windows through which we can gain a better perspective on religious phenomena. Such a view of academic study has been challenged in recent years. The impact of the work of the French philosopher-historian Michel Foucault has been particularly influential in this regard. Foucault argued that the 'discourses' that people use to describe and understand reality do not offer objective accounts of the world as it is, but are specific ways of making sense of the world that have emerged through particular processes of cultural history.[1] After Foucault, then, there has been a growing recognition amongst many scholars that the language and concepts they use in their work are not neutral vehicles for

[1] M. Foucault, *The Archaeology of Knowledge* (London: Routledge, 2002).

understanding truth, but products of cultural discourses that define and structure the world in specific ways.

Thinking about concepts in the academic study of religion as expressions of cultural discourse has important implications. Richard King, for example, has argued that terms such as 'mysticism', and even 'religion' itself, have emerged as concepts through a particular Western intellectual tradition.[2] The concept of 'religion', therefore, does not provide an obvious or taken-for-granted way of looking at the world, but it is a way of thinking about reality that people, particularly in Western cultures, have learnt. Now to suggest that 'religion' is not something that simply exists 'out there', in the 'real' world, and that it is an expression of a particular Western cultural and intellectual tradition, may seem odd or counter-intuitive to some. Yet, when we recognise that 'religion' is a concept developed within Western culture, it is easier to understand why it is so hard to find a widely acceptable definition of religion that fits across all times and places, or why clear divisions between the 'sacred' and 'secular' parts of society make little sense in some cultures.[3] Another relevant example here concerns the concept of 'spirituality'. The meaning and significance of the term 'spirituality' has changed in recent history, and has acquired its current connotations of personally meaningful beliefs through a cultural process since the Reformation in which 'religion' has become an increasingly privatised matter of individual preference and conscience.[4] 'Spirituality' has not always meant the same thing, therefore, but its changing meaning reflects the various times and contexts in which it is used.

In summary, the concepts that are used in the academic study of religion are not neutral or objective ways of defining 'religious' phenomena, but are the products of particular cultural traditions whose meaning changes over time. Furthermore, these concepts do not provide final, authoritative definitions of the world as it is,

---

[2] R. King, *Orientalism and Religion: Post-Colonial Theory, India and the Mystic East* (London: Routledge, 1999).

[3] M. Klass, *Ordered Universes: Approaches to the Anthropology of Religion* (Colorado: Westview Press, 1999).

[4] J. Carrette and R. King, *Selling Spirituality: The Silent Takeover of Religion* (London: Routledge, 2004).

but particular ways of thinking about the world that enable people to make sense of it and act in it in particular ways.

What is the significance of this for a discussion of the subject of conversion, though? If we open many textbooks or research monographs on the subject of conversion, particularly those approaching it from a psychological perspective, we can encounter the assumption that 'conversion' is a clear and unproblematic term. Influenced by a particular tradition of Protestant piety, and more recently by the psychology of religion developed by William James, a frequent assumption is that conversion is a process of radical change in an individual's religious identity grounded in particular experiences and leading to transformations in their beliefs, behaviour and affiliations.[5] The popular icon of this view of conversion is St. Paul and his Damascus Road experience, in which he converted from Judaism to become a follower of Christ. More academic approaches to this subject seek to describe this process of individual conversion in terms of identifiable stages, attempt to measure the psychological effects of such conversion, or to suggest those who are more psychologically inclined to be susceptible to such experiences. From this largely psychologised perspective, then, conversion is a clearly identifiable process and experience within the individual which can be studied in different contexts and in relation to different religious traditions.[6]

Such a clear definition of conversion is problematic, however, and can only be maintained by ignoring the way in which the definition and meaning of conversion changes in different periods and contexts.[7] For example, in normal usage the term conversion

---

[5] See, e.g., K. Loewenthal, *Mental Health and Religion* (London: Chapman & Hall, 1995); R. Hood, B. Spilka, B. Hunsberger and R. Gorsuch, *The Psychology of Religion: An Empirical Approach* (2nd edn.; London: Guilford, 1996); B. Beit-Hallahmi and M. Argyle, *The Psychology of Religious Behaviour, Belief and Experience* (London: Routledge, 1997).

[6] See, e.g., L. Rambo and C. Farhadian, 'Converting: stage of religious change', in C. Lamb and M. Bryant (eds.), *Religious Conversion: Contemporary Practices and Controversies* (London: Cassell, 1999), pp. 23–34.

[7] D. Taylor, 'Conversion: Inward, Outward and Awkward', in Lamb and Bryant, *Religious Conversion*, pp. 35–50.

indicates a movement across boundaries of religious identity. Yet
the boundaries of what constitutes a significant change in religious
belief and identity are not set in stone, but vary in different times
and communities. For many people in contemporary Britain,
changing from being a committed member of a Catholic church to
being a committed member of a Protestant church would not be
particularly problematic and would be unlikely to be referred to as
a process of 'conversion' by anyone around them. Yet in some
parts of Britain (e.g. cities such as Glasgow, Belfast and Liverpool)
such a process might be perceived as far more radical by that person's local community. Similarly, in the two centuries following
the Reformation, 'conversion' from Catholicism to Protestantism
was a highly charged issue which could (e.g. in the context of the
British penal laws enacted in Ireland in the eighteenth century)
quite literally be a matter of life and death.

What counts as conversion does not, then, depend simply on a
process within an individual's soul or psyche, but on the way in
which religious boundaries and identities are drawn up in particular cultural contexts. Furthermore, whether one labels a particular
example of a change in an individual's religious identity and
beliefs as conversion depends on one's particular theoretical and
doctrinal assumptions. What might be described as 'conversion'
by one person, might be seen as 'apostasy' or 'brain-washing' by
another. The idea that one can have a neutral or objective language for analysing conversion is itself a product of the emergence
of a 'science' of comparative religion that has sought to find a
common theoretical language for discussing phenomena across a
range of religious traditions. Furthermore, the very notion of conversion as a process within the soul or psyche of the searching and
choosing individual has acquired its particular meaning and significance in a contemporary culture that has been described by
some sociologists as a 'spiritual market-place' in which individuals
act like consumers choosing between different religious options.[8]

To think about conversion as an event purely within the psyche
of the individual is therefore to neglect the ways in which

---

[8] T. Luckmann, *The Invisible Religion: The Problem of Religion in
Modern Society* (New York, NY: MacMillan, 1967); W.C. Roof, *Spiritual Marketplace: Baby Boomers and the Remaking of American Religion* (Princeton, NJ: Princeton University Press, 1999).

'conversion' is socially and culturally constructed. Conversion is not an unchanging religious phenomenon which can be universally seen across all times and culture. Rather, conversion is a cultural concept whose significance in Western culture has shifted from the conflicts around various forms of Christian identity (Catholic, Protestant, Non-Conformist), to become a term that is applied to different religious traditions through the development of the academic study of comparative religion. More recently, interest and concern with emergence of new religious movements (in particular 'cults') has added a new level of associations to conversion as a potentially unhealthy move away from the secularised norms of mainstream society. Recognising the way in which discourses of conversion have changed at different points in post-Reformation Western culture is important not only for encouraging a greater epistemological humility and self-awareness in the use of this term. But as with any form of cultural discourse, it is valuable to raise the question of what the culturally specific concept of conversion helps us to understand, but also what it obscures or fails to explain adequately.

The term 'conversion' can be helpful in focusing attention on changes in a person's religious identity, beliefs, behaviour and affiliations when they move across particular religious boundaries. These transitions are usually into a form of religious community that are clearly defined in terms of membership, rituals and doctrine, and where the transition itself is usually marked by a specific ritual (e.g. baptism in Christianity, the 'shahadah' in Islam). By contrast, it is unlikely that someone would be described as having converted to 'New Age' beliefs, given that the 'New Age' movement is so diffuse and lacking clear boundaries. The term 'conversion' is therefore generally applied to a person's movement into, say, a Christian, Jewish, or Muslim faith and identity when they were not previously a member of that particular faith community. Conversion, as a concept in the academic study of religion, therefore makes it possible to analyse the way in which people become members of a specific set of established or new religious groups which have clearly identifiable boundaries of belief and membership. This concept can therefore facilitate comparative studies of the psychological and sociological processes involved in this kind of conversion, which can clarify some of the ways in which religious experience and practice can be similar or different within contemporary society.

At the same time, however, this concept of conversion can fail to offer an adequate explanatory language to other kinds of religious transition that are profoundly significant to those experiencing them, but which do not constitute processes or experiences of 'conversion' in the sense just described. One example of this is that of people who have grown up in the Muslim community with a nominal interest in Islam, and who later make an active adult commitment to living according to Islamic teaching and rituals.[9] In this instance, no religious boundaries have been crossed and the ritual for inclusion into the Muslim faith is inappropriate, yet a radical change has taken place in a person's religious outlook. The concept of conversion focuses attention on religious transition at the entry points of the boundaries of certain religious traditions and communities, but this concept neglects the socially, psychologically, and spiritually important transitions that people can make within a single tradition or across religious boundaries to which the label conversion is not applied.

In the second part of this chapter, a more detailed case example will be given of a form of religious transition for which the current academic language of 'conversion' or even 'de-conversion' is not appropriate.[10] This is the transition of moving away from the religious identity and affiliation of being an evangelical Christian. In this section, I will present a theoretical framework for understanding the nature and causes of this particular form of religious transition, before going on to discuss the implications of this kind of transition both for pastoral practice and academic study in relation to changes in religious faith.

II

Evangelical churches and networks have become a significant part of contemporary Christianity in Britain. The most recent English church attendance survey indicated that in 1998, evangelical

---

[9] See S. Gilliat-Ray, 'Rediscovering Islam: A Muslim Journey of Faith', in Lamb and Bryant, *Religious Conversion*, pp. 315–32.

[10] For an example of a definition of de-conversion, see Hood et al., *Psychology of Religion*, pp. 290ff.

Christians made up 37 per cent of those attending church in England on a regular basis.[11] The total number of evangelical Christians counted in this survey (1,391,300) did show a slight (3 per cent) fall on the number of evangelicals in the 1989 survey. Nevertheless, the evangelical wing of the church generally demonstrated a less rapid decline than membership in liberal or Catholic congregations.[12] Theologically and sociologically, evangelicalism in Britain contains some important points of difference and diversity. Notable here are the tensions between those adopting more liberal social ethics and those who are pressing for more conservative theological and ethical teaching in the church. Similarly, the charismatic movement and the emphasis on the gifts of the Spirit remains a divisive issue, with some evangelicals clearly identifying themselves as against the charismatic movement and others warmly embracing it. Alongside this, evangelical churches include a spectrum from traditional congregations and worship services to highly innovative and entrepreneurial experiments in new ways of being church. Given this diversity, it is important not to depict evangelicalism in Britain as an entirely homogeneous phenomenon.

In spite of this diversity, however, there are certain elements which tend to define evangelical theology and culture. Although these elements may carry different emphases in specific networks and congregations, they commonly shape perceptions of what it means to be an evangelical and the way in which issues of faith and practice are talked about in evangelical settings. Bebbington has suggested four such defining qualities of evangelicalism. These are '*conversionism*, the belief that lives need to be changed; *activism*, the expression of the gospel in effort; *Biblicism*, a particular regard for the Bible; and ... *crucicentrism*, a stress on the sacrifice of Christ on the cross'.[13]

---

[11] See P. Brierley (ed.), *UK Handbook Religious Trends 2000/2001 no.2* (London: Christian Research): section 12.3.

[12] Note that the attendance of Anglo-Catholic churches actually showed little decline between 1989 and 1998, but with less than 200,000 people regularly attending such churches this is still considerably less than those attending evangelical churches.

[13] D.W. Bebbington, *Evangelicalism in Modern Britain: A History from the 1730s to the 1980s* (London: Unwin Hyman), pp. 2f.

In practice, these four recurring characteristics of evangelical belief are central elements of a particular discourse that is expressed and reinforced through evangelical worship songs, sermons, Bible study resources and the content of extempore prayers in evangelical settings. This discourse offers a particular hermeneutical structure through which believers conceive of their lives in terms of the following schema:[14]

- God, the source of all goodness, loves me and through an undeserved act of grace he has chosen (through Christ's sacrificial death) to save and redeem me from sin, death and hell.
- God is a loving and positive authority, who continues to offer healing, comfort and guidance in my life, and should be the focus of my worship.
- My appropriate response to God's loving action should be one of love and praise for his saving grace and of commitment to live as an active and faithful Christian disciple.

Conversion, from an evangelical perspective, is typically understood as the process of making a decision to accept this schema as the basis of one's identity, beliefs and actions. Whilst an evangelical conversion experience may often involve a particular mystical or affective element (e.g. a sense of divine presence, an encounter with Christ, a feeling of peace, breaking down in tears), it is actually the adoption of this particular cognitive schema that defines a person as having become an evangelical Christian. Contemporary evangelistic programs in evangelical contexts (such as the Alpha Course) thus normally proceed by attempting to convey the plausibility of this cognitive structure as a framework for understanding life rather than simply trying to generate an emotional response from participants. Indeed, the tone of many evangelical resources which focus on converting others is often to emphasise

---

[14] For fuller discussions and definitions of the concept of cognitive shema in relation to religious belief, see D. McIntosh, 'Religion as schema, with implications for the relation between religion and coping', in B. Spilka and D. McIntosh (eds.), *The Psychology of Religion: Theoretical Approaches* (Colorado: Westview Press), pp. 171–83; E. Ozorak, 'In the eye of the beholder: A Social-cognitive Model of Religious Belief', in Spilka and McIntosh, *Psychology of Religion*, pp. 194–203.

how evangelical faith enables one to make sense of life and find meaning within it.

Again, whilst there can be variations on how this evangelical schema operates in different contexts, it can often function as a 'tight' set of assumptions about the nature of God, epistemology, faith and ethics. The sense of life as being lived under the grace and authority of God is connected to the belief that the Bible is the primary source of knowledge of divine truth and that it offers clear guidance on matters of faith and practice. The schema of core evangelical beliefs thus becomes closely intertwined with a set of norms for personal conduct, in which particular attention is often given to issues of sexuality and sexual relations (e.g. prohibitions on sex outside of heterosexual marriage). This coalescence of theological claims about the nature of divine grace and authority and specific teachings about personal faith and morality is typically mediated through specific individuals who are regarded as credible interpreters of the biblical witness. At a local level, this will include those with a recognised preaching or teaching ministry and at a national or international level, will include pastors, writers and worship leaders who acquire a celebrity status within evangelical circles.

For many people, then, participation in evangelical culture thus involves adopting a tight cognitive schema of beliefs about the nature of God, human experience and ethical standards, a schema which is reinforced by a network of people, structures and resources at a local, national and international level. Again, it is important not to offer this description as a timeless and unchanging account of the essence of evangelical Christianity. Rather it is intended as a broad description of how evangelicalism has functioned in the closing decades of the twentieth century. As debates about 'openness of God' theology have indicated, evangelical beliefs and identity are capable of change and development as much as any other form of cultural identity and discourse.[15]

To understand life within the terms of such a tight cognitive schema can have certain advantages, such as offering a clear framework for interpreting experiences and establishing one's

---

[15] For a further discussion of the openness of God debate, see M. Erickson, *The Evangelical Left* (Carlisle: Paternoster, 1997).

identity. Indeed, if experiences of suffering can be integrated within an existing religious schema of belief, then those beliefs can represent an important resource in coping with trauma.[16] At the same time, however, rigid cognitive schemas are vulnerable in a society characterised by an increasing religious and cultural pluralism. Whether one prefers the term 'late' or 'post' modernity to describe this current cultural context, it is clear that many people face greater exposure to ethnic, religious and cultural diversity in their local communities (particularly if they live in an urban setting), through national and international media and through personal experiences of travel (particularly beyond Western Europe). As Peter Berger has observed, such pluralism makes it much harder for people to imagine that their way of understanding the world is the only possible way.[17] For many people in evangelical settings, this exposure to pluralism can be negotiated in various ways that do not threaten the basic schema of beliefs within which they are operating. Strategies here can include interpreting alternative beliefs and lifestyles as symptomatic of the influence of evil spiritual forces, as well-intentioned and even partial bearers of the truth ultimately expressed in Christianity, or as indicators of social and cultural decline. As with many kinds of tight cognitive schema, people operating within a tight evangelical worldview may also minimise, deny, distort, or simply fail to see evidence of views or experiences that do not fit within this schema.

The degree of investment that individuals place in an evangelical schema for making sense of life can make it difficult and profoundly challenging to reject this schema as a basis for personal identity, beliefs and values. Nevertheless, a substantial number of people are leaving evangelical churches precisely because they find themselves unable to continue to operate within the terms of this schema. As noted earlier, despite the success of evangelistic initiatives such as the Alpha Course during the 1990s, attendance at evangelical churches in England actually fell slightly between 1989 and 1998. Similarly, between 1989 and 1996, although 11,000 new members joined the Baptist Church in New Zealand,

---

[16] See McIntosh, 'Religion as schema'.

[17] P. Berger, *The Heretical Imperative: Contemporary Possibilities of Religious Affirmation* (London: Collins, 1980).

10,118 people left the church during the same period.[18] Alan Jamieson's fieldwork amongst those leaving evangelical churches has suggested that whilst a small proportion of those who left did so because of specific disagreements that left their commitment to the evangelical schema intact, the majority left because they believed that their personal and spiritual development could not be contained within the confines of this schema.[19] This finding is similarly supported by Richter and Francis' survey of church leavers in Britain, which indicated that the most commonly cited causes for leaving included statements such as: I doubted or questioned my faith; I became aware of alternative ways of thinking and living; the church did not meet my needs; I changed; the church failed to connect with the rest of my life; and I grew up and started making decisions on my own.[20]

Many people in Britain (as well as Australia and New Zealand) who have moved beyond an evangelical schema for making sense of their lives have done so by engaging with resources and networks that use terms such as 'post-evangelical', 'post-church', or 'alternative worship'. From my own observation, it is striking that the vast majority of people who are engaged in such post-evangelical networks are white, middle-class graduates. It is possible that middle-class graduates who live in major urban centres are particularly exposed to cultural pluralism through their working and social lives. With greater financial and cultural capital at their disposal, members of this social class are more likely to be consumers of educational, media, and leisure resources that expose them to competing views of the world. Furthermore, members of this social class are also more likely to invest in the values of liberal democratic society, given that they are some of the leading beneficiaries of it. Taken together, this suggests that middle-class, urban-based graduates are more likely to be significantly exposed to cultural pluralism and, at the same time, to be prepared to accept that alternative views of the world have their own integrity and

---

[18] See www.reality.org.nz/articles/32/32-jamieson.html (accessed on 15 October, 2004).
[19] A. Jamieson, *A Churchless Faith: Faith Journeys Beyond the Churches* (London: SPCK, 2002).
[20] P. Richter and L. Francis, *Gone But Not Forgotten: Church Leaving and Returning* (London: Darton, Longman & Todd, 1998).

validity. Exposure to cultural pluralism, and growing regard for alternative beliefs and lifestyles, can lead to considerable dissonance for someone who has functioned on the basis of a rigid evangelical schema which delineates clearly between right and wrong. As Dave Tomlinson has described it:

> [This process] often starts with people's social attitudes, and their attitudes towards the Church sub-culture as well, rather than with theological issues. But I think it is a process that does have inevitable theological outcomes. Once someone, for example, finds that they know gay people and they actually have some sympathy with where they're coming from, although they might be trying to hold tenaciously to a conservative theological view on homosexuality, in reality there's going to be an underlying momentum of change taking place in their beliefs.[21]

The process of moving from a tight schema of religious beliefs and values towards a new and more complex religious schema is often a protracted and challenging one. In Alan Jamieson's fieldwork, some respondents described particular experiences in which they had a sudden insight that they were no longer evangelicals or that they no longer fitted within evangelical churches. For others, the process of disengagement from an evangelical schema and from involvement in evangelical churches was a gradual one, without any specific moments of crisis. For those moving away from an evangelical schema, however, Jamieson suggests there may be a common process of initially deconstructing and criticising this evangelical schema, then developing greater autonomy and self-confidence in one's experience as a basis for personal faith, and finally reconstructing a personalised religious schema drawing on a wider range of resources beyond the evangelical tradition. In many respects, the process identified by Jamieson bears close relation to models of the grieving process developed by writers such as Colin Murray Parkes and William Worden.[22] Their theories of

---

[21] Quoted in G. Lynch, *Losing My Religion? Moving on From Evangelical Faith* (London, Darton, Longman & Todd, 2003), pp. 79f.

[22] See C. Murray Parkes, *Bereavement: Studies of Grief in Adult Life* (London: Tavistock, 1972); J.W. Worden, *Grief Counselling and Grief Therapy: A Handbook for the Mental Health Practitioner* (3rd edn.; London: Brunner/Routledge, 2003).

bereavement suggest that key tasks of grieving consist of being able over time to face and contain the emotional pain associated with the loss and to deconstruct and reconstruct one's cognitive map of the world (including one's sense of personal identity) in the light of the loss. Disengaging from a tight evangelical religious schema of belief can indeed be seen as a form of bereavement. The loss of a cognitive schema through which one has interpreted the world and based one's sense of personal identity is highly significant. Further losses may also be experienced in addition to this, such as the loss of a sense of God as a loving and comforting presence, a loss of social relationships through leaving a congregation, and a loss of close friends or partners where these relationships are unable to bear an individual's move away from evangelicalism. Alternatively, it is possible to see the social and emotional difficulties of disengaging from an evangelical schema of belief in terms of the confusion faced by adult learners whose core ideas and beliefs are challenged through the learning process.[23]

Thinking about this process in terms of grieving or learning is useful in highlighting that movement away from evangelical faith is a transition between different identities and ways of understanding oneself and the world. As with the grieving process, it is possible that a person may become stuck in this transitional process and remain angry (or counter-dependent) towards evangelicalism without making significant progress toward reconstructing a personally meaningful religious worldview. Understanding this transition can also help to make partial sense, psychologically and sociologically, of why some post-church or alternative worship groups are relatively short-lived. Such groups may serve a very useful function for a period of two or three years in helping members to negotiate this transition, but may become redundant as members move on to new groups and networks as they become more confident in their new religious identities and beliefs.

The process of moving away from evangelical faith that has been described here is a deeply significant form of religious change for many individuals in Western society. Yet the terms 'conversion' or 'de-conversion' offer inadequate ways of describing or interpreting it. There is little evidence that those leaving

---

[23] See, e.g., J. Hull, *What Prevents Christian Adults From Learning?* (London: SCM, 1985).

evangelical churches are undergoing 'conversion' to another kind of faith. In Jamieson's study, only 5 per cent of his interviewees described themselves as having become agnostic, 2 per cent moved towards 'New Age' spiritualities, and 1 per cent became atheists.[24] None of his respondents converted to another major religious tradition such as Judaism or Islam. This reflects my own experience of meeting many people who have left evangelical churches and who may have developed an interest in learning more about other religious traditions (e.g. by reading the Qur'an or attending Buddhist meditation classes), but none of whom made the step of formal conversion to another faith. Even the term 'de-conversion' (or more polemical terms such as 'back-sliding' or 'loss of faith') is an inadequate way of understanding this form of religious transition. Jamieson's study, again, indicated that the vast majority of his respondents did not abandon their Christian belief in God when they left evangelical churches, nor did they spend less time on spiritually focused activities, but instead sought to find new ways of thinking about, expressing and practicing their faith.

This case example of disengaging from evangelical faith therefore provides an important illustration of a type of change in religious belief and identity that does not fit within the concept of 'conversion'. As was noted earlier in the chapter, the notion of conversion can be useful in drawing attention to certain kinds of transition across the boundaries of specific religious groups. If academic scholars of religion and leaders of faith communities focus on conversion and neglect other significant forms of religious transition that are obscured by this concept, this will lead both to impoverished understandings of religious faith and identity as well as impoverished educational and pastoral practice within faith communities.

From an academic perspective, it is important to recognise that the kind of religious transition I have described in this chapter is not unique to evangelical contexts, but is representative of wider trends of detraditionalisation in contemporary culture, in which the epistemological balance is shifting away from an emphasis on external religious authorities (e.g. the Bible, the teaching of the church) and toward a greater emphasis on the epistemic

---

[24] Jamieson, *A Churchless Faith*, p. 88.

importance of the self and personal experience.[25] Through studying a wide range of case examples of changes in religious belief and
identity beyond conversion, it will be possible to develop richer
and more complex accounts of how theories such as
detraditionalisation and sacralisation can be related meaningfully
to people's concrete experiences of personal religious change. The
notion of conversion therefore has some role to play in the academic study of the construction and reconstruction of religious
faith and identity, but it needs to be located in a more diverse and
richer theoretical framework for understanding contemporary
religious life.

For faith communities, there are important pastoral and educational issues raised by the kind of religious transition I have
described in this chapter. It is understandably hard for people
committed to an evangelical schema of belief to regard someone's
movement away from that schema in a positive light. There is considerable anecdotal evidence, however, that the way in which
evangelical ministers and congregations sometimes deal with
those who are moving away from evangelical faith can add to the
pain and complexity of that process for those involved. People
negotiating a transition away from evangelical faith need supportive relationships in which their changing faith is accepted and nurtured, and in which they are given sensitive and appropriate
guidance about resources that may help them through this
process. Even if people working in evangelical churches are unable
to provide this kind of support themselves, it is important where
possible that they could offer suggestions about spiritual direction
or counselling support outside of an evangelical context. In addition to these pastoral issues, however, the challenging interaction
between cultural pluralism and a rigid schema of religious belief
raises questions about how evangelical churches and networks
address adult theological education. Whilst some evangelical
theological colleges are engaged in an open and critical engagement with the Christian tradition in a way that allows for a more
complex evangelical cognitive schema, there is little evidence that
this is working through into adult theological education at a

---

[25] For a fuller review of the debate on detraditionalization, see P. Heelas,
S. Lash and P. Morris (eds.), *Detraditionalization* (Oxford: Blackwell,
1995).

congregational or local level. Unless evangelical churches are able to encourage more sophisticated thinking in their membership, people who are exposed to cultural pluralism in their everyday lives will continue to become disenchanted with a rigid and simplistic evangelical schema of belief.

Ultimately, then, this chapter represents an invitation to develop a richer academic language for understanding the construction and deconstruction of religious belief and identity, and more thoughtful ways of responding to religious transitions within and between faith communities. Through this process we can hope to develop more adequate and appropriate ways of interpreting and working with religious change and transition for people as they negotiate the tensions and complexities of life in contemporary culture.

3

The Word of the Buddha and Jesus, the Word

Conversions from Christianity to Buddhism and from Buddhism to Christianity

Elizabeth Harris

I don't think I ever wasn't a Buddhist. Being a Buddhist is being someone who is aware of what is happening around you and anyone who is a real Buddhist is that. I was brought up in a Christian family. And I didn't 'encounter' Buddhism. What I did do was spontaneously begin to practise meditation. Later I discovered that the form of meditation I was practising was a Buddhist form and that it had a name.[1]

The Buddhist interest is in subjective mental states. The other (Christianity) displaces subjectivity into God. I have come to believe that our fulfilment lies in just this displacement. And no matter how much we detect similarities in detail (taken out of context) we have here quite different perspectives on reality, and our highest destiny. We have The Difference. And The Difference demands A Choice.[2]

Introduction

There are numerous ways of describing conversion: a process that includes a personal decision;[3] a journey of discovery; a religious

---

[1] Helen Jandamit quoted in Elizabeth J. Harris, *What Buddhists Believe* (Oxford: Oneworld, 1998/2001), p. 175.

[2] Paul Williams, 'Out of my Head', *The Tablet* (August 5, 2000), p. 1046.

[3] E.g. Andrew Wingate, *The Church and Conversion: A Study of Recent Conversions from Christianity in the Tamil Area of South India* (Delhi: ISPCK, 1997).

emigration;[4] an experience; a cognitive choice; a re-version. Which one 'fits' depends on the person and context concerned. Almost all appear in this chapter, which will focus on conversion from Christianity to Buddhism and from Buddhism to Christianity, in the West. Within the former, I will include those who moved toward Buddhism from a nominal Christian identity or from having had a Christian upbringing. Even so, this means that much is left out. First, by concentrating on Christianity, conversions from Judaism to Buddhism are disregarded. The first Westerner on American soil to take refuge in the Buddha was a Jew, Charles Strauss, in the 1890s, and a significant number of twentieth-century Western teachers of Buddhism were born Jewish.[5] Secondly, by concentrating on the West, Christianity, and the individual, one of the most significant mass conversions to Buddhism must be omitted. On October 14, 1956, fifty-two days before his death, Dr. Bhimrao Ambedkar (1891–1956), constitutional expert and a leader of the Dalits or 'untouchables' in India, publicly converted to Buddhism, taking thousands of Dalits with him. In 1927 he had burned the *Manusmrti*,[6] and in 1935, declared that he would renounce Hinduism because of the inequality it fostered. It took him over twenty years to choose Buddhism as the religion best placed to resolve the caste issue – he rejected Christianity because Christians in India still adhered to caste. In Buddhism he found rationalism, humanism, universalism and morality.[7] Lastly, the history of

---

[4] See Albert W. Jebanesan, *Changing of the Gods: The process and experience of religious conversion among Sri Lankan Tamil refugees in London* (Delhi: ISPCK, 2003).

[5] See Rodger Kamenetz, *The Jew in the Lotus: A Poet's Discovery of Jewish Identity in Buddhist India* (Northvale, NJ: Jason Aronson, 1995), pp. 8–9. Kamenetz, for instance, mentions a roster of Buddhist scholars in America from Jewish backgrounds including: Ann Klein, Alex Wayman, Matthew Kapstein, Charles Prebish.

[6] Lit. The Laws of Manu, the most authoritative Hindu Sanskrit legal text, which lays down social, moral and ethical precepts, and ceremonial rules. It also describes the origins of caste and the duties of the four main caste groups.

[7] See, for instance, K.N. Kadam, *The Meaning of the Ambedkarite Conversion to Buddhism and other Essays* (Mumbai: Popular Prakashan, 1997), particularly pp. 40–44; Indian Bibliographic Centre (Research Wing), *Christianity and Conversion in India* (Varanasi: Rishi Publications, 1999), pp. 203–13.

conversions to Christianity from Buddhism, and to Buddhism from Christianity, in countries such as Sri Lanka and Burma, during the period of British colonial rule must also be omitted.

I shall divide the chapter into three parts: conversion to Buddhism from Christianity or a Christian upbringing; conversion from Buddhism to Christianity; and the 'conversion' that leads to hyphenated or dual identity. I shall draw on published material and interviews, drawn together over a period of ten years. When I am using material that is already published, as in the quotes at the beginning of the chapter, I shall not change the names of the individuals concerned. When using personal interviews, the names will be changed to protect privacy.

From Christianity to Buddhism

Conversion takes place against the background of the previous history of the person and that person's place in history. As Torkel Brekke points out in his survey of conversion in the time of the Buddha, 'Conversion implies movement and we cannot hope to understand it without thoroughly examining *both* the place of arrival and the place of departure in each instance.'[8] So, before looking at contemporary examples of conversion from Christianity to Buddhism, it is worth touching on the first conversions to Buddhism in the West, the historical precedents behind contemporary 'places of departure'.

Early conversions to Buddhism
The first conversions to Buddhism in the West came at the end of the nineteenth century. Darwin's theory of evolution, the growth of positivism with its assertion that science was the only true approach to understanding the world, and the growing availability of material about religions other than Christianity had led to disenchantment with Christianity and the exploration of alternatives. There were at least two key moments. The first was the

---

[8] Torkel Brekke, 'Conversion in Buddhism?', in Rowena Robinson and Sathianathan Clarke (eds.), *Religious Conversion in India: Modes, Motivations, and Meanings* (New Delhi: Oxford University Press, 2003), p. 189.

formation in America of the Theosophical Society in 1875 by the Russian mystic Helena Blavatsky (1831–91) and Colonel Henry Steel Olcott (1832–1907). It was vehemently anti-Christian and looked to the East for truth. At first this was the Near East. Then came Blavatsky's, *Isis Unveiling,* published in 1877, which turned to the wider traditions of Asia as embodiments of a liberative ancient wisdom tradition.[9] The second was Edwin Arnold's poem on the life of the Buddha, *The Light of Asia*, published in Britain in 1879, which presented the Buddha as a romantised, compassionate hero willing to give up comfort and riches for the sake of humanity. Both of these nurtured converts to Buddhism.

One reason why some early Western converts were attracted to Buddhism was that the textual version they knew appeared to offer a rational alternative to Christianity, without the cognitive problems presented by faith in a creator God. For instance, Charles Powell, a person intended for the Christian clergy, who travelled to Sri Lanka at the end of the nineteenth century to join other theosophists there, could declare, when challenged by Sri Lankan Buddhists that he had no faith:

> Buddhism requires no faith from its adherents, and makes no draft upon their credulity. It expressly states in the plainest manner that every man must use his own reason and accept only what that reason approves. On that declaration we take our stand, and we deny anybody's right to dictate what we shall believe. But we do with all our hearts and in all humility accept the Doctrine taught by our Blessed LORD (the Buddha).[10]

The appeal of the rational, however, was not the only reason for these early conversions. For some converts, Buddhism offered the possibility of wisdom with an esoteric flavour, untainted by the imperialism that was surrounding the contemporary spread of Christianity. For others, the key was compassion. For instance, Allan Bennett (1872–1923), the second British person to become a Buddhist monk, taking the name the Venerable Ananda Metteyya,

---

[9] Stephen Prothero, *The White Buddhist: The Asian Odyssey of Henry Steel Olcott* (Delhi: Sri Satguru Publications, 1996), p. 58.
[10] Helen Jandamit quoted in Elizabeth J. Harris, *What Buddhists Believe*, p. 331.

read Arnold's poem when he was eighteen. He converted to Buddhism about ten years later when he travelled to Sri Lanka and experienced Buddhism in practice there.[11] What attracted him was a mixture of the devotion of Asian Buddhists, the practice of meditation, the message of the Four Noble Truths and Buddhism's emphasis on compassion and selflessness. The core of the Buddhist path lay for him in:

> the very humblest, simplest, and most intimate of all directions that the heart of man can turn and travel in ... so does the portal of the Path stand wide for all of us just only when – though it be but for a moment – *we forget our Self; and live, aspire and work for Life at large.*[12]

Not all of these converts moved towards Buddhism from Christian commitment. For instance, although Allan Bennett's mother was a devout Roman Catholic, Bennett rejected Christianity early in life to become a spiritual explorer, working with the esoteric and the occult before Buddhism.

The attraction, therefore, that Buddhism held for Westerners at the end of the nineteenth century and the beginning of the twentieth was not the same for all converts. The same is true for the late twentieth century, and lines of continuity between the two centuries are not difficult to find.

The late twentieth century

I have found the following six factors in contemporary conversion narratives:

- recognition that one was already practicing Buddhist meditation;
- the impossibility of believing in God or Christian doctrine;
- the example of a Buddhist community or the charisma of one Buddhist;

---

[11] See Elizabeth Harris, *Ananda Metteyya: The First British Emissary of Buddhism* (Kandy, Sri Lanka: Buddhist Publication Society [The Wheel Publications No 420/422], 1998), particularly pp. 3–11.

[12] Ananda Metteyya (Allan Bennett), *The Wisdom of the Aryas* (London: Kegan Paul, Trench, Trubner & Co Ltd, 1923), pp. 125–26, quoted in Harris, *Ananda Metteyya*, p. 43.

- the appeal of meditation;
- Buddhism seen as the antidote to selfishness in a violent world;
- an experience of suffering.

One striking example of the first was given to me when I was interviewing for the BBC World Service in 1995–96 in preparation for a radio series, *The Way of the Buddha*, which then became a book, *What Buddhists Believe*. It came from a British woman, Helen Jandamit, who, when I met her, was running a House of Dhamma in Bangkok. Her words are placed at the beginning of this chapter:

> I was brought up in a Christian family. And I didn't 'encounter' Buddhism. What I did do was spontaneously begin to practise meditation. Later I discovered that the form of meditation I was practising was a Buddhist form and that it had a name. What I was doing was exactly what is taught in *vipassana* meditation but I was never taught it. This is what I mean by, 'I think I was always a Buddhist' ... I found out that it had a name when I went to the Buddhapadipa Temple in London because I wanted to find out about Buddhist meditation, not realizing that I was already doing it. They described a method of meditation that I recognized immediately.[13]

This initial experience led to her moving away from the Christian beliefs of her family towards a lifetime commitment to Buddhism. She developed her practice of Buddhist meditation and eventually travelled to Thailand because she wanted to know more than the monks at the Buddhapadipa Temple could teach her. She married and, when I interviewed her in December 1995, had been in Thailand twenty-one years, practicing and teaching Buddhism.

On the same project, I interviewed one other woman, an American, also called Helen, Helen Wilder, who had entered Buddhism through a similar experience. Whilst teaching in Malaysia, she spontaneously began to meditate without seeking to do so. Sufi teachers tried to interpret this for her theistically, but she could not bring herself to believe in God. Eventually, she read a Buddhist text: 'I came across one of the Buddha's *suttas* and in it were the

---

[13] Transcript of an interview made in December 1995. See Harris *Ananda Metteyya*, pp. 175–76.

exact words and the same wording of what I was receiving in meditation. Then, I knew it was Buddhism.'[14]

This also led her to a lifetime commitment to the point of becoming a Buddhist nun, taking the name Sr Nyanasiri. Since she moved into Buddhism from an existentialist position and did not have a Christian background, I will not say more about her. I include her to suggest that Helen Jandamit's experience is not isolated. Buddhists would interpret the experiences as the fruit of actions from a past life. In other words, both Helens were meditators in a previous life and the good fruits generated by this brought them back to Buddhism in the present.

Helen Wilder had never found belief in God possible. Maxine, in contrast, was brought up in a devout Christian Afro-Caribbean household in Britain. But eventually she also found belief in a personal God difficult. In addition, she was alienated by the homophobic attitudes she found in the church, its resistance to gay priests for example. 'But if I had believed in God, I would have stayed', she admitted. From Christianity, she moved into women's spirituality and then New Age groups. Meditation practices appealed to her, particularly because of their link with stress management. And meditation was the trigger that led her to Buddhism. Commitment to Buddhism as a doctrinal system came later. Crucial in this was the example of the Buddhist community, the *Sangha*, which she met through the meditation classes offered by the Friends of the Western Buddhist Order. It was a community that welcomed women as Order members and had nothing against gay and lesbian people. It was seeing people living by the *dhamma* that led her to what could be called conversion. 'It was a gradual process of commitment', she stresses.

For Simon Romer, it was not the community but one individual that led him to Buddhism. He is now a teacher of Tibetan language, ritual, and meditation. He told his story in an article he wrote for a book called *Meeting Buddhists*:

> I was still a Christian when I left the Northeast. I moved to the Midlands from a small coastal village just north of Whitley Bay in order to study English at Birmingham University. That was the official reason anyway. My actual intention, however, was to be a rock star and I

---

[14] Ibid.

supposed that a university campus would prove a fertile ground for like-minded talent.[15]

I was serious about my religion. I had sung in the church choir since I was eight, but my commitment was far more than that of a reluctant choir boy. Following confirmation, I took myself down to the church a half-hour before the service began in order to settle down and pray. I studied the Bible every day and my young life revolved around the church. The vicar was a regular guest at family birthday parties. Rather crossly I found myself thinking: 'I bet I end up a vicar myself.' I had no doubts.

As I grew older, however, I began to sense that some questions could not be answered, or more to the point, that some questions couldn't even be asked. I shut those questions out and tried to forget them.

I will never know now if I could have remained a Christian if I had had suitable guidance at this time, but at university we were encouraged to think, to explore and to challenge. Walking up the Bristol Road in Selly Oak one day, I felt my entire Christian faith drop away in the course of half a minute. Completely.

I was not looking for an alternative but I became particularly drawn by the quality and approach of one of our lecturers. His intelligence and wonder resonated with me and although I had no name for it, I knew that this was good enough for me. It turned out that he was the first Buddhist I had ever met.[16]

In the cases of Maxine and Simon, Christian faith had dropped away before the encounter with Buddhism. For both, it was the example of Buddhists that raised their interest in the religion and nurtured commitment.

For the Venerable Santikaro, a charismatic teacher also played a part in his conversion, but the main trigger was meditation The context was not stress management, as in Maxine's case, but an experience of the selfishness and corruption present in society. He joined the US Peace Corps after graduating from college, wanting to see the world and to find something to write about. He chose Thailand, 'partly because it was a different religious context'.[17] Speaking to me in 1995, he said:

---

[15] Simon Romer, 'The Buddha: A Personal Reflection', in Elizabeth J. Harris and Ramona Kauth (eds.), *Meeting Buddhists* (Leicester: Christians Aware, 2004), p. 94.

[16] Kauth and Harris, *Meeting Buddhists*.

[17] Harris, *Ananda Metteyya*, p. 177.

I came to Thailand as a Christian but then I slowly came into contact
with Buddhist meditation, Buddhist teachings, especially those of the
monk who eventually became my teacher, Buddhadasa Bhikkhu.[18]
But there were also other teachers such as Ajahn Chah.[19] Meditation
and some of the teachings helped me deal with some of the difficulties
I was experiencing in Peace Corps – government corruption, loneli-
ness, having a hot western temper in a culture where that's totally
unacceptable.[20]

After his stint as a Peace Corps volunteer, in 1985 he decided to
become a temporary Buddhist monk, a *bhikkhu,* before returning
to graduate school. The temporary commitment, however,
became permanent. He is still a monk. His relationship with his
teacher, Buddhadasa Bhikkhu, played an important part in this,
but so did awareness of social inequalities and the conviction that
Buddhism had something to offer:

The thing which really affected me in my later Peace Corps work was
the corruption. I was a school teacher but also working in the villages.
I was aware of selfishness – the selfishness of government workers
who took a salary and perks but did very little of service to society and
also the factionalism in the villages which got in the way of people
getting together and solving their problems. I also noticed that I was
selfish in pushing my ideas. It had to be my way. The selfishness I saw
everywhere became a major theme for me. And I have discovered in
Buddhism practical ways to cope with this.[21]

---

[18] The Venerable Buddhadasa (1906–93) was one of the most influential
Thai monks of the twentieth century. He established a forest monastery,
Suan Mokkh, where The Venerable Santikaro eventually stayed. His
teachings became the platform for reformist Buddhism in the country.
His was an engaged Buddhism that took inter-faith dialogue seriously.

[19] The Venerable Ajahn Chah (1918–92) was a Thai monk in the forest
tradition who founded Wat Pah Pong, to which Westerners eventually
came. The founding of Wat Pah Nanachat (International Forest Monastery) followed. It was through Ajahn Chah's Western pupils that
Chithurst Monastery and Amaravati Monastery were established in
England. See Amaravati Publications, *Seeing the Way: Buddhist Reflections on the Spiritual Life by English-speaking Disciples of Ajahn Chah*
(Hemel Hempstead, 1989).

[20] Harris, *Ananda Metteyya*, p. 177.

[21] Ibid.

What Buddhism had to offer the Venerable Santikaro were methods of mind culture designed to cut through and transform selfishness. It was this that also eventually convinced the Venerable Karma Lekshe Tsomo, an American Buddhist nun in the Tibetan tradition, editor of many books on Buddhism and Women,[22] and Secretary of Sakyadhita, an International Association of Buddhist Women. She was born into a strict Baptist family, but began to read about Zen as a child. 'From the beginning', she wrote in 1995, 'Buddhism struck me as a convincing view of life.'[23] At the age of eleven, she declared to her mother that she was a Buddhist, but she continued to attend church, adopting those Christian teachings that she could relate to.[24] She found much that was beautiful, but not the answers to life and death that she was seeking. She travelled – in Japan, Vietnam, Cambodia, India, Nepal, and beyond – and eventually made an adult choice for Buddhism because of its teaching on the eradication of such things as greed, hatred, jealousy and arrogance.[25]

The Buddhist view of life and the spiritual path are summed up in the Four Noble Truths. The first is the Noble Truth of dukkha. Dukkha has been translated as suffering, but its meaning is wider. Many Buddhists prefer the word 'unsatisfactoriness'. The first Noble Truth points to the fact that at the heart of existence is unsatisfactoriness. We are born, grow old and die. Nothing that we own, not even our own bodies, is permanent. We are separated from those we love and yoked with those we do not love.

An experience of dukkha is what has drawn some people towards Buddhism. It might be the death of a loved one, the disintegration of hopes for the future, or witnessing the suffering of others in war or natural disaster. Moira's experience is paradigmatic. She was born into a nominal Anglican family and attended

---

[22] For example: *Buddhist Women Across Cultures: Realizations* (Albany, NY: State University of New York Press, 1999); *Innovative Buddhist Women: Swimming Against the Stream* (Richmond: Curzon, 2000).

[23] Karma Lekshe Tsomo, 'Creating Cross-Cultural Spiritual Identity', in Martin Forward (ed.), *Ultimate Visions: Reflections on the Religions We Choose* (Oxford: Oneworld, 1995), p. 275.

[24] Ibid.

[25] Ibid., p. 276.

a Roman Catholic school. The effect of this was that she ran away from religion. Then, in her thirties, an experience of dukkha came. Rather than return to her Christian roots, she found the answer in the message of Buddhism's Four Noble Truths, which she saw as rational and realistic. For the Truths do not stop with the fact of dukkha. They go on to pinpoint a cause – our craving and our obsession with the self, our greed, hatred and delusion – and to declare that dukkha will end if this cause is removed. The last Truth is the Noble Eightfold Path, which maps out the practice necessary for this, one that combines moral living with the kind of meditation that works on the mind to eradicate the roots of suffering.

For all the people I have mentioned, Christianity failed. For some the stumbling block was belief in a creating and sustaining God. For others Christianity seemed to offer no rational explanation of suffering and evil. Yet others found nothing in Christianity to help them overcome negative qualities within themselves such as selfishness and anger. Claire Disbrey, in her accessible book, *Listening to People of Other Faiths*, offers another factor: an unwillingness among Christians to explore and tolerate dissent. Of her two examples of people who turned to Buddhism after becoming disillusioned with Christianity, one spoke of the 'dogma and regulations, shoulds and shouldn'ts' of her Catholic upbringing. 'My own questioning', she declared, 'was seen as a disruptive force ... so that every query was met with a static, fossilised kind of response'.[26]

Conversions from Buddhism to Christianity

Naomi was invited to a Mahayana Buddhist centre by a friend when she was nineteen. She had had a Roman Catholic upbringing but was not sure where to find God. The friendliness of the people attracted her, as did the peace that seemed to flow from them. She then moved to a Soka Gakkai group, where the main practice was chanting. Moving onwards again, convinced she was a Buddhist,

---

[26] Vagisvari, a member of the Western Buddhist Order, quoted in Claire Disbrey, *Listening to People of Other Faiths* (Oxford: The Bible Reading Fellowship, 2004), p. 116.

she joined the Rajneesh Movement, whose guru, Bhagwan Shree Rajneesh, claimed to draw on Zen Buddhism. For three years she stayed, trusting Rajneesh's promises that she would be led to ultimate truth. By this time, she was thirty. Then, she was invited to a Christian service. Prayers were said for her and she had an overwhelming sense of being made clean. She says of the experience, 'I was cleansed. There was no guilt. There was no need to be ashamed anymore. I was told the blood of Jesus had cleansed me completely and that is what I felt.'

The cleansing involved freedom from some of the hurts and pain that had been there from childhood and also from what she calls 'bad spirits'. She recognises that such healing is an ongoing process, a journey not yet completed. For Naomi, Buddhism failed. 'I had tried to sort out my problems through it', she insists, 'but only more problems came. I would not go back.' Healing came when she allowed the power of the divine 'other' touch her.

Paul Williams made a public conversion to Roman Catholicism from Buddhism in 1999, after practicing Vajrayana Buddhism for twenty years. He is the Professor of Indian and Tibetan Buddhism at Bristol University. In a popular version of his conversion printed in *The Tablet*, he explained how this happened:

> I was converted by Cardinal Ratzinger of the Congregation for the Doctrine of the Faith. Oh yes, I remember it well. I was picked up from the station on my way to a Buddhist meeting. Had I heard that outrageous comment of Ratzinger? The comment about Buddhism being a form of spiritual auto-eroticism? I had not, but Ratzinger (I explained) is a reactionary. No need to worry. That's not really what Catholics think of Buddhism … We drove on in silence. But not the Noble Silence of the Buddha. The trouble was (unlike just about everyone else) I knew exactly what Ratzinger was talking about. He had put into words The Difference. And that difference worried me.[27]

The trigger for Williams was not a 'religious experience' of cleansing or the living witness of a practitioner. It was cognitive. A phrase from a Christian leader struck home and forced him to see a deficiency in Buddhism that demanded a choice. And that deficiency centered, as with Naomi, on 'own-power', the power of the

---

[27] Williams, 'Out of my head', p. 1046.

self, and 'other-power', the power of the divine outside oneself. In other words, Ratzinger's words led him to judge Buddhism's emphasis on 'own-power' as inadequate:

> Buddhism is all about the mind. Mental states are essentially subjective. Buddhism takes as its starting point states of consciousness ... But wait. That may be true of Buddhism, but Catholicism is not all about the mind at all. The Christian religion is all about God, and the salvific actions of God through Christ. Instead of reducing everything to forms of subjectivity – my experiences – everything, but everything, reduces to God. And to the family of God.[28]

Paul converted to Christianity because he was convinced intellectually that the God of Christian faith was the reality, as the quote at the beginning of this chapter indicates. His conversion flowed less from experience than from cognitive assurance and observation of the Christian community, 'the community of those who express that salvation in their lives'.[29] Buddhism had failed for him because it did not speak of God and salvation through grace.

It is significant here that the very factor that drove some converts to Buddhism away from Christianity brought Naomi and Paul to Christianity: belief in or experience of the power of God.

Dual Belonging

For people such as the Venerable Santikaro and Paul Williams, the difference between Buddhism and Christianity demanded a choice. As the reality of one arose, the other dropped away and a new religious belonging was necessary. For Naomi, the experience of cleansing and healing in Christianity convinced her she could never go back to Buddhism. Is this, though, the only option? In the field of Buddhist-Christian relationships, and indeed Buddhist-Jewish relationships,[30] it is not. A growing number of practicing Christians who have encountered Buddhism in depth have not

---

[28] Ibid.

[29] Ibid.

[30] See Harold Kasimow, John P. Keenan and Linda Klepinger Keenan, *Beside Still Waters: Jews, Christians, and the Way of the Buddha* (Boston: Wisdom, 2003), which deals with Jews and Christians who have come close to Buddhism.

converted to the religion, but have drawn something of 'the other' into themselves. In other words, a single religious identity became impossible after contact with Buddhism. The phenomenon has been labelled 'dual belonging', 'hyphenated identity', or 'religious bilingualism', and it occurs far more frequently among those originally Christian than Buddhist.

A key question here is how the differences between the two religions are dealt with. Are they brought into synthesis? Are they transcended? Are they brought into dialogue with each other within the mind? There are a number of models. Ana Schluter is a Zen master and a member of a Catholic religious order. At a presentation she gave at the Parliament of the World's Religions in Barcelona in July 2004, she said:

> The Zen Buddhist and the Christian language are different, but if somebody 'speaks' them authentically, they do not exclude each other. On the contrary, you realize more and more that the fundamental human experience that Zen Buddhism emphasizes reminds Christianity of the roots to be authentic, and the fundamental human experience that Christianity emphasizes reminds Zen Buddhism of the fruits that manifest a true experience of emptiness.[31]

The model here is one of a complementarity that brings greater wholeness to each religion through the influence of the other. Zen can help Christians root its activism in meditation and silence. Christianity can help Zen Buddhists see that an awareness of the emptiness and interconnectedness of all things should lead to acting with compassion. A similar paradigm was in the mind of Peter, a Catholic monk, who told me that he considered himself 'a 100% Christian and a 100% Buddhist'.

Roman Catholic Maria Reis Habito, in an article, 'On Becoming a Buddhist Christian' explains that her first experience of Buddhism was in Taiwan in the late 1970s, when she met a Buddhist nun who had said, 'Buddhists or Christians – it does not make the slightest difference. We are all brothers and sisters.'[32] On a future

---

[31] Ana Schluter, 'Religious Bilingualism', unpublished text given on July 11, 2004, at the Parliament of the World's Religions, Barcelona (7–13 July 2004).

[32] Maria Reis Habito, 'On Becoming a Buddhist Christian', in Kasimow et al., *Beside Still Waters*, p. 203.

visit, to study Chinese language and culture, she met Master Hsin Tao (Shih-fu) and was struck by the radiance of his eyes. She learnt that he believed they had a karmic connection from a previous life. This led to her taking the Triple Refuge in his presence and later to Zen practice under the Jesuit, Father Enomiya Lasalle and others. She finishes the article realising that the process is far from its conclusion:

> My encounter with Buddhism and my close connection to my Buddhist teachers, Shih-fu and Yamada Roshi, have not uprooted me from Christian ground. On the contrary, my Buddhist teachers, together with Father Enomiya Lasalle, have done everything possible to fertilize these roots and to let them grow stronger and deeper. They have taught me how to water them and how to deal with the weeds. They have taught me how to put the knowledge of God from my head into my heart. My deepest gratitude to all of them.[33]

A slightly different model is present here: Buddhism influencing personal practice so that one's Christianity becomes more authentic.

My own encounter has been with Theravada Buddhism. Between 1986 and 1993, I immersed myself in Buddhism in Sri Lanka in an attempt to see the world through Buddhist eyes. The experience changed the path of my life. It was not easy and produced no simple answers about religious choice or religious identity. I would not call myself a Buddhist-Christian. Rather I am a Christian who draws deeply from the wells of Buddhist wisdom. In 2002, I wrote:

> A true crossing over involves immersion in the totality of another tradition, even in what might contradict one's own. Perhaps the most important thing is that the journey continues. Buddhism has given me more than I could have dreamed. At the same time, I am still a Christian. Both are languages of the spirit. They converge in remarkable and life-affirming ways. However, the differences between them remain. They lie, in creative tension, within me.[34]

---

[33] Ibid., p. 213.

[34] Elisabeth Harris 'The Beginning of Something Being Broken: The Cost of Crossing Spiritual Boundaries', in *Spirituality Across Borders* (Oxford: The Way Supplement, 2002/104), pp. 6–17, particularly p. 17.

This is yet another model.

A position on the Buddhist side that touches the three that I have mentioned above is that of Thich Nhat Hanh (1926–), Vietnamese Buddhist monk in exile in Europe, Zen master, founder of Plum Village in France, and pioneer of engaged Buddhism. He encountered what he calls 'the beauty of Jesus' teachings'[35] not in Vietnam but in America in the 1960s, through friendships with people such as Martin Luther King, Dutch woman Hebe Kohlbrugge and Heinz Kloppenburg. The experience led him to draw something of Christianity into himself and to explore the touching points between the two religions. He could write in 1995 after speaking of his friendship with these Christians:

> On the altar of my hermitage in France are images of Buddha and Jesus, and every time I light incense, I touch both of them as my spiritual ancestors. I can do this because of contact with these real Christians. When you touch someone who authentically represents a tradition, you not only touch his or her tradition, you also touch your own.[36]

Related to this but not identical is the experience of some of the converts to Buddhism in this chapter, who, over time, have found that they were able to look with more understanding and sympathy on the religion they had rejected. This is the case with Moira, who after a Buddhist commitment of several decades, is now able to see Christianity in a far more positive light than in her youth. She is much involved in inter-faith activity as a representative of her Theravada Buddhist centre and does not feel alienated by a Christian act of worship. As for Karma Lekshe Tsomo, she found, after becoming a Buddhist nun, that she was drawn back into contact with her Christian roots through inter-monastic dialogue when she was invited to meet some Benedictine contemplatives in Dharamsala, India. She found their open-mindedness made 'communication on a very deep level possible', leading to friendships that have continued down the years.[37]

---

[35] Thich Nhat Hanh, *Living Buddha, Living Christ* (London, Sydney, Auckland, Johannesburg: Rider,1995), p. 5.
[36] Ibid., pp. 6–7.
[37] Tsomo, 'Creating Cross-Cultural Spiritual Identity', p. 277.

Concluding Thoughts

According to Brekke, the paradigmatic elements of Buddhist conversion are: 'the rapid and overwhelming realisation that life is suffering and the dramatic break with life in the world to seek salvation'.[38] He continues to argue that the early texts of the Theravada canon present a much more complex picture than this. The appeal of rational argument is combined with the effect of a charismatic teacher, and volition is combined with determinism. This chapter has shown that these factors are still at work, drawing people to Buddhism, expressed in a different context and era. Added to this, in the case of movement from Christianity to Buddhism, are perceived failings in the Christian worldview and Christian practice, particularly in relation to theism and mental culture. Where the convert was coming from was just as important as where they arrived. And the remarkable stories of the spontaneous practice of Buddhist meditation must not be forgotten.

Accounts of conversion to Christianity often focus on personal experience. Naomi fits classically into this. Paul does not. His conversion was rooted in the cognitive. But again, where both came from was a decisive factor in where they both arrived.

The narratives in this chapter invite much more analysis and reflection than a short article allows. All I have done is touch the surface of movements that reach into the heart of what it is to be human.

---

[38] Brekke, 'Conversion in Buddhism?', p. 188.

4

Becoming Pagan Having Been Christian

Graham Harvey

In an article on Maori religion that contains my favourite definition of religion, Te Pakaka Tawhai provides a model of how scholars might write about their own religion.[1] He writes of the sense of
danger that he may be misunderstood and insists that his presentation of Maori traditional knowledge and religious activity is
moulded by the given purpose of explaining such matters to outsiders. Since this is not the purpose of Maori religious activity, he is
worried that it may distort the telling and the understanding.
Nonetheless, he is not seduced into converting Maori religion into
something entirely alien to the experience of his people, Ngati
Uepohatu (a Maori *iwi*, perhaps 'tribe', on the east coast of
Aotearoa, New Zealand) and other Maori. Such people are familiar with speech making that refers to traditional knowledge and
religious activity. They expect an orator on a *marae* (meeting
place) or in a *wharenui* (meeting house) to bring such discourses
and practices to bear on contemporary, particular, contingent,
and even everyday concerns. So, Tawhai takes traditional knowledge and oratorical themes (sometimes labeled 'myths') and uses
them to say something about the forms by which 'Maori religion'

---

[1] Te Pakaka Tawhai, 'Maori Religion', in Stewart Sutherland and Peter
Clarke (eds.), *The Study of Religion, Traditional and New Religion*
(London: Routledge, 1988), pp. 96–105, reprinted in Graham Harvey
(ed.), *Readings in Indigenous Religions* (London: Continuum, 2002), pp.
237–49.

is conveyed and expressed among his Maori relatives and friends. The point of my reference to Tawhai's work is that I have a similar concern. Pagans (contemporary practitioners of a nature centred spirituality) do not typically engage in evangelism, do not seek or expect converts, and only rarely tell one another how they became Pagans. On the other hand, Pagans do often explain elements of their tradition to outsiders. The question, like that confronting Tawhai, is how one makes such explanation fit in with the more usual kinds of Pagan discourse and practice. It is also important to face the difficulty of saying something about Paganism without suggesting that one is saying everything about it or that one is speaking for all Pagans.

I have felt tempted to provide an account of my own path out of Christianity and into Paganism. More accurately, I would have to describe a path that was simultaneously a leaving and an arrival. While it probably took me some years of small steps departing from Christianity (first shifting from one denomination to another, then seeking a different kind of Christian practice and understanding altogether), those very same steps are now visible to me as Pagan steps. There was no 'Damascus Road' experience, no sudden revelation, no abrupt transformation. Although there was a moment when I realised I had ceased being Christian, the fact that I had become a Pagan only dawned on me later. Furthermore, discovering that I had been Pagan for some time did not reveal to me the moment at which the transition had occurred. In fact, I am fairly sure that there is no single moment – as if between steps on my life's journey – where the change occurred. Like many Pagans, my sense is that I 'came home' to the knowledge that much of what has always appealed to me – and sometimes satisfied, intrigued and inspired me – has always been Pagan. I can now survey that phase of my life when I considered myself and was considered by others to be a Christian and recognise some desires, affinities and even practices that are recognisably Pagan (too). This is not to say that I was a heretic, although perhaps towards the end I became that. It is to acknowledge that Paganism overlaps considerably with many other religions, philosophies, worldviews and life-ways. There is little or nothing that is uniquely Pagan except the whole package deal. And even that varies in the mix celebrated and lived by particular Pagans. As I say, I have been tempted to narrate my life story. While I could justify this by the verifiable assertion that my 'coming home' to Paganism is an entirely typical Pagan experience or realisation, anything more than this sketch would be entirely personal and of interest only to myself. However, to tell this story would not be to say anything about Paganism and might, rather, offer the misleading impression that Paganism is a confessional religion.

The one fact so far noted that is entirely of a piece with Pagan practice and discourse is the affirmation of 'coming home'. This should resonate with the implications of terms like 'ecology', 'indigenous', 'spirit of place', and, perhaps, 'Earth Mother'. Words like these suggest something of what Pagans are engaged in and enthused by. The implication that Paganism is, like other religions, a walk or path, a journey or way, finds roots (and routes) here too. Among journeys that have destinations, Paganism seeks to find 'home' and to know how to live there with grace, gratitude and respect. Unlike many other religions where 'home' is elsewhere, in Paganism 'home' is here, in this small blue-green planet, in each person's dwelling place and environment. If this is what 'ecology' means (the study of home and dwelling places), it is also what 'Pagan' means: living respectfully in a place. But such explanations, again, are slippery, tempting us away from the kind of stories Pagans tell around fires, in seasonal ceremonies or environmentalist actions, or in pub gatherings and initiatory rituals. I have chosen, then, to imitate a bit more of what Tawhai does in his article: I summarise some Pagan stories that may be told for a host of purposes. For this time only, I use them to say something about becoming Pagan and leaving Christianity.

Specifically, I discuss three questions asked at key moments in three stories of quests for the Holy Grail. These legends are told in many forms, arising from a rich historical literature and touching many other mythologies. They have become sources of entertainment as film-makers have seen their visual and narrative potential. They have inspired ritual enactments that serve initiatory and bonding purposes (i.e. they touch individuals and groups). They are claimed by members of more than a few religions since, having attained 'classic' status, they are available for anyone to appropriate, interpret, contextualise and elaborate. I am not about to argue that they were first told by Pagans because I am fairly certain that they were not. Although I do not find the question of origins particularly interesting, I am thoroughly engaged by questions about uses, ramifications and elaborations. Anyway, my purpose is better served by the recognition that what began as entirely Christian stories can be told with equal pleasure (if different understanding) by Pagans. Very little change in the telling or dramatisation is required, more matters of emphasis and implication.

The Question of Purpose

In the various tellings of Perceval's story, the young knight fails to ask a question when he sees a procession bearing the Grail past him. This seems the more remarkable because he and the other knights of Arthur's royal court are supposed to be on a quest to find that Grail. It is not just that he is overawed by the experience, as if he was confronted by the life-changing kind of experience Rudolf Otto calls 'numinous',[2] but because he is obeying his mother's instruction not to ask questions. Otto taught humility and self-effacement, as did Perceval's mother. However, a question was needed. Precisely what that question should have been varies as different authorities tell the story to suit their purposes. He could have asked about the meaning of the procession or the nature of his host's illness. The former is a question about the nature of the Grail; the latter knows what the Grail is for (healing in this telling) but offers compassionate sympathy to the afflicted. In another telling, the Grail question is 'Who does the Grail serve?'

Pagans, Christians, Humanists, Baha'is and many other people are able to ask questions that seek justice, liberty and/or morality. Similarly, their religious traditions may inspire them all, equally, to seek the well-being of others, to provoke them to offer compassion, or to engage in activism for particular causes. There is nothing in this aspect of the Grail story that is uniquely Christian or Pagan or anything else. The paths that seek improvements in

---

[2] Rudolf Otto, *The Idea of the Holy* (New York, NY: Oxford University Press, 1968). Melissa Raphael, *Rudolf Otto and the Concept of Holiness* (Oxford: Clarendon, 1997).

people's well-being are the common ground of humanity. I believe that C.S. Lewis somewhere alleges that 'imitating nature' is no basis for an ethical system and that divine revelation is required to lift us from mere and brutish animality. Whether or not this was Lewis's view, it is inadequate not only because it relies too heavily on a particular (nasty and simplistic) kind of Darwinism, but also because it underestimates the abilities of humans and other animals to act well towards one another. Even if it were not wrong in these ways, it is certainly wrong in imputing to those who's religions do not rely on alleged revelations an attempt to 'imitate nature' as theists might attempt to imitate their deities. All of this is to say that Pagans and Christians may walk together and appear indistinguishable in questioning the value of facets of contemporary life, challenging those who benefit from the status quo and proffering solutions that may benefit others. It is, however, likely that for most Pagans today, the process of becoming Pagan entails a growing appreciation of what kind of questions are most Pagan, what domains of justice are most Pagan, and so on. They are likely to find themselves engaged, to one degree or another, in questions that might be labelled 'environmentalist'. It is not at all that ecology is of no interest to Christians, or that it has no place in Christianity, but that it has a central place, near the heart of being Pagan. Perhaps, then, questions in this area have a call on Pagans that they do not on Christians. In my own experience, and that of many other Pagans, part of the process of becoming Pagan and leaving Christianity was a sense of frustration at the marginality and inadequacy of environmentalism in Christianity.

A second thread is discernible in the question of Perceval. It is worth considering the possibility that Perceval's mother taught him not to ask questions because she deemed this to be polite behaviour and good etiquette. At the centre of any communal, social way of life it is possible to find notions about appropriate ways of meeting, greeting and treating others. Usually these aspects of a culture's etiquette are unspoken, taken-for-granted and assumed. Children, like Perceval, may have to be told how to behave when entering wider society. Christian denominations have long traditions of teaching particular ways of addressing the divine, exemplified in discourses about confession and prayer (whether to do them, how to do them, who to do them for, to whom to address them, etc.). While Paganism draws on ancient resources, it is still young in this regard. Pagans are still finding fitting ways of addressing significant other-than-human persons around them. In the transition from a modernity rooted in Protestantism and the Enlightenment toward a Paganism infused by the flavours of more ancient and more indigenous cultures, the question of etiquette is likely to become more urgent. At present, most Pagans continue to enact ceremonies influenced by the traditions of high ritual magic or esotericism. For all their distinctive colour, these practices are continuous with the wider modern culture. For example, they continue to privilege spirit over matter, intent over action, ideas over forms, discourse over performance, meaning over doing, inner over outer, will over embodiment, and so on. Similarly, the underlying unity of the divine and a degree of pantheism are clearly referenced in many Pagan ceremonies. However, there are signs that a more radical polytheism and/or an even more pluralistic animism is growing. Pagans who once bid 'hail and welcome' and later 'hail and farewell' to the 'Spirit of Place' may now say 'hello' to 'all those who live in this place'. Pagans who once viewed trees as symbols richly associated with corresponding colours, directions, moods, purposes, goals, and so on, may now address particular oaks, ashes, yews, and so on as respected co-inhabitants of particular places. I think it is possible to discern in these and similar moves, some steps away from Christianity and its tutelage toward something that is more closely akin to the pre-Christian traditions of Europe and elsewhere.

However, the importance of questioning and of etiquette is small in comparison to another issue raised by Perceval's question. It is commonplace to note that Christianity is a religion of belief, so much so that it is frequently referred to as a 'faith'. (Other religions have now adopted this discourse, or have been so labelled, but with little or no justification.) If belief plays a central role in the construction and maintenance of Christian identities, pervading the entirety of Christian discourse and praxis, its correlative, doubt, is equally significant. If Christians are supposed to believe certain teachings about God, Christ, salvation, and so on, doubting the veracity of these teachings, or particular understandings of them, is at least partially generative of the diversity of ways of being Christian. It is almost certain that doubt must play a part in anyone's departure from the Christian path. There is nothing automatic in that process: doubt and the questioning that it provokes may well reinforce or establish stronger faith. One mechanism that seems to ensure that doubt plays this supporting role in Christianity is doubt's twin, guilt. Doubt alone may lead to theological reflection, philosophical clarification and apologetic precision. Guilt prevents doubt transgressing too far beyond the boundaries of what is thinkable, do-able, or appropriate. If nothing else, this demonstrates that Christianity is not 'merely' a set of teachings, dogma, or creeds treated as ideas. Guilt arises because Christianity, like other religions, is relational. To question the core teaching of one's denomination or of scripture is to doubt one's teachers and, ultimately, one's deity and putative saviour. Guilt is the whistle of doubt's safety valve that calls for immediate measures to rebuild one's relationships and one's faith. Nothing in Perceval's story suggests doubt. In fact, he suffers guilt because of a failure to ask questions. Nonetheless, the entanglement of questioning, faith, doubt and guilt in Christianity deserve some reflection. If it has seemed necessary to devote some space to the point, this grows from a feeling that inadequate attention is paid to doubt in regard to Christian identities and performances. More to the point, doubt is almost certainly party to the process by which some people have left Christianity to become Pagans.

On more than one occasion I have heard Pagans who have previously been Christians suggesting the establishment of a 'Christians Anonymous' group. This joke derives almost entirely from two perceptions held by many ex-Christian Pagans. First, many such people talk about the necessity of dealing with guilt in order to feel free to leave the Christian path. Secondly, some of these people consider that baggage carried out of Christianity slowed down their engagement with what they come to consider Paganism to be about. The first issue says more about Christianity than about Paganism. As if to reinforce this, it may be noted that Jews who become Pagan rarely consider themselves to be ex-Jews or suggest that their transition was much to do with belief or doubt. This is not to say that other, more orthodox Jews would welcome the affirmation of ancient Israelite Goddesses alongside the God of Israel, but that some people affirm the possibility and satisfaction of a Jewish and Pagan identity. That this is so may be related to the second perception arising from the 'Christians Anonymous' joke. Pagans are rarely, if ever, bothered by questions of belief. It is entirely possible to mix with Pagans of differing paths (e.g. Druids, Witches, Heathens, Goddess-feminists) without much concern about whether any deity is a 'real' one. Pagan writers regularly list possibilities such as that deities may exist as beings in their own right (much as hedgehogs do), that they are symbols of natural and/or cultural processes, that they are archetypes of psychological processes, and more. Similarly, the question of the number of existing deities is of only small importance to many Pagans. Options vary from one to many, and from two to none. (That is, some Pagans 'believe in' a single creative deity; others are radically polytheist; some affirm the existence of a male and a female deity – perhaps manifesting an underlying unity, perhaps eternally co-existent, perhaps entirely symbolic – while others see no need or evidence of deities at all.) It is not only possible for Pagans with different understandings of these matters to celebrate together, but it is quite common for Pagans to suggest different understandings as they participate in different kinds of discourse or practice. Theological belief, creedal affirmation and dogmatic teaching play little, if any, role in any contemporary Paganism. If beliefs are rarely debated, doubt and guilt play no role at all in Pagan discourse. Any Pagan doubting the reality of a deity can be an atheist Pagan. A Pagan doubting the efficacy of a way of doing magic, or of magic itself, can develop a different method or even jettison the idea that magic is a necessary part of Paganism. I imagine that there may come a point where someone feels that they have left Paganism behind, but I doubt that they will experience guilt in the process.

In various ways, the first Grail question is about purpose. This has generated a series of short reflections about activism, etiquette and doubt in Christianity and Paganism. The next question reveals another turn of the spiral.

The Question of Passions

The second Grail question is told in the story of Gawain and the Loathly Lady (the popularity of which is attested by the multiple versions that survive). For a variety of complex reasons which need not matter here, Gawain faces a trial that will affect the rest of Arthur's Court. He has to go on a quest to answer the question, 'what do women most desire?' The answer he finds and presents to the Court is that women desire obedience. What they desire is that their desires should be acknowledged, honoured and satisfied. However, it is not enough that Gawain braves the wilderness and the seasons as he collects answers that inform and form his report to the Court. When he does return to announce his success, he is put to the test: is he merely parroting an answer or will he act on it? For Gawain, this test takes the form of the eponymous 'Loathly Lady' or hideous hag and her desire for marriage. The Court is at stake, but so, too, is Gawain's reputation. In private, Gawain is presented with a choice of whether the lady will use her transformative powers to be beautiful at night when they are alone in the bedroom but hideous and uncouth when they are in public, or vice versa. When Gawain asks the Loathly Lady to make that choice herself, he demonstrates that he has really learnt the lesson of his quest. He willingly accedes to women's desires.

It is not the precise nature or content of women's desires that is important in my reflections on leaving Christianity and becoming Pagan. Nor is it precisely the question of feminism. It is possible to be a Christian feminist or a Pagan feminist and celebrate or oppose similar issues, ideas and acts. There are significant communities of Christians and of Pagans that define themselves as feminist, as women's groups addressing women's concerns, values and desires for the world. It may well be that feminism fits more easily within Paganism, or some branches of Paganism, than within most types of Christianity. There is, for instance, no great burden imposed by inheriting the use of male pronouns to refer to the divine. It is probably still the case that the majority of Pagans use 'the Goddess' as an easy, everyday reference to deity – even when some of them mean what others would mean if they said 'Goddesses and Gods' or even 'all living beings'. (This may be changing as polytheism and animism become stronger within Paganism, perhaps overtaking pantheism and monotheism.) It is, however, entirely possible for Christian feminists to speak in the same ways about deity as Pagan feminists do. Certainly some people reach a point along the Christian path where they become exhausted by talking against the grain of the tradition merely to be inclusive. Some certainly decide that the burden is unnecessary and prevents engagement with more vital issues. Some, then, do leave Christianity because Paganism can make it easy to speak inclusively and so get on with the larger implications of acts of justice.

There is more to it than this, however. The question of women's desires is wrapped up in the first Grail question, 'who does it serve?' Who is served by the diminishment of desire in authoritative Christian discourses? Who is served by the focus on desires in normative rituals of repentance and penitence? Who is served by the easy link made between women, desire, and sin in traditional Christian theologies? Again, Christian feminists can and do challenge these master narratives. For many of us ex-Christian Pagans, it is remarkable to see this happening. We may respect the attempt to change the tradition from within, and we suspect that, as outsiders, we are likely to provoke a deeper entrenchment of whatever we might oppose. Perhaps we have not been brave or persistent enough, but we do wonder if that struggle is worthwhile. The second Grail question encourages us to face our desires, to own them and to seek their fulfilment.

Just to talk about desire is to challenge the inheritance of the fathers and apostles. In telling Gawain's tale, the storytellers reached toward the limits of Christianity and pointed toward the fertile soil in which Paganism would grow. In various forms of Christianity, the world and embodiment are rejected and vilified in favour of something transcendent and spiritual. In contemporary Paganism these entangled aspects of materiality are found to be loci of liberation. The Pagan revival began among poets, novelists and storytellers for whom nature (earth, moon, seasons, bodies, desires, passions) was a fecund womb of valued possibilities repressed by wider culture. Whatever the first self-identified Pagans in recent centuries thought they were doing, they inspired others to seek their desires in relationship with nature. Gerald Gardner ('father of modern witchcraft') and Ross Nichols (founder of the Order of Bards, Ovates and Druids), for example, shared a passion for both naturism and naturalism. Not many Pagans now follow this example too closely, but neither have many found any reason to jettison the notion that a celebration of nature might, indeed should, include a celebration of embodiment. Elsewhere I have argued that ultimately Paganism may be characterised as an affirmation of life in all its ordinariness, its messy and profligate diversity, and its excess.[3] Paganism is not always an ecstatic religion, any more than it is always an ecological one, but there is something at its core that calls its practitioners toward the kind of activist and embodied engagements that Shaw calls 'ecoerotic'.[4] Whether they are attracted by celebrations of 'nature' or by eco-activism, Pagans are likely to find that the world is increasingly significant as both a physical/material reality and a relational/processual community. They are invited by their predecessors on Pagan paths to find themselves so deeply and viscerally immersed in acting fully within this world that there is little if any room left for notions like temptation, sin, or salvation to resonate at all. It then becomes possible to ask 'what do women – or men or hedgehogs or oaks or salmon or wrens or plankton – most desire?' without a shred of the slippery old feeling that there is something less than right and proper about any kind of desire.

The Question of Preferences

So we come to the third Grail question. This is the one that explains, enables and energises the previous two. All three questions are part of quests for the Holy Grail, but this one clarifies something about what the Grail is and what it does. The question of preferences comes nearest to the heart of why I and some others have left Christianity and become Pagan. Apart from anything else, even the mode of its transmission is more Pagan than that of the previous questions.

---

[3] Graham Harvey, *Listening People, Speaking Earth: Contemporary Paganism* (London: Hurst; Adelaide: Wakefield Press, 1997), simultaneously published by New York University Press as *Contemporary Paganism: Listening People, Speaking Earth*. I extrapolate ideas from Gayatri C. Spivak, *In Other Worlds: Essays in Cultural Politics* (London: Routledge, 1987) as meditated in Shannon Bell, 'Tomb of the sacred prostitute: the Symposium', in Philippa Berry and Andrew Wernick (eds.) *Shadow of Spirit: Postmodernism and Religion* (London: Routledge, 1992), pp. 198–207.

[4] Sylvie Shaw, 'The Body and the Earth', *Ecotheology* 8.1 (2003), pp. 85–99.

The third and greatest Grail question comes from the epic *Monty Python and the Holy Grail.*[5] In order to cross a perilous bridge over a deadly chasm, Arthur and his knights have to answer three questions. After several knights give wrong answers that lead to their being cast into the chasm to certain death, one correctly answers two easy questions: 'What is your name?' and 'What is your quest?' The tension mounts as he awaits the third question – the one that I here assert to be the foundational and ultimate Grail question. The bridge keeper asks, 'What is your favourite colour?' The knight answers correctly and crosses the bridge. In case anyone misses the importance of this, the next knight rides up with considerable confidence and answers the first two questions with ease. However, when asked 'What is your favourite colour?' he gives the same reply as the previous knight and is thrown to his death. Why? Because the correct answer is always and only about particular preferences. This is not a question of dogma, orthodoxy, universal truth or rationalist objectivity. It is a matter of celebrating whatever one considers most beautiful. Of course, the celebration of preference is not in the least simple, especially in the context of discussions of religions or of modernity.

Granted that the scene is intended as comedy, how does it aid our understanding of the process by which some people leave Christianity and become Pagan? First, the question of preferences reveals something about the Grail itself. Secondly, the celebration of preferences reveals something about Paganism and its diversity. Finally, the recognition of our partiality for particular preferences, even as they change, tells us something about why some people prefer Paganism to Christianity. Brief elaboration of each of these follows.

What is the Grail? In the most Christian tellings the 'Holy Grail' is a container of some shape. It may be the cup used at Jesus' Last Supper and then used to collect his blood as he died on the cross. It may be a platter or vial that served a similar function: a conduit for the saving blood of Christ. The way many Pagans tell it, Jesus' Grail is an echo of more ancient cauldrons and/or horns of plenty. The cauldron of Ceridwen, for example, is considered

---

[5] Terry Gilliam and Terry Jones, *Monty Python and the Holy Grail,* DVD CDR14164 (Columbia Tri-Star Home Video, 2002 [1975]).

by some Pagans to be a tool used by a Goddess in a transformative ritual. In it she brews up a potion that gives wisdom. It may also be a womb-like vessel of rebirth. Myths, mystics, and esotericists elaborate other possibilities. What many Grail stories have in common, however, is that when it appears, in whatever shape or form, accompanied by whatever signs and wonders, and leading to whatever salvations or transformations, the Grail is always accompanied by the gift of the food and drink which the observer most desires. Medieval chivalry may have required abstinence and chastity from quest knights, but the achievement of the Grail was always accompanied by a feast of stupendous quality. We can con-clude that we are being offered a tautology: the Grail that one seeks is the grail one seeks. If one seeks transformation or salva-tion or wealth, that is what one will pursue and, most likely, achieve to some degree. These are, after all, myths – where people are rewarded for questing rather than frustrated by nature, society, fate or deity. If Christianity is a religion of salvation, Bud-dhism a religion of enlightenment and Judaism a religion of sancti-fication – and none of these are entirely equivalent, and all require different practices – Paganism is a religion of embodied knowl-edge. Its Grail, cauldron, or horn of plenty proffers a celebration of coming home to being embodied, sensual dwellers in ecologies, earth's various places now discovered to be home.

Secondly, the question of preferences casts some light on the pluralism that is endemic to Paganism. While there are rifts, polemics and divisions, the majority of Pagans recognise and cele-brate the plurality of ways of being Pagan. Denominational differ-ences are generated not by divergent interpretations of central truths that, in turn, cause hostility and violence (verbal or physi-cal), but by questions of preference and experience. If a Pagan does not find what they like in one group or on one path, they may find it elsewhere. This is not to deny that Pagans indulge in what some call 'bitchcraft', nor to pretend that the different Pagan paths are really the same at some level. The diversity has reached a point where observers and some Pagans alike are talking about 'Paganisms', plural, rather than 'Paganism'. Nonetheless, for the most part, Pagans embrace differences with some ease and grace.

Thirdly, the third Grail question – the question of preference – says something important about why some of us have left

Christianity and now identify ourselves as Pagans. Admittedly, some of us spend a while regretting time spent worshipping the Christian God, preaching salvation, fellowshipping in one denomination but not others. My experience is that most ex-Christian Pagans get through this phase fairly fast and settle down to a recognition that there was some purpose in that part of their life's journey. Or, if not a purpose, then at least it might become possible to recognise that, for a while, Christianity was a preference and, thus, an appropriate path at that time. This, in turn, permits some of us to recognise that, having once been Christian and now being Pagan, it is not clear what we might yet become. For now, however, there is great satisfaction in seeking to deepen relationships with all those, our relations, with whom we share this small, beautiful, fragile, diverse, exciting, blue-green planet home. For now, it is enormously satisfying to seek to improve our understanding of the meaning of life (here and now), our performance of respectful etiquette towards all life, our neighbours, and our sharing of delight in the manifold preferences that all living beings express.

5

Conversion and Judaism

Jonathan Romain

Conversion is one of the issues in which Jewish thinking has made a total volte-face over the centuries, initially being very proactive, then becoming totally opposed to it, and only now beginning to change to a marginally more accommodating attitude. In its original biblical form, Judaism was an avowedly missionary faith, convinced in its superiority over the surrounding gentile faiths. Thus, Abraham is adamant that his son Isaac should not marry a Canaanite woman lest he fall under the influence of the local faith and goes to great lengths to ensure this does not happen,[1] while the Israelites were later commanded by Moses to destroy all vestiges of the local cults.[2] The very first chapter in which Abraham appears takes only five verses to leap from God's revelation to the patriarch to mention of the converts Abraham had made in Haran. This, at least, was the rabbinic interpretation of the strangely worded phrase 'the souls that they had gotten in Haran'.[3] Even if that could have been seen instead as a reference to the servants he had acquired, the fact that Jewish tradition chose to view it as converts indicates its mindset and the assumptions that it held.

Historically, it was often the case that that when the Israelites defeated tribes, they would be forcibly converted, as happened with the mass conversions during the conquests of John Hyrcanus I

---

[1] Gen. 24:1–67.
[2] Deut. 7:1–5.
[3] Gen. 12:5.

between 135 and 104 BCE.[4] It was a policy that was partly a common technique of strengthening political control, but also reinforced by an underlying religious vision, which saw the Jews as 'light to the nations'[5] and which envisaged many nations flocking to the 'mountain of the Lord'.[6] It was in similar spirit that the biblical canon included a book which took as its heroine the Moabite Ruth, whose declaration 'Your people shall be my people, and your God my God'[7] became the rallying cry of subsequent converts. Moreover, there could be no higher signal of the honour due to a convert than the fact that David was her direct descendant and that from her stemmed both the most successful king and the messianic line.[8] It was little wonder that Matthew complained that the Pharisees, one of the main Jewish sects of the first century and subsequent leaders of Judaism thereafter, were so imbued with a missionary spirit that they would 'traverse sea and land to make a single proselyte'.[9] While there was a degree of hyperbole to the remark, it was a depiction that would largely have rung true to Matthew's readers.[10] It also reflected the rivalry between Judaism and Christianity at the time, as the two faiths vied with each other for the interest of the growing numbers in the Hellenised world for whom the ancient gods had lost their appeal.[11]

It was that same battle with Christianity that caused a major change in Jewish attitude to proselytisation. With the conversion of Emperor Constantine to Christianity around 313 CE, the Church changed from a minority sect to the official religion of the most powerful empire in the world. It also led to a series of edicts protecting the church, which included punishing those who converted from Christianity to Judaism. Missionary activity became

---

[4] Josephus, 'Jewish Wars', 1:54ff.; 'Jewish Antiquities', 13:229ff.
[5] Isa. 42:6.
[6] Isa. 2:2.
[7] Ruth 1:16.
[8] Ruth 4:17.
[9] Matt. 23:15.
[10] Dirk Herweg and Rachel Monika Herweg, 'Conversion in Antiquity and the Talmudic Period', in Walter Homolka, Walter Jacob and Esther Seidel (eds.), *Not By Birth Alone* (London: Cassell, 1997), p. 19.
[11] Hyam Maccoby, *Revolution in Judea* (London: Ocean, 1973), pp. 235–38.

dangerous not only for the individuals concerned, but also for the Jewish community at large, resulting in fines and arrests.[12] The same situation was to occur later in Islamic countries, for although the Jews did not experience the same persecution that they suffered in Christian lands, converting a Muslim was banned under pain of death.[13] Thus it was external political circumstances, rather than internal theological developments, which caused a major revision to Jewish mission. The effect of this enforced brake quickly led to a change of attitude within the Jewish community, initially seeing attempts to convert others as unsafe, and then as undesirable, and ultimately, as the passing centuries turned innovation into tradition, as un-Jewish. It was also underpinned by the notion that Christianity and Islam were forms of monotheism, and so, unlike the pagans in biblical times, did not need to be converted. By the time of the Babylonian Talmud in the fifth century, the teaching of Joshua ben Hananiah – 'the righteous of all nations have a place in the world to come'[14] – had become the standard Jewish view. Thus (in stark contrast to the more exclusivist concept that 'no one approaches the Father except through the Son') it was held that there were many paths to God, and that heaven is not reserved for Jews alone. While Judaism was still seen as the faith chosen by God to first reveal his existence to the world, there was no insistence that only Jews were assured of divine favour. It meant that there was no longer any motivation for conversion and it gradually disappeared from the Jewish lexicon.

Events in Britain exemplify the situation.[15] The Jewish community, which was established in the wake of the conquest by William I, was well aware of the penalties associated with conversion and never sought to win over any souls. There was also a major social divide between Jews and Christians that meant any Christian

---

[12] H. Graetz, *History of the Jews,* Vol. II (New York, NY: Hebrew Publishing Co., 1919), pp. 402–407.
[13] Salo Baron, *A Social and Religious History of the Jews*, Vol. III (New York, NY: Columbia, 1957), pp. 139–150.
[14] *Babylonian Talmud*, Sanhedrin: 13:2.
[15] For an overview of British Jewry, see Cecil Roth, *A History of the Jews in England* (London: Oxford University Press, 1941) and V.D. Lipman, *A History of the Jews in Britain since 1858* (Leicester: Leicester University Press, 1990).

changing faith not only risked the charge of heresy but would be totally alienated from their family and the rest of society. Those who did attempt to cross the divide met a fate that did not provide encouragement to others: a deacon whose own studies of the Bible led him to renounce the church and adopt Judaism was burned at the stake in Oxford in 1222.[16] Robert of Reading, a Dominican friar, also perished in the same way.[17] A charge levelled against the entire Jewish community was that they encouraged Jews who had converted to Christianity to return to their former faith.[18] There were indeed a few such cases, largely of those who had converted out of convenience rather than conviction, but who consequently found themselves in a social no man's land, treated with hostility by Jews and viewed with suspicion by Christians. Although the real reason that Edward I expelled the Jews from England in 1290 were economic and political considerations, officially the edict was justified in part by the reversion of Jewish converts.[19] When British Jewry was readmitted to England almost 400 years later in 1656, there was a long-standing but totally unfounded myth that it was on condition that they did not 'Judaise' – an assumption for which there was no evidence, but which both lay and religious leaders were content not to deny. In fact, they were so nervous of public criticism if anyone should convert to Judaism that it became routine for almost a century to refuse all applicants, and any that insisted were sent abroad to convert so that at least it took place on foreign soil and could be blamed on others.[20]

As Jewish confidence in the security of their position in Britain grew, conversions were conducted domestically, but such instances were few and never the result of any missionary effort, but activated by the individuals themselves. Today, the reluctance to engage in proselytising activity has been reinforced by three other considerations. First, the distaste felt by the Jewish community at attempts by Christian missionary groups to convert Jews, ranging from those who targeted impoverished Jewish immigrants

---

[16] Roth, *History of the Jews*, p. 276.
[17] Ibid., p. 83.
[18] Ibid.
[19] Ibid., p. 85, n. 2.
[20] Benjamin Artom, *Sermons* (London: 1876), p. 275.

from Eastern Europe who arrived here in the1880s to those in
recent times who sought out Jewish students at university who
were living away from their families. Jews objected to what were
seen as assaults on their community, as well as to the underhand
tactics used to ensnare the vulnerable, and developed an even
greater antipathy to anything that might lay them open to the same
charge.[21] A second factor was the increasingly 'right-wing' tendency amongst the Orthodox rabbinate. This affected many areas
of Jewish life, including conversion, for it led them to hold that
unless a convert observed Jewish law 100 per cent, it was better
that they remained non-Jewish and not be guilty of breaking
any of the commandments.[22] The third new objection to conversion arose from the steep rise in the number of Jews marrying non-
Jewish partners since the 1930s. Most rabbis oppose mixed-faith
marriages on the grounds that it endangers the survival of the
faith. They regard conversion as a backdoor to intermarriage and
fear that, unless admittance procedures are very demanding, it will
result in Jews marrying non-Jews who have officially converted
but in reality are indifferent to the faith.[23]

This negative legacy has remained a hallmark of the Orthodox
rabbinate. Thus the former Chief Rabbi, Immanuel Jakobovits,
declared that during his term of office in the 1970s and 1980s, he
was faced with 400–500 applicants for conversion a year, but only
accepted 1 per cent of them.[24] The figure, which he quotes with
approval, would horrify many a Christian minister, who would be
more likely to have welcomed the other 99 per cent too. It is only in
the Reform and Liberal movements (collectively known as Progressive Judaism) that a more positive approach is slowly emerging. Whilst there has been no return to actively seeking converts,
those who enquire of their own accord are often accepted. This

---

[21] Lloyd P. Gartner, *The Jewish Immigrant in England 1870–1914*
(London: Simon, 1960), p. 165.
[22] Norman Cohen, 'Trends in Anglo-Jewish Religious Life', in Julius
Gould and Shaul Esh (eds.) *Jewish Life in Modern Britain* (London:
Routledge & Kegan Paul, 1964), pp. 43–46.
[23] Louis Jacobs, 'The Beth Din: The Jewish Ecclesiastical Court', in *The
Lawyer* 5.1 (1962), p. 23.
[24] Lawrence Epstein, *Readings on Conversion to Judaism* (New Jersey:
Jason Aaronson, 1995), p. 141.

difference in approach stems from two causes: first the philosophy of Progressive Judaism is much more accommodating to individual variations in practice. Its essence is to marry the best of the traditions of the past with the realities of modernity. Judging where to draw the line in terms of ritual observances is a mixture of tradition, communal consensus and personal conscience. There is, therefore, much less insistence on the 'correct' way to behave and much greater willingness to tolerate converts who, for instance, may not adhere to all the dietary regulations but still wish to identify with Judaism.[25] Second, conversion is regarded as one possible solution to the rise in mixed marriages (alongside efforts to encourage Jews to marry within the faith). By bringing the non-Jew into the Jewish fold and encouraging the born-Jew to maintain their religious identity, it effectively turns a mixed-faith marriage into a Jewish-Jewish one.[26]

The practical details of the conversion process exemplify many of the wider issues associated with it. The act of even enrolling onto a conversion course can often prove very difficult. There is a long-standing tradition that applicants be refused three times and are only admitted if they still maintain their interest. Officially, this is to replicate the experience of Ruth who was turned away thrice before being allowed to become Jewish, but in reality it is symptomatic of the reluctance of many rabbis to take on candidates, as chronicled above. As is often noted, Judaism is not just a faith, but a way of life, and the conversion course is designed to facilitate entry into that way of life, involving not just changing beliefs, but joining a people and adopting a culture. The convert to Judaism has to acquire a range of new skills never previously encountered, ranging from home cooking to learning Hebrew. The study period can last from a minimum of twelve months (Reform and Liberal) to several years (Orthodox), depending on which denomination one has approached. In addition, males are required to be circumcised, as has been the custom for all Jews since the time of Abraham.[27] Both male and female applicants also

---

[25] Michael Curtis, 'The Beth Din of the Reform Synagogues of Great Britain', in Dow Marmur (ed.), *Reform Judaism* (London: Reform Synagogues of Great Britain, 1973), p. 136.
[26] Ibid., p. 138.
[27] Gen. 17:10.

have to undergo immersion in flowing water, be it natural water, such as the sea or a river, or in a specially designed chamber (*mikveh*) which has water flowing in and out of it.[28] The idea also found its way into the church in the form of the baptismal font. It serves as a physical expression of an inner change of direction and acts as a powerful psychological marker, not only taking on a new identity, but also letting go of aspects of one's past. At the end of the tuition, candidates have to appear before a Beth Din – an examining board of three rabbis – so as to justify their request for acceptance and prove their knowledge and their sincerity. They are asked about their background and motivation, as well as being presented with factual questions about Jewish life and tradition. The assumption is that they will usually pass, otherwise their teacher would not have recommended them, but for the candidate concerned it is still a daunting experience.[29]

The total number who become Jewish in Britain per annum is estimated at around 200 adults.[30] They tend to differ markedly from those joining other faiths in several key ways, notably gender, situation and age. In terms of gender, the percentage of women who convert to Judaism is far higher than those joining other religions, being a ratio of 5:1 in Judaism, compared to 2:1 in Christianity and 6:4 in Islam.[31] This is owing to two reasons: first, Judaism is a matrilineal faith, with religious identity being transmitted through the female line and inherited automatically at birth. This acts as a powerful incentive towards conversion for non-Jewish women marrying Jewish partners who wish to gain Jewish status for their children. Many such men are not worried greatly by their partner's religiosity per se – after all, they were attracted to them as non-Jewish individuals – but they are concerned that their children be Jewish. Some rabbis strongly object

---

[28] For a history of the origins and development of the *mikveh* see *Encyclopaedia Judaica* (Jerusalem: Keter, 1972): col. 1534ff.

[29] Curtis, 'The Beth Din', pp. 133–34.

[30] This figure is based on the reports from the main rabbinic courts in Britain, from that of the United Synagogue (ca. 25), Reform Synagogues of Great Britain (ca. 100), Union of Liberal and Progressive Synagogues (ca. 50).

[31] Jonathan Romain, *Your God Shall Be My God* (London: SCM Press, 2000), p. 21.

to women who have little or no loyalty to Judaism converting for the sake of their offspring, regarding it as meaningless and hypocritical. Others are more tolerant, viewing it as generous and selfless, and certainly a better option than not converting and thereby ending the Jewish line of that family unit. Conversely, the tradition of matrilineal descent means that there is much less pressure on the male partners of Jewish women to convert, as any children would have full Jewish status anyway. Many such men are philo-Jewish and happy for their wives to organise a Jewish home life, but are not sufficiently committed to convert themselves. Secondly, a number of men who might otherwise convert are deterred by the necessity for circumcision, fearing both the physical pain and the effect on their sexual ability. In reality, the ceremony is performed in a matter of minutes, usually involving just a local anesthetic and with few after-effects. However, such rational considerations are not uppermost in the mind of most men when thinking about surgery on their sexual organ and are outweighed by concerns as to what it will look and feel like afterwards. Many men who would have been happy to undertake a course of instruction and willing to change religious status to please their partner, balk at such a step.

The personal situation of converts to Judaism also stands out, in that over 75 per cent are drawn to Judaism because of a relationship with a Jewish partner, whereas those adopting Christianity are more likely to do so as a result of a religious experience or through the influence of a circle of friends.[32] Within this figure, the motives can vary greatly: for some conversion is a way of mollifying prospective parents-in-law who object to their son or daughter 'marrying out'; for others it is a way of achieving a 'white wedding' in synagogue rather than settle for a registry office one; for others it is to unify the family unit so that they are both 'heading in the same direction' and can provide a stable religious background for children; for others it is because, having come into contact with Judaism by chance through a partner, they then found that it appealed to them and wished to adopt it for themselves without any pressure being brought upon them. In all such cases, most would never have considered adopting a Jewish identity had it not

---

[32] Ibid., p. 91.

been for becoming involved with a Jewish partner. The fact that marriage is the main trigger to conversion to Judaism is not surprising in view of the absence of a strong missionary impulse over the better part of the last two millennia. Moreover, although it may seem paradoxical, many rabbis prefer a conversion because of marriage to one motivated purely by religious factors. The reason is purely practical: someone who marries into a Jewish family automatically has a support group, with a spouse and in-laws who can involve them in Jewish home life and festivals. It is a major advantage and helps the newcomer integrate within the community. A person who comes to Judaism alone has to start totally from scratch and has no guidance. Judaism is very much a home religion and a family faith, full of domestic rituals and involving celebrations which are designed to be shared. It can be very lonely lighting candles by oneself or singing alone. A convert who comes out of personal faith may be more sincere than one who comes with a Jewish partner in hand, but the latter has much greater chance of feeling at ease within Judaism. Moreover, the 'romantic motive' should not necessarily be taken as detracting from the person's sincerity, as most non-Jews with Jewish partners do not convert, and it only applies to those who feel some degree of affinity with the faith. Marriage may be the main motive for those who convert, but it is still only by a minority of those who are married to Jews. It is also notable that of those with a Jewish partner, a majority convert after marriage rather than beforehand. This suggests that they are not rushing into conversion for the sake of a synagogue wedding, but doing so after they had time to experience Jewish family life and find themselves at home in it. The age at which people convert to Judaism is also different in that they tend to be older than those joining other faiths, with a majority of Jewish converts being in their late twenties or early thirties. The peak age of conversion to Christianity is late teens, while converts to Islam are most often in early- to mid-twenties. This reflects the marital situation of many converts to Judaism.[33]

Within these overall characteristics, there is still a wide range of conversion scenarios, with some individuals coming to Judaism without any personal attachments, inspired by their own study of

---

[33] Ibid., p. 24.

the faith. In some cases, it is because they have no faith of their own, not having been brought up in a religious household, but feel a spiritual vacuum in their lives and wish to fill it. For those coming from a Western culture – who may not be Christian, but have a sense of its values and may be vaguely familiar with the Bible – Judaism is a relatively easy step, involving not too great a cultural leap, and associating with a tradition and ethic that are recognisable territory. In other instances, applicants do come from a faith background, but no longer feel at home in it. Those brought up in the church sometimes find that their belief in God is complicated by concepts such as the virgin birth and the Trinity. For them, Judaism offers ethical monotheism free of all the Christian doctrinal difficulties. For others, again from a Christian background, it is the sense of roots that appeals to them, yearning to be part of the ancient trunk itself and not just one of its offshoots. There are also those who convert in later life, having the time to turn to matters of faith that they lacked earlier or motivated by thoughts of mortality.

As a generalisation, that which attracts people to Judaism is that it offers communal camaraderie and personal identity at a time when family values and local ties are under siege and many feel that they do not belong anywhere. Some of these are real differences from other faiths. If one goes, for instance, to a Sabbath morning service in synagogue looking for meditation and tranquillity, the seeker will probably not find it, but will get noise and back-slapping and 'a good nosh' at the communal snack that often takes place afterwards. In many cases, though, the differences are merely perceived ones, with each of those characteristics in every faith, but not always emphasised or appreciated. For some people, therefore, the religious grass on the other side looks greener and they have not explored their own heritage sufficiently well to discover in it what they can see so obviously in another faith. A new trend is for non-Jews who already have a non-Jewish partner to wish to become Jewish, presenting a problem for rabbis in that accepting them will create a mixed-faith marriage. This development mirrors the increasing tendency in society at large to see religion as a private hobby that one member of the family may pursue but is not binding upon anyone else, rather like train-spotting or stamp collecting. There are also occasional examples of a husband

and wife both converting to Judaism together, having each thought of such a move independently but not telling the other for some time for fear of upsetting the domestic applecart until they both realised that they shared the same wish.

With the Jewish community slowly becoming more open to converts, an issue that has arisen is what to call them. According to rabbinic tradition, once a person has become Jewish they should not be described as a convert.[34] This is because they are to be regarded as fully Jewish, and therefore no different from any other member of the community. However, there are those who see no reason to play down their change of faith and deliberately opt to call themselves 'a Jew-by-choice'. They feel proud to be Jewish by conscious decision and 'Jew-by-choice' has become a fashionable term.

However pleased converts may be at their new identity, the existing Jewish community is not always so ecstatic. The centuries-old reluctance of rabbis to accept converts has had a negative effect on the views of many ordinary Jews. It should be noted that there are also born-Jews who are welcoming, appreciate the commitment made by converts, and regard their conversion as a compliment to Judaism.[35] Nevertheless, others can be very prejudiced against those joining the faith and take the attitude that only those born Jewish are 'real Jews'. Delving beneath the surface, this reveals a number of different motivating factors. Sometimes it is a form of racism, or at least tribalism, seeing non-Jews as different and resenting their attempts to become part of the community. Sometimes it is out of a misplaced sense of elitism, that Jewish history and suffering are unique, and so only those who have been the product of it can truly carry the name of being a Jew. Sometimes it is because born-Jews, particularly those who are non-observant or fairly ignorant Jewishly, feel threatened by converts, who display an enthusiasm and knowledge that they feel puts them to shame. The result is that, instead of being welcomed, converts can be treated disdainfully or even shunned. Such reactions can be very painful to those who had taken considerable effort to

---

[34] *Babylonian Talmud*, Baba Metzia: 58b.
[35] John Rayner, 'Counting the Commandments', in Walter Homolka, Walter Jacob and Esther Seidel (eds.), *Not By Birth Alone* (London: Cassell, 1997), p. 100.

become Jewish. This sense of hurt can be compounded if converts had encountered resistance from their own families at making a religious change. This may have been because they were seen as abandoning the family faith and therefore abandoning the family too. Alternatively it could have been specifically because they were converting to Judaism, with negative associations about Jews still lingering in some circles. Equally, the hostility could be a projection of the parents' fear of the unknown, along with worries that they would lose contact with their son or daughter, or be unable to relate to any grandchildren. This, in turn, can produce a sense of guilt in the convert at the hurt their decision is causing the family. Thus, contrary to popular perceptions of conversion being a time of joy and fulfilment, it can also be enormously fraught and even painful.

Despite occasional personal upsets, the general consequences for the Jewish community of the growing number of converts are largely positive. The few that drop out after a while are outnumbered by those who take their commitment to Judaism seriously and, proportionately, they play a more active role in synagogue life than born-Jews. This is particularly noticeable in the number of converts who become teachers in religion schools.[36] Having learnt about Judaism as adults, they often have a deeper knowledge than those who finished their Jewish education at thirteen after they had their bar/bat mitzvah. If there are any negative impacts, they might be in terms of identification with causes that are often automatic to Jews, but not necessarily to those converting because they break the link between faith and ethnicity. Thus converts to Judaism may not feel the same loyalty to the land of Israel as do most born-Jews. Whereas the latter tend to regard it as an ethnic homeland in which they have a personal stake, the former will see it merely as the geographical location of important religious events that has great interest but no personal relevance. This can also have repercussions for charitable giving, for whilst many born-Jews will give to charities in Israel or domestic Jewish charities, feeling a need 'to support our own', converts are more likely to be motivated by the nature of the charity irrespective of

---

[36] Jonathan Romain, 'How are we Handling Conversion Right Now?', *Manna* 67 (Spring 2000), p. 13.

where it is and whether or not it is Jewish based. It is significant that they may feel guided in this by Jewish principles to help all who are in need and to see all people as equal in the sight of God. Some fear that the gulf between faith and ethnic identity will mean that converts will not have strong enough roots within their new communities to maintain their own long-term commitment and certainly not that of their offspring. Thus Jonathan Sarna, Professor of Jewish History at the Hebrew University, warns that 'many of today's converts will be one-generation Jews – Jews with non-Jewish parents and non-Jewish children'.[37] Others would reject this view as alarmist and point to the personal commitment and practical involvement converts display towards their new faith, which are exactly the ingredients needed if their children are to grow up valuing the faith into which they are born. It is often said that 'religion is caught not taught', and converts may succeed in enthusing their children in a way in which their own parents often failed to enthuse them. In addition, they can often stimulate their born-Jewish partners to take a greater interest in their own faith, especially as they are usually obliged to attend the conversion course too and thereby develop their own Jewish awareness.

The Jewish community also needs to acknowledge that the religious traffic is heading in both directions, with some Jews converting away from Judaism. The most obvious faith to join is Christianity. This is partly because it is the most available alternative, with churches in every city, town and village, and so a natural place to turn for those dissatisfied with their Jewish heritage. In previous centuries, when the church dominated national life to a far greater extent, conversion to it was sometimes seen as a way of advancement and 'a passport to society'. It was for this reason that Isaac Disraeli had his young son Benjamin baptised, without which he would never have been able to prosper in political life in later years. The future prime minister was never known for his religiosity and was to describe himself as 'the blank page between the Old Testament and the New'. Today, however, Jews who join the church do so for reasons of faith and often because they have come into contact with Christian friends who have drawn them into

<hr />

[37] Epstein, *Readings on Conversion*, p. 128.

their religious fellowship. The fact that so much of Christianity is based on the Hebrew Bible may make the transition easier, but is rarely the determining factor. Instead, it is the spirituality often found in church and the sense of personal salvation that lifts one above the limitations of the human condition. It is one of the strengths of Christianity and is in contrast to the much more 'this-worldly' atmosphere to be found in Judaism. However, despite these personal journeys and the intense efforts of Jews for Jesus and other Christian missionary organisations, it is estimated that a maximum of seventy Jews turn to the church each year.[38] This is partly because the long history of hostility between the two faiths has made Jews wary of associating with the church, with the cross being for them a symbol of persecution rather than of redemption. It is also because those dissatisfied with Jewish tradition can feel that Christian teaching is too closely allied to be sufficiently appealing. The result is that they either drop out of religious life altogether or seek a home in one of the eastern faiths, which has the advantage of novelty and being free of any associations with the Judeo-Christian heritage. In recent years, there has been a marked tendency of Jews leaving their faith to become Buddhists. It is estimated that 10 per cent to 20 per cent of converts to Buddhism are Jewish – attracted by its emphasis on inner calm and self-knowledge, and without any theological and ritual demands. There they are free of miracle stories disbelieved since childhood and dietary laws that were equally resented. Their prominence in the movement has even led to a generic name, with them being affectionately referred to as a 'Ju-Bu'.[39]

It is clear that the assumption once held that people will stay in the same faith in which they were born can no longer be taken for granted. British Jewry, like all other faith groups, needs to be aware of the swirling religious currents that sweep away existing members and bring new recruits.

---

[38] Romain, *Your God Shall Be My God*, p. 101.
[39] Ibid., p. 74.

6

The Social Construction of Evangelical Conversion

A Sideways Glance

Derek J. Tidball

Meredith McGuire defines conversion as 'a transformation of one's self concurrent with a transformation of one's basic *meaning system*. It changes the sense of who one is and how one belongs in the social situation.'[1] In stressing the element of transformation and change, she, together with most sociologists working in the area, tend chiefly to research conversions that are from one religious faith to another, from a position of non-faith to committed faith or from mainstream conventional religion or conventional secularism to a deviant cult. Yet many conversions, as she admits, are 'less extreme' than this suggests and 'are an alteration of self and meaning system representing a reaffirmation of elements of one's previous identity'.[2] This paper looks at a particular group of 'converts' with a view to understanding the nature of conversion as experienced by evangelicals today.

The preaching of conversion lies at the heart of the evangelical understanding of the Christian faith.[3] The imagined public

---

[1] Meredith B. McGuire, *Religion: The Social Context* (3rd edn.; Belmont, CA: Wadsworth, 1992), p. 71.

[2] Ibid., p. 72.

[3] See D.W. Bebbington, *Evangelicalism in Modern Britain: A History from 1730s to 1980s* (London: Unwin Hyman, 1989), pp. 5–10 and

rhetoric of evangelical preaching frequently suggests that conversion is a dramatic life change captured in the biblical images of being 'born again' or 'the Damascus Road'. This paper suggests that though evangelicals are keen to date their experience of becoming disciples of Jesus, the reality is that 'conversion' is overwhelmingly a process of socialisation rather than a dramatic reorientation of life. This is consistent with George Rawlyck's research into recent Canadian evangelicalism in which he concluded that, 'The sudden, traumatic, transforming New Birth in itself is in the 1990s no longer the key defining evangelical experience' that it was in the previous century.[4]

Survey of Data

The London School of Theology (LST) is a leading educational institution in British evangelicalism.[5] It is a non-denominational college and embraces a wide range of evangelicals rather than catering for any particular segment of the evangelical family. As such it closely identifies with the work of the Evangelical Alliance that seeks to unite mainstream evangelicals of different denominations and emphases. Thus it may be considered a place that offers an important window into the evangelical world.

The fact, however, that it is concerned with students who are studying their faith in some depth and that many of them are going to enter ministry, missionary work, or religious education as a vocation *may* skew the responses in particular ways and make them not exactly representative of the wider evangelical family. A research project asking the same question of a sample who have not applied to a Bible college would be required to establish that with certainty.

Tidball, *Who are the Evangelicals?* (London: Marshall Pickering, 1994), pp. 116–36.

[4] G. Rawlyk, *Is Jesus your Personal Saviour? In Search of Canadian Evangelicalism in the 1990s* (Montreal & Kingston: McGill-Queens University Press, 1996), p. 118. He believed that witness to the faith, a high view of the Bible and the centrality of the cross were more important.

[5] The school, founded in 1943, was formerly known as London Bible College. Its history and significance is set out in Ian Randall, *Educating Evangelicalism: The Origins, Development and Impact of London Bible College* (Carlisle: Paternoster, 2000).

Approximately 360 students are registered at the school to read for university-level qualifications, ranging from Certificates in Higher Education to PhDs. The main group is following a three-year path leading to a Bachelor's degree in theology. Students come from approximately forty countries and represent over forty Christian denominations. There is an unusual student profile in the school when compared with an average university department, since theology has frequently been a 'second career' subject. Consequently, the average age among undergraduates in 2003–04 was thirty, with 34 per cent already holding another university degree. The gender balance in the school as a whole was 51 per cent female to 49 per cent male.

On application to the college, entrants are requested to answer the question 'Please explain briefly how and when you came to faith in Christ.' This survey analyses the answers given to that question by 180 students who were continuing their studies at undergraduate level in the summer of 2004. The data may, therefore, be considered to be representative of the undergraduate student population and generally indicate, with certain caveats that will be mentioned, the mindset of the wider evangelical church.

The data is slightly biased towards females, with eighty-two male and ninety-eight female respondents. The gender balance has changed in favour of women in recent years, since the introduction of a joint degree in Theology and Counselling has led to a greater proportion of female applicants. The fact that this course is available on a part-time basis means that several housewives undertake it, and so it is understandable that they should be slightly over-represented in the survey. However, this makes the gender distribution roughly what the split is thought to be in the church as a whole.[6]

The data was provided by 129 British students and fifty-one overseas students, which is reasonably consistent with the total student body in recent years. The denominational background of the applicants has been categorised as shown in Table 6.1.

---

[6] Peter Brierley, *Christian England: What the English Church Census Reveals* (London: Marc Europe, 1991), p. 80.

Table 6.1

Denomination	Students
Baptists	35
Evangelicals (Independent or FIEC)	33
Church of England	41
Methodists	10
New Churches (almost wholly charismatic)	26
Pentecostal (traditional)	18
Presbyterians	10
Others (1 Salvation Army; 1 URC;3 ethnic churches; 1 overseas denomination, 1 Free Methodist)	7

These figures are consistent with the usual denominational representation at LST. Methodism may be considered to be underrepresented, but this would be a true reflection of their place in wider non-denomination evangelical activity since (i) the Methodist Church operates on a more centralised basis than any other and (ii) they have their own vibrant evangelical institutions such as Easter People and Cliff College. Similarly, few Salvation Army people have trained at LST, since they train their own officers. The United Reformed Church has a smaller evangelical constituency than other denominations.

The question to which applicants were responding has certain limitations when trying to interpret an evangelical understanding of conversion. In looking back and asking for an account of past experience it must be assumed that a respondent is almost inevitably going to reinterpret their past experience in the light of their present faith framework.[7] In asking how applicants 'came to faith in Christ' this question aids them in reconstructing their experience in a particular way. It is intended to be fairly open-ended and non-directive, rather than asking about 'conversion' or 'being

---

[7] McGuire, *Religion*, p. 73.

born again'. Even so, the wording tends to assume a definite time or experience when faith was first placed in Christ, and that impression is emphasised by the addition of the word 'when' to the word 'how' in the question. Perhaps it is for this reason that there seems an overwhelming desire on the part of the applicants to date their initial steps of faith, with only fifteen of the one hundred and eighty not giving a fairly specific time when these steps occurred. The vast majority of respondents give their age at the time their coming to faith occurred. In several cases they provide the actual date and in one case the respondent replied, '7.45 on 9/11/76'. A few admitted a difficulty in answering the question 'when' because in reality the date was so far back in childhood that it was lost in the mists of time, but most made a stab. Five of the fifteen who did not state a date or age were honest enough to record that they could not 'pinpoint a specific date or moment', that there was 'no one occasion I can pinpoint' or that they believed 'for as long as I can remember'.

Though coming to faith is clearly in all but very exceptional cases a process that deepens and matures as time passes – only one person mentions a 'Damascus Road experience' at the age of forty-eight and one other refers to their conversion at University as 'dramatic' – the desire to specify a spiritual birthday may still reflect the traditional evangelical view of conversion as an event.[8] In other respects, the data underlines the desire to specify the 'event' in which conversion occurred with many referring to particular conversations with friends or family members, attendance at youth events, children's clubs, beach missions, students' camps and evangelistic meetings. Billy Graham rallies, Spring Harvest, Soul Survivor and Alpha are all mentioned in this connection more than once. Curiously, two mentioned funerals as a significant turning point, but more of that later.

---

[8] Research undertaken by Bible Society into public confession of faith by adults concluded that 69 per cent came to faith as a result of a process and only 31 per cent saying their faith was 'dateable'. Members of evangelical churches reported a higher rate of sudden conversion at 39 per cent. See John Finney, *Finding Faith Today* (Swindon: Bible Society, 1992), p. 24.

Conversion or Socialisation?[9]

Consistent with the *Finding Faith Today* report, it is clear that friends and family play the most significant part in establishing faith.[10] Forty-six out of 180[11] explicitly refer to the role that a named parent, relative, or friend played in their coming to faith, though at least one hundred and nine of them are nurtured in a believing family and this must have played at least a supportive role, and probably more, in their coming to faith. In a general way, then, faith seems to be socially constructed and 'conversion' more a matter of socialisation than crisis experience.

The age breakdown on their reported coming to faith is fascinating (see Table 6.2). Most are converted as young people, and for that reason age cohorts that relate to school education have been used.

Table 6.2

Age	Number coming to initial faith	Number identified as Christian families
Pre-school	10	9
Primary/Junior School (yrs 1–6)	55	53
Secondary School (yrs 7–14)	53	36
Student years (ages 18–25)	35	9
Post-25 years	27	8

The column recording whether or not the respondent identified their family as Christian needs careful interpretation. The fact that a respondent did not mention that they were not Christian

---

[9] For an overview see H. Paul Chalfant, Robert E. Beckley, and C.E. Palmer, *Religion in Contemporary Society* (3rd edn.; Itasca, IL: Peacock, 1994), pp. 63–78.

[10] Finney, *Finding Faith,* pp. 36–47.

[11] In some cases, whether the family was a practicing Christian family or not is unclear. See more below.

does not mean to say that they were not. In some cases it may be safe to assume they were but the evidence is unclear. Twenty-two explicitly state their families to have been anti-Christian, non-Christian or at most nominal Christians. Seven had Roman Catholic backgrounds and so, although they were con-verted to the evangelical church from Catholicism, they clearly had a Christian foundation. Four, all overseas students, came from families belonging to other faiths. In one case this led the convert to being disowned by his family. Reference to family background naturally decreases with age and therefore the figures for eighteen years plus are not really significant. It is possible that in more cases than explicitly reported, a faith ini-tially nurtured in the family was being revived. Nonetheless, as might be expected the importance of the family in bringing chil-dren to faith is incontrovertible.

Among the fifty-five who confessed faith before they were aged eleven, seventeen stated that they drifted away from God in teenage years and came back to faith in mid or late teens. The figure is not as high as anecdotal evidence would lead one to believe in its suggestion that childhood conversions almost always lead to a phase of teenage rebellion. Perhaps not all reported their lapse. Most who do speak of it use the vocabu-lary of 'recommitment' or 'rededication' in one form or another. One said, 'I shifted back to God'; another 'I discovered my desire for God'; and a couple talked of life being empty or wasted without God. In spite of their recognising the authentic-ity of their childhood faith, it is evident that it is the teenage commitment that many regard as 'the real thing', helping them to move out from under the 'shelter' of their parents' faith and find a faith of their own. This is consistent with the need to affirm their own adult identity.

On the basis of this evidence, 'conversion' would frequently appear to be a matter of 'primary socialisation' which, as Peter Berger and Thomas Luckmann suggest, has 'a peculiar quality of firmness' about it which is explained 'at least in part, by the inevitability of the individual's relationship to his very first sig-nificant others. The world of childhood', they write, 'in its luminous reality, is thus conducive to confidence not only in the persons of the significant others but in their definitions of the situation. The world of childhood is massively and indubitably real.'[12] Religious faith is 'internalised' in this way.[13] True, the reality of the meaning system is tested out in the pluralistic world of the adolescent, leading to periods of uncertainty about faith. It is evident in the testimonies of applicants that when this happens, youth workers, pastors, peers and others regarded as significant play a crucial role in legitimising the faith in the way Berger has suggested.[14] The responses frequently spoke of working through intellectual questions and doubts with others who were able to answer their queries satisfactorily and provide the support needed. In some cases it involved a change of church or youth group and it was the new group who served as an adequate plausibility structure.

These responses remind one of Peter Berger's comment that 'the experience of conversion to a meaning system that is capable of ordering the scattered data of one's biography is liberating and profoundly satisfying. Perhaps it has its roots in a deep human need for order, purpose and intelligibility.'[15] Whatever the motivation, the experience of joy is certainly evident as applicants reported conversion overcoming the emptiness of life and experiencing peace, love, excitement and wonder at 'knowing Christ'. One even repeated the old hymn, ''Tis so Sweet to Trust in Jesus.'

---

[12] Peter L. Berger and Thomas Luckmann, *The Social Construction of Reality* (Harmondsworth: Penguin University Books, 1971), p. 155.

[13] The balance of evidence, I believe, points in the direction of internalisation of religious worldview, contra the standpoint of Long and Hadden who argue that to speak of internalisation is to use a faulty model of socialisation. See Theodore Long and Jeffrey Hadden, 'Religious Conversions and the Concept of Socialisation: Integrating the Brainwashing and Drift Models', *Journal for the Scientific Study of Religion* 22 (1983), pp. 1–14.

[14] Peter L. Berger, *A Rumour of Angels* (Harmondsworth: Pelican, 1971), pp. 50–51 and for a wider debate Berger and Luckmann, *Construction,* pp. 110–22 and Peter L. Berger, *The Social Reality of Religion* (Harmondsworth: Penguin University Books, 1973), pp. 153–54.

[15] Peter L. Berger, *Invitation to Sociology* (Harmondsworth: Pelican, 1966), p. 77.

The Vocabulary of Faith

Rhetoric of commitment

My original interest in this area was sparked some years ago when it was my responsibility to process applications for London Bible College, as it was then called. In those days the question regarding personal faith gave a little more scope for a fuller answer and I used to read the replies to the relevant question and guess the denominational background of the applicant before checking whether I had guessed correctly or not elsewhere on the form. Different denominations and segments of evangelicalism articulate 'conversion' or 'coming to faith' in different ways in spite of sharing a common core of beliefs. In other words, it is not only that a general faith position is socially constructed, but also particular interpretations of faith experience are socially constructed. To what extent, then, were such 'regional accents' of faith evident in the responses of current students?

Overall, while some differences are evident, the more significant picture is of a common vocabulary being spoken across the evangelical family suggesting a more generic social construction of faith. This may be the result of living in a 'post-denominational age' and an age that has seen the triumph of inter-denominational enterprises like Spring Harvest, moulding and shaping the experience of evangelicalism across the board.

Meredith McGuire speaks of converts constructing their 'story of conversion, drawing on a socially available set of plausible explanations' and she mentions rhetorics of choice, rhetorics of change and rhetorics of continuity.[16] What 'rhetorics' did an analysis of the language used by applicants to LST reveal? I engaged in a language analysis of each response and recorded all significant phrases and factors mentioned. These were then grouped into common themes for further analysis. An individual's response nearly always contributed more than one expression and provided more than one insight into their coming to faith and they were therefore listed in several of the categories chosen. The results were as follows.

---

[16] McGuire, *Religion*, p. 73. McGuire consistently refers to 'rhetorics' in the plural.

The dominant rhetoric used is the rhetoric of commitment. Thirty-five out of the 180 applicants said that at a certain time they 'gave their lives to Christ' or 'made a commitment'. Only one used the language of 'surrender' that used to be fashionable vocabulary in some evangelical circles. Other fashionable words in post-war evangelicalism were those of consecration or dedication. None used this vocabulary to describe their initial experience, and the only time anyone got near it was a teenager who, after slipping away from Christ, in late teens spoke of 'rededicating' her life to Christ. One spoke of 'devoting myself to Christ'. Sometimes the 'commitment' was qualified with 'personal', highlighting the evangelical distinctive that faith has to be individually acquired rather than simply received as part of one's family. But other words that qualified 'commitment', like 'initial' or 'serious', were just as numerous. Both of these indicate that the applicant was aware that faith was not just a 'one-off' moment, but led to a life of discipleship.

Closely akin to the language of commitment was the language of decision. It was never used in reference to 'a moment of decision'[17] as provoked by the itinerant evangelist, but always in reference to deciding on a course for one's life, a decision to follow Christ from that time on. It is synonymous with the language of commitment. People used one or the other but not both. The ten people who used this language show some evidence of supporting the Rational Choice theorists' explanation of belief when they argue that making religious decisions is similar to economic behavior, in that people subjectively weigh up rewards and costs and opt for the answer that seems most to maximise their benefit. There is also support in these testimonies for the Rational Choice theorists' view of the significance of supply-side religion, namely that religious groups prosper when they market themselves with a view to winning converts. Furthermore, the testimonies give weight to their concept of household economies and the religious capital and loyalties amassed by families.[18]

---

[17] Billy Graham's long-running TV program is called 'The Hour of Decision' and his news magazine is called *Decision*.

[18] Rodney Stark and Roger Finke, *Acts of Faith Explaining the Human Side of Religion* (Berkley, CA: University of California Press, 2000), pp. 85–88 and Laurence Iannaccone, 'Rational choice framework for the

The theory has been subject to much criticism. A collection of papers edited by Lawrence Young raises some pertinent queries about the suitability of using economic behaviour as a model for religious behaviour, especially from a feminist perspective.[19] Its most vociferous critic is Steve Bruce, who has mounted a major attack on the theory in his work *Choice and Religion*. He is right in saying that we should be suspicious of 'single theory of everything' approaches, especially as they neglect the significance of the cultural context.[20] He produces a mass of historical evidence to counter the thesis and concludes that its basic fault is that it does not really understand the people it is seeking to explain[21] because it applies economic rationality to religious behavior.[22] He dismisses the theory as lacking explanatory rigor. Like any metaphor, if pushed to its logical conclusion it does not stand up and the theory does need greater rigor. Its proponents are, however, constantly modifying the theory in the light of criticisms and further research.[23] In spite of Bruce's attempted demolition, the general orientation of Rational Choice theory has much to commend it and, in my experience, as well as that of the evidence of the testimonies we are examining, it does yield a true insight into the way people make religious choices and the significance of the religious economy.

One applicant wrote, for example, that one afternoon when he was sixteen and his youth worker was witnessing to him: 'I sat in front of the TV and weighed things up. I decided I had nothing to lose and said a prayer and for the first time ever I truly believed it.'

Scientific Study of Religion' in L.A. Young (ed.), *Rational Choice Theory: Summary and Assessment* (London: Routledge, 1997), pp. 25–45.

[19] Young, *Rational Choice Theory*. See especially Mary Jo Neitz and Peter Mueser, 'Economic Man and the Sociology of Religion', pp. 106–16.

[20] Steve Bruce *Choice and Religion: A Critique of Rational Choice* (Oxford: Oxford University Press, 1999), pp. 40–44.

[21] Ibid., p. 121.

[22] Ibid., pp. 125–30.

[23] The latest version of the theory, for example, in *Acts of Faith*, dispenses with the earlier idea of compensators, one of the specifics that Bruce has criticised.

Having explored the matter with him since, he insists it was as cool and rational as it sounds, which he proves by saying he can even recall the score in the football game that was being broadcast at the time! Some of the others who use this language clearly weighed up costs and rewards and decided that the bottom line led them to belief. Another, from a Muslim background, was well aware of the cost element in discipleship, but wrote of how it became 'impossible not to follow'. A female said, 'it was the best decision I ever made'. The choice of 'decision' vocabulary shows no distinctive pattern as to age, gender, or nationality.

A further twenty-three used the language of 'acceptance' or 'receiving' – as in 'I accepted Jesus as my Saviour and Lord', or 'I invited Jesus to come into my life', or 'I received Jesus as Lord.' Only three of these also used the vocabulary of commitment and for the most part this is an alternative expression for the same phenomenon, especially where the emphasis falls, as it often does, on accepting Jesus as Lord. Again the language is used by young and old, male and female, British and overseas students without distinction.

Putting these three groups together leads us to conclude that the dominant paradigm of conversion is not of encountering God or of his initiative in people's lives, or of conviction of sin, as once would have been considered the 'evangelical' view of conversion, but one of making a life choice. It is the human element that is uppermost. Admittedly, this may be aided by the wording of the question, but it confirms the picture gained generally from hearing testimonies and conversations in evangelical churches. It also endorses the conclusion that, however much influenced by others, the role of a person coming to faith is an active one. Lofland's earlier view, since revised, that converts are passive – putty to be moulded by others – is not supported by the evidence.[24] Bible College applicants may be more socialised into the faith than dramatically converted, but they claim to have chosen to make certain

---

[24] Cf. John Lofland and Rodney Stark, 'Becoming a World Saver: A Theory of Conversion to a Deviant People', in American *Sociological Review* 30 (1981), pp. 862–74 and John Lofland, 'Patterns of Conversion', in Eileen Barker (ed.), *Of Gods and Men: New Religious Movements in the West* (Macon, GA: Mercer University Press, 1983), pp. 1–24.

commitments and, were the research field widened, it would be possible to find others who had experienced the same process of socialisation but had chosen to make other commitments.

Rhetoric of encounter

Elements of encountering God certainly exist. Twenty-four spoke of 'meeting Jesus' or 'experiencing him'. With the exception of two of these, in which the human element remains dominant, it is evident that they see the initiative here as lying with God, who comes into their lives so that they cannot avoid him and for some does so overpoweringly. One recorded that as a fourteen-year-old girl 'God's love overwhelmed me and I went down on my knees.' A man, thirty-two at the time, spoke of struggling with sin for three months 'until one glorious day ... when the heavens opened and I had a personal encounter with Jesus'. A lady, as mentioned before, recorded her 'Damascus Road experience' at the age of forty-eight. Another speaks of a 'profound experience of God', and still another of a dramatic conversion. The more profound encounters are recorded mainly by older applicants without distinction of gender or nationality. For the most part, however, the encounters are expressed more vaguely as when people wrote 'Jesus met with me' or 'God spoke to me.' The variety of meaning given to 'encounter' language also probably explains why no denominational pattern is discernable in those who use it. Every denominational category is covered by this language in rough proportions to the size of the denomination in the sample. A slight bias to Pentecostal or newer charismatic churches might be thought to be present but it is not significant.

Particular attention was paid to specific mentions of the Holy Spirit. The question related to 'faith in Christ' and so a reference to the Holy Spirit was not required and is likely to indicate a particular interpretation of a conversion experience if it occurred. Twenty-six mentioned the Holy Spirit. Most who did so had some dramatic experience in mind and there were references to healings, visions, prophecies and revelations. In this case the denominational background was significant: four came from Pentecostal churches, six from Anglican churches (five of which are known to me as charismatic), nine from newer charismatic fellowships and two from a Methodist holiness background. Only four came from backgrounds where it would not be expected that there would be an emphasis on the Holy Spirit or on his dramatic action today. But there may well be local factors, such as the spiritual experience of the pastor, that encourage an interpretation of spiritual experience in terms of the Holy Spirit, especially as two of these churches were overseas. The gender balance was exactly split in the middle. Eight out of the twenty-six were overseas applicants, which means that overseas students were slightly under-represented in this category, but it is probably not significant.

Rhetoric of relationship

The next most important group of responses use the rhetoric of relationship. Seven speak of coming 'to know the Lord' or beginning a 'personal relationship with Jesus'. Four out of the six were young children when the relationship commenced, and in one case at least it was quite sentimental and a response to an invitation from a speaker to children to know 'Jesus as their special friend'. Another child 'convert' spoke of Jesus becoming 'my buddy, my Father, my companion, someone I could lean on' at the age of eight. A further thirteen used the language of the heart, eight of whom were female. In two cases it was used in reference to knowledge about the faith moving 'from head to heart' in the sense of something become a personal conviction rather than mere head knowledge, but in all other cases it had more emotional overtones. In these cases, giving one's heart to Jesus is like a falling in love. One female teenage 'convert' spoke of her early months of Christian experience leading her to become 'so in love with Jesus' and added, 'but I am even more so now'. Another, converted in her early twenties after a family break-up, wrote of becoming 'a special loved child'. While the age profile seems significant in terms of Jesus becoming a friend, and the gender profile is significant in terms of the language of the heart, there seems to be no significance as far as nationality or denomination is concerned.

Rhetoric of theology

Since the application form was to a Bible College that enjoys a reputation for academic standards, one might have expected that applicants would try to frame their response to the question in more 'theological' language or aim to introduce a theologically impressive comment into their responses. This does not seem to have happened. The statements are almost wholly personal rather than theological. Twenty-one speak of some personal difficulty, such as divorce, sickness, or bereavement, or a major transition in life, like moving overseas, as precipitating their faith commitment. To that extent Lofland's 'value-added' approach to the process of conversion in which he emphasises the element of 'tension, strain, frustration, deprivation, or the like' as a factor that predisposes people to conversion is confirmed.[25] Others will no doubt have been experiencing an adolescent identity crisis that is resolved by their faith commitment and is either no longer remembered or not considered significant enough to report. The element of problem-solving, though significant, is clearly not a universal factor since only 12 per cent of the sample refer to it.

Less people comment theologically. Sixteen mention an awareness of sin as a problem that needed to be dealt with and of receiving forgiveness. But in several cases it is spoken of as a fairly routine transaction between them and God. Only three of these speak about being 'under conviction of sin', only one speaks of 're-pentance' and one other uses the strong language about her 'very nature of rebelliousness toward God'. These few alone betray any of the classic signs of angst in their approach to a holy God. None mention guilt, as such. *Finding Faith Today* commented that 'the picture of guilt-ridden, self-accusatory people finding psychological release by turning to Christianity is sometimes painted. If it is true at all, it is true only for a tiny minority – the great majority of the story the participants told did not fit this pattern.'[26] In that report a larger proportion spoke in terms of consciousness of sin and guilt[27] than in the data we are examining, and it was the younger element who spoke of guilt more frequently than the over fifties. That does not seem to have been confirmed here where our respondents are biased towards the young. Interestingly, ten out of the sixteen who mention the problem of sin were men. The denominational background of those who referred to sin is evenly spread

---

[25] John Lofland, *Doomsday Cult* (New York, NY: Irvington, 1977), p. 35.

[26] Finney, *Finding Faith*, p. 34.

[27] 18 per cent reported 'specific guilt' and 21 per cent 'general guilt', p. 33.

across the main denominations represented in the survey, with the exception of the Methodists, but in each case the particular church in which the 'conversion' took place can be identified as among the more conservative wing of evangelicalism.

Central to evangelical theology is the cross of Christ, but only thirteen out of the one hundred and eighty respondents mentioned it – seven men and eight women. Most write about understanding the significance of Christ dying for them but do not articulate it further. A few go further. One speaks of it as 'an atoning death', another of it making 'peace with God' and still a third of it as 'a full and sufficient payment for (my) sin'. It was generally those who came to faith later who spoke in terms of the cross and usually those from a more conservative evangelical background where the cross would have been frequently preached.

Another central plank of evangelical theology is the authority and inspiration of the Bible. What part, if any, did it play in these applicants coming to faith in Christ? Ten specifically mentioned reading the Bible as crucial. Again, each can be identified as coming from the more conservative wing of evangelical churches where the importance of the Bible would be emphasised. Once again, therefore, there is some evidence that faith is socially constructed by the community in which it is born and nurtured.

A powerful incentive to conversion, at least as presented in the popular stereotype of evangelicalism, is the fear of hell. Significantly, in spite of the dominant rhetoric being about forging a positive relationship with God, the fear of judgement is not altogether absent. Eight mention it as a significant factor in provoking a commitment. All but one were female. In one case a reaction had been triggered by a sermon on hell, in another by the evangelist urging a response 'before it is too late', and in two by attending funerals at which eternal destiny was mentioned. In other cases it was a general awareness of the fate of those who did not believe or a desire not to be separated from friends and family in eternity.

Nine respondents mention baptism, mostly as a natural follow on from their having 'committed' their lives to Christ. Those who mention baptism come from a range of churches and almost half of them from churches that are not know for practicing 'believers' baptism'. At this point, then, the natural follow-on from commitment seems to be constructed by the general evangelical subculture rather than any particular denominational stream within it. Only three mentioned confirmation, and all did so as a public confession of the faith commitment they had entered. One older respondent was affected by the 'rites of passage' in a different way. His initial contact with the church came when he and his wife wanted their oldest child baptised. This led to the vicar explaining the meaning of baptism and to his reading the Bible (the church was a conservative evangelical church) shortly after which 'God opened my eyes to the gift of salvation' and this 'led me to give my life to the Lord'.

Conversion Motifs

In a seminal article in 1981, John Lofland and Norman Skonovd identified six different conversion 'motifs' (perhaps better termed paradigms) in relation to 'new religions'.[28] The 'motifs' were determined by 'those aspects of a conversion which were most memorable and orienting to the person "doing" or "undergoing" personal transformation – aspects that provide a tone to the event, its pointedness in time, its positive or negative affective content, and the like.'[29] The patterns were distinguished on the basis of degree of social pressure, temporal duration, level of affective arousal, affective content and the belief-participation sequence involved.

The six motifs were as follows:

1 *Intellectual.* It was considered comparatively rare and involved a convert privately investigating faith options.
2 *Mystical.* By mystical, Lofland and Skonovd have a 'Damascus Road' type experience in mind. It involves a high level of arousal but may be of short duration.
3 *Experimental.* This type of conversion stresses conversion as a process where the convert gradually reaches a conclusion, having adopted a pragmatic approach and having asked others to show the way.

---

[28] John Lofland and Norman Skonovd, 'Conversion Motifs', *Journal for the Scientific Study of Religion* 20 (1981), pp. 373–85.
[29] Ibid., p. 374.

4 *Affectional.* Here conversion takes place over time due to attachments a convert has. Both social pressure and affective arousal are moderate. The key characteristic is that belonging precedes believing.

5 *Revivalist.* Revivalist conversions are defined as those where the 'central feature consists of profound experiences which occur within the context of an emotionally aroused crowd'.[30] While considering such conversions to be 'far from absent' in the world, the authors do consider them in decline in modern societies.

6 *Coercive.* This motif includes forced means of conversion using techniques such as brainwashing, programming, mind control and thought reform. Obviously, the level of social pressure and affective arousal concerned is high and it is thought that the newly acquired identity endures over the long term.

In practice it is quite difficult to assign people neatly to one or other of these categories. Categories 2 and 5 in particular lack clear boundaries. For example, those who respond at a Billy Graham Rally fit into category 2, according to Lofland and Skonovd's definition, but may equally fit within the Revivalist classification.

Taking a fairly rigorist approach by trying to identify the key element in each case yields the following result. Only two LST applicants could be said to fall clearly within the category of 'intellectual' conversions, though six others speak of a significant intellectual component in their coming to faith. The 'mystical' motif, as defined in terms of a 'Damascus Road experience' or being 'born again' applied to two. Only two are clearly 'experimental', testing Christianity out against other faith experiences. Only one demonstrates a true 'revivalist' motif – though many others might fit this category depending on one's definition of revivalist. None fit the 'coercive' motif. The dominant motif, whether explicitly stated or implicitly implied is 'affectional', so much so that it could be considered the 'evangelical motif'. As noted, Lofland and Skonovd explain, in 'affectional' conversion the degree of social pressure is

---

[30] Ibid., p. 380.

medium since there is a long-term influence rather than heavy persuasion; the duration of such conversions appears long; the level of
affective arousal varies somewhat, but is usually on the low side;
and participation precedes belief. In several cases there is explicit
mention that it was when a teenager changed church or youth
group and was involved in the activity, for example, in the worship
or drama group, that 'commitment' occurred. Participation defi-
nitely preceded belief.

5. Conclusion

Those who apply to study at LST *may* possess peculiar characteristics that mark their faith journey out as different from a general
evangelical population. The language of 'commitment' *may* be
more dominant because of the element of vocational choice they
are making. It *may* be that those who are the children of believers
nurtured in the faith from a young age see the vocation of full-time
Christian service as more desirable than 'first-generation' converts. Without researching the stories of those who have not
chosen to attend a Bible College we cannot be sure. But, as mentioned at the beginning, there is sufficient about this sample to
suggest it is not altogether unrepresentative of the wider evangelical church. If so, the language of 'conversion' ought perhaps to be
replaced by the language of 'socialisation' and the moment of so-
called conversion seen more as an affirmation of commitment, one
of several, which those maturing in the faith will experience.

7

Pentecostal Perspectives on Conversion

William K. Kay

The Pentecostal movement is a vast, diverse and global phenomenon that has now been in existence for about one hundred years.[1] There are enormous variations within Pentecostalism in different parts of the world but the basic origins and orientation of the movement are sufficiently clear to allow generalisations to be made.

Although any analysis must take account of contextual factors that promote variation between different cultures, it is still true to say that running through Pentecostalism is an experientialist orientation coupled with a basic evangelical doctrinal substructure. These two factors combine to produce various shifting configurations of belief and practice that are stabilised by traditions dating back to the doctrinal statements adopted by Pentecostal denominations at their inceptions.

This chapter will begin by analysing historical antecedents of Pentecostalism as a way of providing an understanding of the different components that contribute to Pentecostal belief and practice, especially in the area of conversion. Although these beliefs

---

[1] V. Synan, *The Holiness-Pentecostal Tradition: Charismatic Movements in the Twentieth Century* (Cambridge: Eerdmans, 1997); W.J. Hollenweger, *The Pentecostals* (London: SCM Press, 1972); A. Anderson, *An Introduction to Pentecostalism* (Cambridge: Cambridge University Press, 2004); W.K. Kay and A.E. Dyer (eds.), *Pentecostal and Charismatic Studies – A Reader* (London: SCM Canterbury Press, 2004).

and practices were modified during the twentieth century, the main changes concerned the integration of healing praxis within a relatively untouched evangelical framework. The chapter will then consider the impact of the charismatic movement on Pentecostal doctrine before finally turning to contemporary evidence from a large-scale survey of Pentecostal ministers in the UK.

Antecedents

According to the generally received account, the Pentecostal movement grew out of a matrix of Methodist and holiness groups that had formed in the United States by the end of the nineteenth century.[2] Within this sub-culture by the end of the century – and especially in England – must be included independent gospel halls, exotic offshoots of Methodism, Baptists, Brethren, Salvationists, Congregationalists and missionary-minded evangelicals within established churches like the Anglican, A.A. Boddy.

Revivalism had been endemic to the North American religious scene at least since the time when Methodism had arrived in 1766[3] and, in the figures of Charles Finney (1792–1875) and D.L. Moody (1837–99), had reached national prominence and a degree of respectability. When the Welsh revival broke out in 1904 the revivalist Evan Roberts achieved brief worldwide fame.[4] When the Azusa Street revival broke out in 1906, it was not so much the revival that was extraordinary but rather its interracial, glossolalic and spontaneous character. When T.B. Barratt transplanted

---

[2] 'This impulse which climaxed in the rise of revivalism, coalesced with burgeoning Methodism to lay the foundations of the evangelical religious and cultural synthesis that was to dominate pre-Civil War America … the dominant force on the eve of the Civil War as a coalition of "revivalistic Calvinism" and "Evangelical Arminianism" – a coalition of dominated by Methodist-like ideas, including the doctrine Christian perfection', taken from D.W. Dayton *Theological Roots of Pentecostalism* (Metuchen, NJ: Scarecrow Press, 1987), p. 64; see also V. Synan, *Holiness-Pentecostal*.

[3] V. Synan, *Holiness-Pentecostal*, p. 7.

[4] W.K. Kay, 'Revival: Empirical Aspects,' in A. Walker and K. Aune (eds.), *On Revival: A Critical Examination* (Carlisle: Paternoster, 2003), pp. 185–204.

Pentecostalism to Europe, he did so by means of revival meetings in Oslo City Mission, a church that enjoyed Methodist connections.

Methodist theology in John Wesley's hands was fiercely Arminian, that is, he was prepared to emphasise the role of human free will in the apprehension of salvation on the grounds that 'if man were not free, he could not be accountable either for his thoughts, words, or actions' (sermon 58).[5] Wesley was not prepared to preach that salvation was entirely a matter that flowed from the initiative of God whose saving of one person and damnation of another lay behind a barrier of inscrutability. His argument was altogether more theologically subtle: since, strictly speaking, God does not foreknow things (because all time is simultaneously present before the divine mind), the notion of foreknowledge is simply a human way of speaking about divine knowledge of what is only future from our own perspective. With regard to predestination, Wesley considered that the term does not speak of causes and effects but rather of divine order.

This emphasis on human freedom and responsibility was compatible with a doctrine that, in its completed state, sanctification culminated in Christian perfection. Wesley's own teaching about Christian perfection differed from that of the important though less well-known John Fletcher, as is made clear in this extract:

> You will find my views on this matter in Mr Wesley's sermons on Christian perfection and on scriptural Christianity; with this difference, that I would distinguish more exactly between the believer baptised with the Pentecostal power of the Holy Ghost, and the believer who, like the Apostles after our Lord's ascent, is not yet filled with that power.[6]

So, even in the 1770s, the notion of Christian sanctification was being connected with a post-conversion crisis experience of baptism in the Holy Spirit. The Arminian element within this view of sanctification ensured that, when Pentecostalism arrived at the turn of the twentieth century, the post-conversion experience was

---

[5] Sermons: Second Series: On Predestination (LVIII).
[6] Quoted by Dayton, *Theological Roots*, p. 50.

one to which Christians might feel entitled. Indeed, the Arminian theme within conversion produced the kind of 'altar theology' that led to public avowals of repentance within church and tent meetings at which new and penitent believers might publicly accept Christ. It was a short step from this voluntaristic conception of conversion to an almost equally voluntaristic conception of spiritual empowerment through the baptism in the Holy Spirit. Indeed, it is arguable that the template of conversion-plus-crisis sanctification that was found in revivalistic Methodism was simply transferred to Pentecostalism in the form of conversion-plus-baptism in the Holy Spirit. Once it was agreed that there was an important experience for Christians after conversion, it became relatively easy for Pentecostals to adjust the Wesleyan tradition to their theological scheme.

Pentecostalism Begins

Actually, it was not as simple as that because of the complexity of the religious culture of the United States at the dawn of the twentieth century. While there were those who believed in a sanctificatory crisis, there were also others for whom sanctification was much more likely to be a gradual experience. The issue here was that sanctification should not simply be 'claimed' but must be acquired by long spiritual discipline and sustained holiness of life. Consequently, the two-stage model of salvation was not the only one being defended. A three-stage model of conversion, sanctification and then baptism in the Spirit also came circulate in early Pentecostal circles. That it did not predominate was largely due to the ministry of W.H. Durham (1873–1912). From around 1910 onwards, Durham argued cogently for 'the finished work of Calvary,' that everything necessary for salvation was received at the new birth, at conversion, so that sanctification could be achieved on the basis of the atonement and endowment with power by Spirit baptism could also be appropriated on the same basis.[7] Of course, there might be a delay in the way that these

---

[7] E.V. Blumhofer, 'William H. Durham: Years of Creativity, Years of Dissent', in J.R. Goff and G. Wacker (eds.), *Portraits of a Generation: Early Pentecostal Leaders* (Fayetteville, AR: University of Arkansas Press, 2002), p. 136.

stages unfolded in an individual's life but, in principle, everything a Christian needed was given at the cross and nothing stood in the way of a Christian's progress from regeneration to an Acts 2 experience.

So, when Pentecostals formed themselves into denominations in the first part of the twentieth century and drew up the doctrinal statements by which they defined themselves, it was common to find propositions like: 'We believe in salvation through faith in Christ ... [T]his experience is also known as the new birth, and is an instantaneous and complete operation of the Holy Spirit upon initial faith in the Lord Jesus Christ.' (This is taken from the current 'fundamental truths' of Assemblies of God in Great Britain and Ireland.)

The assertions here are right in line with evangelical culture.[8] Salvation is through faith in Christ and this is identified with the 'new birth' of John 3 and is instantaneous and complete. What is asserted here is that the moment of salvation occurs as someone, anyone, puts their faith in Christ for the very first time. Once this happens, the Holy Spirit causes the individual to be born again, or born from above, in a process that is as complete as natural birth: the entire life of individual is changed in every important respect in the sense that this individual now stands in a different relationship towards God while being forgiven of sin and justified. The words 'every important respect', however, imply that debts, marriage vows and other obligations remain intact at conversion. Thus conversion spoken of here is vital, not nominal, and presumes sufficient intellectual understanding by the participant for him or her to know something of the Christ in whom faith is exercised. Or, to put this by way of deliberate contrast, the conversion spoken of here does not depend upon a religious ceremony, the faith of others or any other set of beliefs apart from those that explicitly concern Jesus Christ himself. It would not, therefore, be possible to be 'an anonymous' Christian,[9] someone who belongs to a religious faith other than Christianity who was nevertheless a

---

[8] G. Dorrien, *The Remaking of Evangelical Theology* (Louisville, Kentucky: Westminster John Knox Press, 1998).

[9] See K. Rahner, 'Christianity and the Non-Christian Religion', in his *Theological Investigations*, Vol. 5 (trans. by K.-H. Krueger; New York: Crossroad Publishing, 1983).

participant in salvation brought by Christ, nor would it be possible to be a Christian simply by virtue of persistent and prolonged attendance at religious services.

Pentecostal accounts of conversion follow the type of 'twice born' religious reorientation described in William James's *Varieties of Religious Experience* (1902). Such accounts are consonant with those going back in church history and most famously illustrated in the works of John Bunyan. The sense of guilt, perhaps fear of God, the acceptance of Christ and the joyful release from anxiety are well documented. Yet, in providing this account of Pentecostal conversion, there is insufficient smell of the sawdust trail or of the television studio. Pentecostal evangelism was, in the period before the mid-1940s, characterised by large indoor meetings within city halls and church buildings at which the gospel was preached, appeals for salvation were made and those who wanted healing came forward for prayer. In the UK George Jeffries conducted impressive crusades in most of the major cities and regularly filled the Albert Hall in London for Easter service for many years in the 1930s. In the United States, in the period after 1945, Pentecostal evangelism gradually moved from the great circus tents of Oral Roberts to radio and television and, again, huge meetings were held which, in the 1950s, were televised. In 1960s a rather different style emerged where religious programs were made that contained a variety of singing and testimony features as well as a low-key preaching. All these meetings and all these means of communication presumed the reality of vivid conversion, the possibility of miraculous healing to 'confirm the word' (Mark 16:20[10]) and might make reference to the fullness of Holy Spirit.[11]

Pentecostal and charismatic variants are dramatically illustrated in David Wilkerson's *The Cross and the Switchblade* (published in paperback 1964). He worked in the 1960s among drug addicts in New York and took these young people into youth hostels where, isolated from drug intake, they went through 'cold turkey' in an atmosphere of prayer so that, soon afterwards, many

---

[10] All Bible quotations in this chapter are taken from the New International Version.

[11] D.E. Harrell Jr, 'Healers and televangelists after World War II,' in V. Synan (ed.), *The Century of the Holy Spirit* (Nashville, TN: Thomas Nelson, 2001).

went through evangelical conversion and an experience of the baptism of the Spirit. In Wilkinson's view it was the baptism in the Spirit that finally broke the habit of drugs and released people from their cravings.[12] This bestselling book brought the reality and power of the Holy Spirit to wide notice and illustrated that the doctrine had practical importance.

The Biblical Material (First Phase)

Many of these historically debated issues are more clearly illustrated by direct reference to the biblical material. The Pentecostal movement, as the name implies, identifies itself strongly with the original Day of Pentecost when the early church was launched. The key events are recorded by Luke so that the combined Lukan corpus, his Gospel and the Book of Acts, are often seen as the main text from which Pentecostal theology is primarily derived.

Along with evangelicals, Pentecostals would argue that the disciples were 'saved' prior to the crucifixion both because Jesus says to them 'rejoice that your names are written in heaven' (Luke 10:20) and because to deny this would be to create an enormous logical problem over the salvific status of Old Testament saints. This means that saving belief in Jesus, even without a full understanding of the doctrine of the atonement or the full historical information concerning the crucifixion, is possible. Elsewhere in the Gospels saving belief in Jesus is associated with an appreciation of his identity as Son of God or Messiah (Matt. 16:16).

Once this is granted, it is logical to ask what happened on the Day of Pentecost itself. This, Pentecostals would argue, is the day when disciples were filled with, or baptised with, the Holy Spirit. This demonstrates that conversion and the baptism of Holy Spirit are separable. Other features in Acts are thought by Pentecostals to confirm this position. The narrative of the Samaritans in Acts 8 falls into this category. Philip goes to Samaria and preaches to the city and, as a consequence, evangelical salvation takes place (v. 4). The Samaritans believe in Jesus, find physical healing and are baptised in water (v. 12). But, only after this, do the apostles Peter and John come down

---

[12] Quoted in W.K. Kay and A.E. Dyer, *Reader*, pp. 153–57.

from Jerusalem and lay hands on the new believers for them to receive the Holy Spirit (v. 17). So, again, salvation and baptism in the Holy Spirit occur on different occasions.

In Acts 10 the two processes occur in quick succession. Here the members of the household of Cornelius receive the message of Jesus preached by Peter and believe and, almost simultaneously, the Holy Spirit descends on them and they begin speaking other tongues in the same way that the disciples did on the Day of Pentecost some years before (vv. 44–46). After this combined process, Cornelius' household is baptised in water.

So, using the Acts as a template and then drawing normative patterns of doctrine from it, Pentecostals argued for separability and subsequence: separability implying the notional separation of salvation and baptism in the Spirit and subsequence implying that, after salvation, there is a further experience of Holy Spirit in store for Christians. This experience, drawing on the words of Jesus in Acts 1:8 ('you will receive power when the Holy Spirit comes upon you; and you will be my witnesses') is purposive: it is missiological, and it equips for service.

Indeed, conversion usually takes place in the context of preaching and often in the presence of healing or other spiritual manifestations. Philip goes to Samaria and we are told that 'many paralytics and cripples were healed' (Acts 8:7). Similarly, on Paul's missionary journeys preaching and healing often coincide (e.g. Acts 14:10). This is seen as a logical outcome of the promised Holy Spirit and of the linkage between being a witness of Christ and being 'clothed with power' (Luke 24:48, 49). In this respect Pentecostal views are that conversion is, from every angle, influenced by the Holy Spirit. The gospel should be preached by a man or a woman filled by the Holy Spirit; reception of the gospel message leads to a new birth that follows faith in Christ and is effected by the Holy Spirit; healing may take place at the same time, and occasionally involve the new convert, as was the case with St. Paul himself when he was healed of blindness (Acts 9:18). Prophecy, inspired by the Spirit, may also manifest itself, as it did when the disciples of John the Baptist made the transition to fully fledged Christians (Acts 19:6). In short, Pentecostals take pulsating and exciting spiritual activity from the pages of the New Testament and fervently seek to apply it to the contemporary world.

The Charismatic Movement

The broad outlines of the Pentecostal position on conversion remained much the same from the 1920s right up until the 1960s. Pentecostalism existed as a separate force within Christianity and only interacted with other streams within the Christian tradition in limited circumstances. Within the United States, Pentecostalism gained in respectability and was a founding member of the National Association of Evangelicals in 1942,[13] and this tacitly implied that Pentecostalism amounted to 'evangelicalism plus tongues' which, in terms of the earlier discussion, could be seen as an acceptance of second blessing theology as a kind of 'optional extra'.

Once the charismatic movement began, the situation changed. The changes are complex and can only be described in broad outline. We may distinguish three basic positions which, to some extent, correspond with three basic stages unfolding in the 1960s and 1970s. First, there were those who accepted the Pentecostal position without any great reflection on its larger implications.[14] Since the charismatic movement swept through Methodist, Baptist, Anglican, Congregational, Presbyterian, Lutheran, Roman Catholic and other branches within Christianity, and since this movement began with a fully fledged doctrinal package that had been worked out when Pentecostal denominations were formed, it appeared to be simple enough to accept the baptism with the Holy Spirit as a revitalisation of spiritual experience that could be easily accommodated within the doctrinal systems of the various denominations that included charismatics. This is because the Christians within the various groups that became charismatic did so through informal prayer meetings or at interdenominational conferences. They were largely unaware of theological refinements and had no great investment in the historic positions that their denominations had worked out, often with much pain,

---

[13] E.V. Blumhofer, *Assemblies of God: A Popular History* (Springfield, MO: Radiant, 1985), p. 105.

[14] Indeed, Harper seemed happy to combine a Pentecostal view with an evangelical view. As he points out, 'nowhere is the coming of the Holy Spirit coincidental with water baptism', meaning that there is no need to assume the Holy Spirit is given at infant baptism. See M. Harper, *As at the Beginning* (London: Hodder & Stoughton, 1965), p. 98.

during the course of church history. They were attracted by experiential Christianity and repelled by propositional logic-chopping.

Second, a position was worked out by Anglicans and some Roman Catholics that blended Pentecostal theology with existing sacramental theology concerning Christian initiation. Thus, a theological position that accepted that babies at christening or baptism received the Holy Spirit needed to find another terminology to explain what happened when these babies grow up and spoke in tongues. Simon Tugwell, a Dominican, argued that the Spirit was 'released' at the point when baptism in the Spirit occurred.[15] This meant that the baby or young person who had been admitted into Christian family had indeed received the Holy Spirit at that point in time but that, only during the subsequent crisis experience, had the Spirit been fully manifested. The result of this theology was that it was possible to argue for the validity of sacramental forms of Christian initiation and, at the same time, to avoid dividing Christians into first- and second-class categories. All Christians had received the Spirit but, in some, spiritual gifts were operative, and they were so as result of the grace of God and not because of the superiority of Pentecostal theology or ecclesiology.

This second position might be pressed with more or less divisiveness. Larry Christenson,[16] writing as result of a Lutheran consultation, was happy to hold the notion that the appropriation of the Holy Spirit may be one that conforms to sacramental and evangelical theology or to the Pentecostal theology of second-blessing without necessarily adjudicating between the two since, in pastoral terms, the results may be very similar. Peter Hocken,[17] writing as a Roman Catholic, is willing to develop the thinking of the first Malines document of 1974[18] and to avoid collapsing

---

[15] S. Tugwell, *Did You Receive the Spirit?* (London: Darton, Longman & Todd, 1971).
[16] L. Christensen, *Welcome, Holy Spirit* (Minneapolis: Augsburg, 1987).
[17] P. Hocken, *The Glory and The Shame* (Guildford: Eagle Publishing, 1974).
[18] The Malines documents were a series published by Cardinal Suenens to provide theological-pastoral foundation and orientation for the charismatic renewal. The earliest of these were cooperative efforts by teams of scholars and consultants. See www.rc.net/org/cka/books/html/introduction.html (accessed December 2005).

baptism in the Spirit into ritual initiation (whether evangelical conversion or Catholic baptism-confirmation) and to avoid positing two baptisms, one in water and one in the Spirit. What matters is the trans-confessional character of the experience of the Holy Spirit and the 'visibly invasive' sense of the immediacy of the divine persons, whether of the Spirit himself or of the ascended Christ.

Third, an altogether more sophisticated theological debate took place concerning the role of the Holy Spirit within the salvation. The debate concerned whether the Spirit was portrayed differently within the writings of Paul and Luke, whether it was permissible to construct doctrinal formulae on the basis of narrative portions of scripture, whether, indeed, systematic theology either from an evangelical or from the Pentecostal side was excessively sharp in its terms and boundaries – as the Lutheran Larry Christenson implies it was – and exactly how the different elements within the process of Christian initiation ought to be assembled and in what timeframe.[19] This debate also concerned discussion of what should be thought of as normative or paradigmatic in Christian experience and what was transitional, exceptional and unrepeatable.

Fourth, and finally, the old debate about dispensations within Christian history surfaced from time to time. The debate attempted to dismiss all the elements of Pentecostalism that were distinctive to it and to assert that the Christianity of the Reformation in its barest and most restrained form was normative Christianity.[20] Such a view might be linked with a functionally deistic worldview that denied the possibility of any supernatural or non-empirical invasion of the sensory world and which, by way of subsidiary argument, argued for a dispensational account of Christianity that confined miracles and revivalistic phenomena either to the apostolic phase of church history or to occasional and exceptional periods that were, preferably, a long time ago and somewhere else.

---

[19] L. Christenson, *Welcome*, p. 83.

[20] For example, V. Budgen, *Charismatics and the Word of God: A Biblical and Historical Perspective on the Charismatic Movement* (Welwyn: Evangelical Press, 1985). .

The Biblical Material (Second Phase)

James Dunn in a classic book, *Baptism in the Holy Spirit*, focuses on the main texts in the Book of Acts already briefly discussed, but he did so after considering the account in Luke's Gospel of the baptism in water of Jesus and the descent of the Holy Spirit upon him.[21] Dunn considers that this event is pivotal to church history and initiates a new age. For this reason the parallel between Jesus' baptism and the events of the Day of Pentecost are to be seen as similarly initiatory. In his view the Day of Pentecost marks the opening of the next stage in Luke's threefold salvation history. Pentecost inaugurates the era of the church and ought to be seen as a paradigm not of second blessing but of becoming a Christian.

The narrative in Acts 8 is in Dunn's view the discussion of a defective response to the gospel. The Samaritans at the start of the chapter are thought to be trusting in Philip rather than in Christ and so, only when the Apostles come down from Jerusalem to lay hands on them, do the Samaritans properly become Christians. Here is a story contrasting true and false Christianity.

The account of the conversion of Cornelius in Acts 10 shows, according to Dunn, that the Spirit fell when the household heard Peter speaking about faith and forgiveness so that, at the moment Cornelius trusted in God for forgiveness, he received the Spirit. For this reason 'the baptism in the Spirit is God's act of acceptance, of forgiveness, cleansing, and salvation'.[22]

John Stott argued that, since all Christians received the Holy Spirit at conversion, no second blessing is needed.[23] In his earlier publication he stressed the difficulty of obtaining doctrine from the narrative part of Scripture and the need to use the doctrinal parts to interpret the narrative parts. The same basic passages of Scripture are revisited by Stott but his view, for example, of Acts 8 is that the Apostles came down from Jerusalem specifically in order to heal the Samaritan schism, which had lasted for centuries. The apostles, by laying hands on the first Samaritan converts,

---

[21] J. Dunn, *Baptism in the Holy Spirit* (London: SCM, 1970).

[22] Ibid., p. 82.

[23] J. Stott, *Baptism and Fullness* (2nd edn.; Leicester: Inter-Varsity Press, 1975) and J. Stott, *The Message of Acts* (Leicester: Inter-Varsity Press, 1990).

demonstrated the unity of the Jewish church with the new Samaritan church.

In two books coming from a genuine heavyweight within the field of New Testament scholarship, Max Turner took many of the elements within Dunn's view but also sought to integrate Johannine and Pauline accounts of the Holy Spirit with those of Luke.[24] The discussion ranges widely and goes back into the inter-testamental period and to Jewish messianic expectations outlined in Isaiah. Turner's view is that the Spirit has four functions: he is the source of prophecy, of charismatic wisdom, invasive prophetic speech and invasive charismatic praise. As a source of charismatic wisdom the Spirit functions soteriologically (that is, to effect salvation) by showing how the believer can enter and remain in the community of salvation.[25] Turner though also writes, 'I should clarify that I am not claiming the evidence of Acts "absolutely refutes" the majority traditional Pentecostal view on initial tongues (even less am I attempting to diminish the theological significance of glossolalia).'[26] What he wants to say, however, is that there is only 'one gift of the Spirit, given at conversion-initiation',[27] even if, at the same time, he does not wish to collapse the missiological and charismatic dimensions of the Spirit into conversion.

It is not possible to give a blow-by-blow account of Pentecostal responses to Dunn, Stott and Turner, as well as others, but these may be read within the writings of Stronstad, Ervin, Petts, Shelton, Menzies.[28] These are well summarised by Atkinson

---

[24] M. Turner, *Power from on High: The Spirit in Israel's Restoration and Witness in Luke-Acts* (Sheffield: Sheffield Academic Press, 1996a) and M. Turner, *The Holy Spirit and Spiritual Gifts: Then and Now* (Carlisle: Paternoster, 1996b).

[25] M. Turner, *Power*, p. 445.

[26] Ibid., p. 447.

[27] Ibid., p. 450, original italics.

[28] R. Stronstad, *The Charismatic Theology of St Luke* (Peabody, MA: Hendrickson, 1984). H. Ervin, *Conversion-initiation and the baptism in the Holy Spirit* (Peabody, MA: Hendrickson, 1984); D. Petts, 'Baptism in the Holy Spirit in relation to Christian initiation' (unpublished MTh dissertation; Nottingham: University of Nottingham, 1987); J. Shelton, *Mighty in Word and Deed* (Peabody, MA: Hendrickson, 1991); R.P. Menzies, *The Development of Early Christian Pneumatology* (Sheffield: JSOT Press, 1991).

who concluded that 'Dunn's depiction of the gift of the Spirit initiating its recipients does not accurately reflect the Lukan portrayal. The Pentecostal emphasis on empowering for service is more accurate'.[29] The debate continued with contributions, among others, from Pawson, Menzies, Chan, Menzies, and Menzies and Menzies.[30]

Many of the differences turn out to be more theoretical than practical. Pentecostals, on one side, wish to preserve the distinctiveness of second blessing theology on the grounds that, unless they do so, the reality of such a blessing will eventually diminish and be lost. Evangelicals, on the other side, wish to retain what they believe to be a robust biblical balance that, at same time, leaves the possibility of charismata open without being obligatory. Both sides sometimes speak in private as if their view were obviously correct, which probably explains which there is continued argumentation in the academic arena.

Empirical Data on Conversion

During a research project on Pentecostals in the United Kingdom I collected data from 907 Pentecostal ministers in four denominations: Assemblies of God, Elim, the Apostolics, and the Church of God.[31] The data were used to construct four categories of Pentecostal ministers. There were those who had remained within the denomination in which they had been brought up. There were

---

[29] W. Atkinson, 'Pentecostal responses to Dunn's Baptism in the Holy Spirit: Luke-Acts', *Journal of Pentecostal Theology* 6 (1995), pp. 87–131.

[30] J.D. Pawson, 'Believing in Christ and Receiving the Spirit: A Response to Max Turner', *Journal of Pentecostal Theology* 15 (1999), pp. 33–48; R.P. Menzies, 'Paul and the Universality of Tongues: A Response to Max Turner', *Asian Journal of Pentecostal Studies* 2.2 (1999a), pp. 283–95; S.K.H. Chan, 'A Response to Max Turner', *Asian Journal of Pentecostal Studies* 2.2 (1999), pp. 279–81; R.P. Menzies, 'The Spirit of Prophecy, Luke-Acts and Pentecostal Theology: A Response to Max Turner', *Journal of Pentecostal Theology* 15 (1999b), pp. 49–74; W.W. Menzies and R.P. Menzies, *Spirit and Power: Foundations of Pentecostal-Experiences* (Grand Rapids, MI: Zondervan, 2000).

[31] W.K. Kay, *Pentecostals in Britain* (Carlisle: Paternoster, 2000).

those who had been brought up as church attenders but who had switched to Pentecostalism. There were those who had non-churchgoing parents but who had, nevertheless, switched from the denomination in which they had undergone a formal religious rite at the beginning of their lives. And there were those who had no churchgoing connections at all and had undergone no religious rite in babyhood. In each instance the ministers were asked whether they had converted in childhood or after childhood and whether their religious commitment had been gradual or sudden.

The results showed that nearly one in five (19 per cent) of the total sample had not switched denomination at all; that those who had come from a churchgoing background and switched denomination amounted to over half of the total sample (54 per cent); those who had come from a non-churchgoing background and switched denomination amounted to one in five (19 per cent); and those without any religious rite attending birth amounted to less than one in ten (9 per cent).

The study showed that Christian commitment overwhelmingly began in childhood for those ministers who are brought up in the denomination where they now minister. In other words, these ministers had grown up within their denominations, in most cases being taken to church by both parents, had made a commitment early in life and had followed this commitment through by joining the denomination of which they were part and by becoming its ministers. In nearly three quarters of these cases (72.8 per cent) the commitment to Christianity had been gradual. We may therefore assume that in these instances the person had been inducted into Christian beliefs and practices which, over time, became personal convictions. A similar gradual commitment to Christianity occurred in nearly two-thirds of those who had switched denominations (64.2 per cent). Whereas, among those who had switched denominations without having churchgoing parents (presumably these young people had churchgoing grandparents or had simply been baptised as infants without any religious commitment on the part of their immediate families) the figures were almost reversed, in that nearly two-thirds (64.5 per cent) had been converted suddenly. Of those who had become Christians out of a completely irreligious beginning a similarly large percentage (58.9 per cent) had been converted suddenly.

In general terms, ministers with a churchgoing background made a gradual commitment to their faith while ministers without a churchgoing background made a sudden commitment. This sudden commitment is likely to fit the standard pattern of evangelical conversion described by William James and assumed by the Methodist/holiness debate of the nineteenth century. And this is significant because, when we look at the ministry of these ministers, it is evident that it is this group that is most likely to preach in such a way as to elicit sudden conversion from their hearers. In some ways this is hardly surprising since those who have undergone an experience must surely be most likely to convey this experience to others. Nevertheless, what this implies is that ministers who have undergone a sudden conversion experience are an important point of growth within Pentecostalism. It is they who, in general terms, are most likely to press a conversionist gospel upon the next generation. This group amounts to 42.1 per cent of the total number of ministers in the sample. Perhaps more surprisingly, but equally in line with the experientialist dimension of Pentecostalism, 62.3 per cent of all ministers said that they had been healed physically in answer to prayer.

Conclusion

Four general conclusions may be drawn from the foregoing discussion. First, the debate about stages within Christian conversion-initiation is likely to continue. The debate existed at the beginning of Pentecostalism as result of the plethora of opinions prevalent within the late nineteenth-century religious matrix. The debate was further refined as a consequence of the interaction between Pentecostals and charismatics in the period after the 1960s. It is unlikely that the debate will be resolved one way or the other, particularly as Pentecostalism interacts with more and more streams within Christianity and with streams stemming from the charismatic movement itself.

Second, although the theological emphases within Pentecostalism and the charismatic movement are important, the vast majority of churchgoers have little interest in many of these topics and are much more likely to prioritise their own religious experience or the teaching of their own particular minister. Whether there are two or three stages within Christian initiation and whether these are simultaneously experienced or experienced in a sequence with brief intervals between the stages is much more of a pastoral matter than a theological one.

Third, the nature of Pentecostalism as a form of Christianity that values experience and conveys this experience through personal testimony or public narrative is likely to perpetuate the importance of dramatic conversion accounts. Moreover, when this narrative is accompanied by accounts of conversion out of slavery to drugs or crime, theological considerations recede even further into the background. When a man stands up in tears before congregation and solemnly says, 'I was once a heroin addict but Jesus saved me and filled me with the Spirit and now I'm free' preachers will be encouraged to declare the merits of Christ's death and the glories of the baptism in the Holy Spirit.

Fourth, given the nature of Pentecostalism, it seems probable that Pentecostal evangelists will continue to stress salvation in Christ, the baptism in the Spirit, and the possibility of divine healing. In other words, there may well continue to be a practical division between Baptist evangelists like Billy Graham and Pentecostal evangelists like Oral Roberts in that they will conduct their meetings in a quite different way. For Billy Graham the climax of the meeting is the appeal to come to Christ. For Oral Roberts the climax of the meeting was almost invariably the healing line – and the same differentiation occurs between more up-to-date examples of evangelical and Pentecostal evangelists.

Part Two

Understanding Conversion to Christianity

8

Paul

Archetypal Convert and Disputed Convert[1]

Stephen J. Chester

The Paradox of Paul and Conversion

'If you were to ask the average person, "What is conversion?" chances are that he or she would reply: "It's what happened to St. Paul on the Damascus road."'[2] Paul is the archetypal convert of popular imagination. His story as told in Acts and the images of conversion contained in his letters also inform, either consciously or subconsciously, much scholarly work on the subject. The reader of Timothy Yates's helpful review of twentieth-century studies of Christian conversion certainly finds significant numbers of unacknowledged Pauline (and Johannine) images being employed by scholars in their analyses and definitions of conversion.[3] In his book, *Paul the Convert*, Alan Segal highlights the

---

[1] For further discussion of the themes and issues discussed in this essay, see S.J. Chester, *Conversion at Corinth: Perspectives on Conversion in Paul's Theology and the Corinthian Church* (London/New York: T&T Clark International, 2003).

[2] Richard V. Peace, *Conversion in the New Testament: Paul and the Twelve* (Grand Rapids, MI/Cambridge: Eerdmans, 1999), p. 17.

[3] T. Yates, 'Christian Conversion 1900–2000: William James to Lewis Rambo' in M. Percy (ed.), *Previous Convictions: Conversion in the Present Day* (London: SPCK, 2000), pp. 124–37.

prominence of the metaphor of transformation in both Paul's letters and contemporary social-scientific studies of conversion.[4] It seems that, to some degree, a convert in the contemporary world is someone whose experience is deemed to conform in important ways to that of the Damascus Road, and/or someone of whom it is appropriate to use Paul's imagery. It is therefore all the more striking that, within New Testament scholarship, the subject of Paul and conversion continues to spark strong disagreements. Was Paul a convert at all, or should his experience be described in other terms? If it was a conversion, did his experience provide all that is central in his theology or was its influence insignificant compared to his subsequent experience of mission to the Gentiles? What status should be given to his own biographical comments in answering these questions? Moreover, how did Paul think about the conversion of others? Did he think that his own experience and that of his Gentile converts should be identical? In contemporary scholarship, Paul is thus *both* the archetypal convert and a disputed convert. This essay will explore the apparent contradiction, examining what its different aspects mean for our understanding of Paul himself and, just as importantly, teasing out their implications for the study of conversion in today's world.

Paul and Definitions of Conversion

In the various debates that cluster around the subject of Paul and conversion, it is our understanding of conversion that is at stake just as much as our understanding of Paul. This is nowhere more apparent than in the most fundamental challenge to Paul's status as the archetypal convert.

Was Paul a convert?

Krister Stendahl famously answers this question in the negative for two principal reasons.[5] First, Paul was called, not converted. In Galatians 1:15 Paul uses the verb καλέω (call) to describe his

---

[4] A. Segal, *Paul the Convert: The Apostolate and Apostasy of Saul the Pharisee* (New Haven: Yale University Press, 1990), pp. 28–29.
[5] See K. Stendahl, *Paul Among Jews and Gentiles* (Philadelphia: Fortress, 1976), pp. 7–23.

experience. 'When God, who set me apart from birth and called me by his grace, was pleased to reveal his Son in me so that I might preach him among the Gentiles, I did not consult any man.' This language has its background in the prophets. 'Paul describes his experience in terms of a prophetic call similar to that of Isaiah and Jeremiah. He felt hand-picked by God after the prophetic model to take the message of God and Christ to the Gentiles.'[6] This leads Stendahl to the conclusion that 'if, then, we use the term "conversion" for Paul's experience, we would also have to use it of such prophets as Jeremiah and Isaiah. Yet we do not speak of their conversion, but rather of their call.'[7] Conversion and calling are here defined as opposites rather than equivalents. Secondly, Paul's experience in coming to faith in Christ did not lead him to reject Judaism, and so 'here is not that change of "religion" that we commonly associate with the word *conversion*'.[8]

Neither of these claims stands up to close scrutiny, and in both cases for the same reason. Stendahl introduces implicit definitions that pre-determine the answer to his question as to whether Paul was a convert. Paul's vocabulary in Galatians 1:15 is indeed undoubtedly drawn from Isaiah 49:1–6 and Jeremiah 1:5, and calling is undoubtedly a prophetic concept, particularly evident in second Isaiah. Yet the Septuagint contains not a single narrative relating the commissioning of a prophet that employs the verb καλέω.[9] Scholarship uses the term 'call narrative' to describe the commissioning of a prophet by God, but the prophetic texts themselves do not.[10] It is difficult to see that this scholarly usage is in any sense illegitimate if the concept

---

[6] Ibid., p. 8.

[7] Ibid., p. 10.

[8] Ibid., p. 7 (his emphasis).

[9] Jer. 1 is certainly included by scholarship among prophetic call narratives, but it should be noted that it provides no exception to the rule. It does not itself speak of the calling of the prophet. The contribution of Jer. 1:5 to Paul's language in Gal. 1:15 is the idea of being set apart. Earlier in Old Testament history, God is said to 'call out' to Moses and Samuel but in these cases καλέω refers to the audible sound of God's voice, not the commission given to the prophet. See Ex. 3:4, 19:3, 19:30 and 1 Sam. 3, where the verb is used eleven times to describe God speaking to Samuel.

[10] The vocabulary of calling is most commonly applied to Israel as God's people. The only individuals said to have been called are Abraham

of calling offers genuine assistance in the accurate interpretation of the narratives concerned. So long as scholars are aware of the steps of analysis involved, calling can be construed as compatible with, indeed explicative of, the terms that are used in the narratives. Similarly with Paul and conversion, there is no requirement to define calling and conversion as opposite categories. Indeed, Paul's own use of the verb καλέω would lead us to equate the two rather than to define them over and against one another. In his undisputed letters it refers to the beginning of the Christian life on no fewer than seventeen occasions.[11]

Further, the suggestion that conversion must involve a change of religion begs important questions about definition. What is meant here by 'religion'?[12] As Christianity did not yet, at the time of Paul's experience, understand itself as a clearly separate 'religion' from Judaism, could anyone leave Judaism to enter Christianity? Feeling the force of this question, most Pauline scholars agree that Paul did not, from his own perspective, in any straightforward sense, reject Judaism. Yet fewer are prepared to deny that he was a convert. Paul's sudden reversal from persecutor of the church to advocate of its gospel, and his change of communities within Judaism from Pharisaism to Christianity, are regarded as adequate grounds on which to apply the label 'convert' even though Paul continued his adherence to Israel's God.[13] Stendhal's definition of conversion thus appears

---

(Is. 51:1–3), Cyrus of Persia (Is. 46:11), and, if he is properly to be understood as an individual rather than as a personification of the people of Israel, the mysterious figure of Isaiah's servant songs (Is. 49:1, 6).

[11] Paul uses the aorist tense fourteen times, and the perfect tense, which denotes the present state of being called but does so on the basis of God's past action, three times. For the aorist, see Rom. 8:30 (2); 9:24; 1 Cor. 1:9; 7:18, 20, 21, 22 (2), 24; Gal. 1:6, 15, 13; 1 Thess. 4:7. For the perfect, see 1 Cor. 7:15, 17, 18.

[12] We should note that in Stendhal's definition of conversion, the term 'religion' is used as if its own definition was entirely clear and unproblematic.

[13] See J. Ashton, *The Religion of Paul the Apostle* (New Haven & London: Yale University Press, 2000), pp. 75–79; B. Gaventa, *From Darkness to Light: Aspects of Conversion in the New Testament* (Philadelphia: Fortress Press, 1986), p. 40; Segal, *Paul the Convert*, p. 6 and ch. 3; J. Ziesler, *The Epistle to the Galatians* (London: Epworth Press, 1992), p. 10.

inadequate,[14] something confirmed by the observation that Paul twice specifically applies the concept of calling to both Jewish and Gentile Christians (Rom. 9:24; 1 Cor. 1:24). As the latter have abandoned the Graeco-Roman gods to follow Christ, presumably they could qualify as converts on Stendahl's definition. When Paul applies the concept of calling to Gentiles it would function as equivalent to conversion, when he applies it to Jews as the opposite. The unsatisfactory nature of such a procedure is further illustrated by Paul's questions in 1 Corinthians 7:18: 'Was a man already circumcised when he was called?' The concept of calling here clearly refers to the beginning of the Christian life for both Jew (the circumcised) and Gentile (the uncircumcised).

Yet, for all that Stendahl's definition of conversion is problematic, formulating an alternative is no easy task. As pointed out above, it is the scale of the change that Paul experienced from persecutor to advocate, and from one community to another, that convinces many that he was a convert. Segal, in particular, suggests that conversion 'can denote moving from one sect or denomination to another within the same religion, if the change is radical'.[15] The issue here is that of the question: from whose perspective is a change of community deemed radical? And how radical does the change have to be for a person to qualify as a convert? Paul's repeated submission to physical punishment at the hands of synagogue authorities (2 Cor. 11:24) suggests a perception on their part that he had significantly violated the boundaries of Judaism, even as it bears witness to Paul's own determination to deny that his activities did so.[16] It is one thing to

---

[14] The issue of circularity also arises here. Peace suggests that 'Stendahl's assertion that what Paul experienced was a call, not conversion, is tied to Stendahl's definition of conversion. And Stendahl gets that definition not from the Bible but from the same Western society he decries in his article' (*Conversion in the New Testament*, p. 29).

[15] Segal, *Paul the Convert*, p. 6.

[16] Whether this means that synagogue authorities perceived Paul as no longer Jewish is a complex question. J.M.G. Barclay comments that 'Such punishment represents the response of a synagogue to an erring member, not quite the expulsion and ostracism of one judged wholly apostate. But if Paul continued in the practice which earned him this punishment, the synagogue authorities must eventually have decided to ostracise him (cf. 3 Maccabees 2:33 and 3:23)' (*Jews in the Mediterranean Diaspora: From Alexander to Trajan* [Edinburgh: T&T Clark, 1996], p. 394).

assert that Paul was, after all, a convert, but quite another to give an adequate account of what we mean by 'conversion'.

Defining conversion in contemporary scholarship

The question of whether or not Paul was a convert thus confronts us with the use of the term conversion as a conceptual tool, which, while it may aid us in our attempts to explore a vital dimension of religious experience, is always defined in relation to the perspectives and interests of the researcher. How much change is necessary for the term conversion to become applicable is only one example of this phenomenon. Another dimension of it can be seen in the manner in which older studies often define conversion to the advantage of some religious traditions and the disadvantage of others. For example, A.D. Nock's classic text, *Conversion*, defines conversion in such a way that it is only in Christianity and Judaism among the religious traditions of the ancient world that conversion existed.[17] Prophetic religion is contrasted with traditional religion, faith and creed with ritual and myth, exclusive worship with supplements to ancestral piety, and moral reformation with a desire for knowledge of the secrets of the universe. In each of these contrasts, conversion belongs with the first of the two opposites, as do Judaism and Christianity. Conversion only exists in some religious traditions, the implication being that its presence is a mark of superiority. Paul is here the archetypal convert, but conversion is itself a Judaeo-Christian concept and experience.[18]

More recent studies are usually aware of the potential bias involved here, but a desire to avoid it has failed to produce a

---

[17] A.D. Nock, *Conversion: The Old and the New in Religion from Alexander the Great to Augustine of Hippo* (Oxford: Clarendon Press, 1933), pp. 1–16.

[18] Nock by his definition of conversion as belonging specifically to Christianity *and* Judaism, is enabled to emphasise both the radical change experienced by Paul and the continuity with his past. On the one hand, Paul was the first Christian to become so by conversion. The twelve in Jerusalem perceived their faith in Jesus as the completion of their previous Jewish religious traditions but Paul was different, having opposed the church in the name of Judaism. 'For him to become a Christian meant in the first instance a complete change of face.' Yet, on the other hand, Paul had 'an imperious inner need to discover an interpretation and reconciliation of the old and the new in his religious life' (Ibid., p. 191).

common alternative approach. L.R. Rambo argues 'most studies of conversion to date have been too narrow in orientation, employing ... assumptions too deeply rooted in religious traditions'.[19] He instead offers a descriptive, seven-stage model of the conversion process capable of application to a multitude of different varieties of conversion in a multitude of contexts. 'More specialised, normative definitions of conversion are the preserve of particular spiritual communities.'[20] The problem of potential bias pushes Rambo towards a wider definition. In contrast, similar concerns drive medieval historian Karl Morrison towards a narrower focus:

> It is a confusion of categories to use the word *conversion* as though it were an instrument of critical analysis, equally appropriate to any culture or religion. The word has a profound, mystical sense in the West for which some great religions and languages of the world have no equivalent. Even in the history of the West, it has displayed different connotations at different moments. Thus, the word is more properly a subject, rather than a tool of analysis.[21]

Morrison therefore offers a highly detailed exploration of the hermeneutics of conversion current within twelfth-century monasticism. The different approaches of Rambo and Morrison thus leave the student of conversion with a dilemma: should we seek to develop a universal definition of conversion, or one that is as historically and culturally specific as possible?

The study of Paul as convert provides a useful perspective from which to approach this question. For Paul's position at the start of the Western tradition of understanding conversion raises certain problems for Rambo's approach. A Western scholar may be able to avoid the more obvious forms of bias when constructing a broad definition of conversion, but can he or she wholly avoid Paul's pervasive influence? The intention may be to explore conversion in terms of what a group or person studied says that it is, but can a model of the conversion

---

[19] L.R. Rambo, *Understanding Religious Conversion* (New Haven/London: Yale University Press, 1993), p. 4.
[20] Ibid., pp. 3–4.
[21] K.F. Morrison, *Understanding Conversion* (Charlottesville: University of Virginia Press, 1992), p. xiv.

process be that neutral? It is noticeable that transformation, the very metaphor that Segal points to as characteristically Pauline,[22] figures significantly in Rambo's discussion and is claimed by him as a universal need.[23] Further, people do not experience conversion in relation to a neutral definition of the phenomenon. Conversions take place to, or within, particular religious traditions, and, as we already have seen, cases of conversion are always labelled as such from particular perspectives. It is *not* the case that Paul himself, the synagogue communities offended by his ministry, or contemporary scholars, would necessarily answer the question of whether he was a convert in the same way, or that, even if they did, they would necessarily imply the same things by the same answer.

The case for the kind of careful explorations of particular understandings of conversion urged by Morrison is therefore strong. Even here, however, the issue of definition is not easily resolved. One may decline to develop a definition of conversion as an analytical tool by which to categorise people as converts or non-converts, but it is difficult to see that conversion can be treated entirely as the subject of analysis. As in any branch of study, pre-conceptions play their part. Even careful studies of particular understandings of conversion are partly shaped by the choices made, and the questions posed, by the researcher. In Morrison's own case, it seems that it is the desire to find a conception of conversion as far removed as possible from that proposed by Nock that partly shapes his decision to restrict his examination of conversion in the Middle Ages to twelfth-century monasticism.[24] More generally, it could be the case that the questions about conversion posed by Western scholars tend to be shaped by Pauline concepts. Questions may appear suitable because they

---

[22] Segal, *Paul the Convert*, pp. 28–29.

[23] Rambo, *Understanding Religious Conversion*, p. 4.

[24] Morrision comments that 'in Nock's view, conversion was largely a change of mind or behaviour marked by a single, identifiable event in history ... Conversion, in other words, was a turning point or peripety' (*Understanding Conversion*, p. 3). He contrasts this with the twelfth-century monastic view that 'the idea of conversion described continuing and danger-filled transformation, rather than abrupt and permanent change' (p. 66).

make sense in relation to existing, rather Pauline, understandings of conversion.

Equally, however, similarities between experiences of conversion in different social, historical and religious contexts should not be ignored because a neutral, universal definition of conversion is not possible. Certain dimensions of change in conversion are present so widely that the student of conversion will be unwise to ignore them, even while acknowledging that the content of such common dimensions, and the relationship between them, varies enormously from context to context. Sensitivity to changes in experience and belief, of community and morality, as well as to any rituals that may mark them, will rarely, if ever, be deficiencies in conversion research. Those studying conversion, including Paul's own, should look at all these areas, but do so recognising that to apply the label convert to a person, or the label conversion to an experience, is to make a statement about what someone is or has experienced *in relation to* an overt or implied definition of conversion formulated from a particular perspective. Definitions of conversion can be used fruitfully in research to generate appropriate questions to address to the evidence, but their own particularity must not be evaded. When we say that Paul was a convert, 'In whose eyes?' is the necessary supplementary question.

Paul and the Conversion Account

The way in which scholarship defines conversion is not the only crucial issue confronting those who would study it. We are naturally interested in the perspectives of those we term converts, and scholarly definitions of conversion are partially shaped by accounts of conversion given by converts themselves. This leads to what has been, alongside the question of definition, perhaps the most pressing methodological issue in recent study of conversion. When studying conversion, can one rely on the accounts that converts themselves provide of their experience? Do they give accurate information about the event or process of conversion and its consequences? Once again, Paul himself provides an apposite illustration.

Did Paul's conversion shape his theology?

Entering on a description of his conversion, Paul says about his gospel that 'I did not receive it from any man, nor was I taught it; rather, I received it by revelation from Jesus Christ' (Gal. 1:12). Given that Galatians addresses a crisis concerning the very legitimacy of Paul's law-free gospel for Gentiles, this statement seems at face value to suggest that the essential elements of Paul's theology can be attributed to his conversion and that they emerged in its immediate aftermath. Within recent scholarship, just such a position is vigorously defended by Seyoon Kim.[25] It is disputed with equal vigour by Heikki Räisänen,[26] especially in relation to Paul's antithesis between justification by faith and justification by works of the law. Räisänen suggests that the later practicalities and problems of mission to the Gentiles were much more influential for Paul's theology than his experience of conversion.[27] Beverly Gaventa goes one step further and suggests that it is this later theology that then moulds Paul's accounts of his conversion and not vice versa: 'Paul does not construct his theology out of the content or experience of his conversion. Indeed, the reverse is true. It is Paul's understanding of the gospel that brings about a construction or re-imagining of his past.'[28] The implication that we cannot take Paul's accounts of his conversion at face value is unmistakable.

One feels that, as with Stendhal's contrast between calling and conversion, false opposites are being constructed here. On the one hand, it is reasonable to claim that our perspectives on past events decades after their occurrence are affected by subsequent experiences. Paul could not, decades later, relate his conversion experience to his theology as if his years of missionary experience had

---

[25] S. Kim, *The Origin of Paul's Gospel* (2nd edn.; Tübingen: J.C.B. Mohr, 1984).

[26] H. Räisänen, 'Paul's Conversion and the Development of his View of the Law', *New Testament Studies* 33 (1987), pp. 404–19.

[27] H. Räisänen, *Jesus, Paul and Torah: Collected Essays* (Sheffield: Academic Press, 1992), pp. 17–44.

[28] B. Gaventa, 'Galatians 1 and 2: Autobiography as Paradigm', *Novum Testamentum* 28.4 (1986), pp. 309–26 (313). Gaventa expresses a different and rather more balanced attitude towards the significance of Paul's conversion experience for his theology in *From Darkness to Light*, pp.

not taken place. What he says about his conversion in his letters is not necessarily the same as that he would have said a day, a week, or a month after it had happened. Yet, on the other hand, human beings are interpretative creatures, for who to have an experience is to interpret it. There is no access to raw experience divorced from interpretative considerations. Were we somehow able to interview Paul the day after his conversion, we would still only have access to his interpretation of the experience, and not to the experience itself. The theological concerns shaping the account then offered might be different from subsequent ones, but the account would not be inherently superior for being early. Whether it should be regarded as a fresh account in comparison to later stale accounts, or as an ill-considered response compared to later mature ones, would itself be a matter of interpretation.

Thus, although the retrospective self certainly develops, it does not therefore *necessarily* distort, either with regard to the experience of conversion, or to its consequences for the beliefs of the convert.[29] If Paul provides us with accounts that suggest that his conversion experience had certain theological consequences, then there is no prior reason to doubt that the connection is genuine. His strong claim to have received his law-free gospel through a revelation must be taken seriously. The question of how great a period elapsed between Paul's conversion experience, and the reflections upon it which gave rise to such consequences, is a related but *different* one. We can allow that the theology of his letters is not necessarily the same in every important respect as that which he held in the immediate aftermath of his conversion without drawing the conclusion that his conversion held little significance for Paul's theology.[30] Similarly, one does not necessarily

[29] For an argument that it does, see P. Fredriksen, 'Paul and Augustine: Conversion Narratives, Orthodox Traditions and the Retrospective Self ', *Journal of Theological Studies* 37 (1986), pp. 3–34 (33). In relation to Paul, the same is rather implied by F. Watson, *Paul, Judaism and the Gentiles: A Sociological Approach* (Cambridge: Cambridge University Press, 1986), p. 30: 'All we know of Paul's conversion is how he chose to understand it in polemical contexts many years later.'

[30] The assumption that such an implication does follow is one of the shared misconceptions marking the fierce debate between Seyoon Kim and Heikki Räisänen referred to above. Kim assumes that all of the

have to draw that conclusion if one allows that subsequent experiences played a part in the development of Paul's theology. Doubtless the problems and practicalities of mission did influence him but, whatever these were, one doubts that they were unique to Paul. Other Jewish Christians, who did not respond by advocating a law-free gospel, also faced such problems and practicalities. Paul's distinctive attitude is best explained in relation to his experience of conversion,[31] which was therefore indeed significant for his theology.

We thus find ourselves in a complex situation with regard to Paul's own brief biographical statements. In the period between his conversion and the writing of these accounts, he may have been confronted with issues in mission his response to which was different from that of other Jewish Christians because of his conversion experience. However, these subsequent episodes presumably then became part of Paul's perspective on his own conversion. His understanding of that experience and its significance has developed as a result of its interaction with new situations. These new

---

essential elements of Paul's theology must have arisen in the immediate aftermath of his conversion if they reflect its influence. Räisänen assumes that if Paul's views were the subject of development, especially those on the Law, then they cannot be regarded in any significant sense as a consequence of Paul's conversion. Despite this misconception, should the different conversion accounts with which Paul provides us prove to be consistent, it would seem reasonable to conclude that that the elements of his theology influenced by his experience had reached a settled form by the time he wrote his epistles. Apart from the possible exception of 1 Thessalonians, this is accepted by Räisänen, 'Paul's Conversion', pp.404–406.

[31] Nock, *Conversion*, pp.190–91: 'The Twelve in Jerusalem, and no doubt most of their early adherents, had found in the Gospel of Jesus and the Gospel which took shape around Jesus the integration and completion of the religious traditions in which they had always lived. For them he came to fulfill, and not to destroy. Paul, on the other hand, had regarded them and theirs as apostates and had thrown himself heart and soul into the struggle to suppress them.' Watson argues that Paul began preaching a law-free gospel to Gentiles in reaction to the failure of mission to Jews, but offers no explanation as to why the reaction of Paul and his colleagues was so different from that of other Jewish Christians (*Paul, Judaism and the Gentiles*, pp. 31–36).

situations may now also hold significance for Paul's identity. On the one hand, Paul's conversion experience shapes his theology; on the other hand, his theology in turn influences his perspective on his conversion. As one might expect, he is actively engaged as he moves through life in an ongoing process of reflection on the experience that was the defining event of that life. When we read Galatians 1:11–17 (or indeed Phil. 3:4–11, or Rom. 7) we need not suspect Paul of misleading us, but we do need to be aware that the presentation of biographical information in such texts will reflect subsequent experiences and concerns. Paul recounts his past experience but does so in the present and for present purposes.

The conversion account in contemporary scholarship

This defence of the reliability of Paul's statements about his conversion recognises his activity as an interpretative agent, reflecting upon his own experience and its significance in creative ways. That it does so is a partial application to Paul of recent developments in social-scientific discourse about conversion that have replaced older patterns. The discussion of the status of Paul's conversion accounts helps to exemplify the change. However, as usual, Paul is more than an example. The apostle and his conversion are part of the argument about the nature of conversion, not simply objects of study to which the outcomes of such debates are applied. For sociologist James Richardson speaks of a traditional paradigm of conversion derived from a long-standing common interpretation of Paul's conversion that emphasises its sudden, dramatic and emotional quality, with Paul transformed by the irresistible power of God. Later secular theorists replaced the Christian God with other irresistible forces, such as unconscious psychological drives, or social deprivations that must be satisfied, but the paradigm remained intact.[32] While this traditional paradigm does persist today, both in religious and academic discourses, an alternative paradigm has developed which understands the convert as an active agent in his or her own transformation. Converts may seek religious change, trying out several

---

[32] J.T. Richardson, 'The Active vs. Passive Convert: Paradigm Conflict in Conversion/Recruitment Research', *Journal for the Scientific Study of Religion* 24 (1985), pp. 163–79 (164–66).

groups, and may experience an extended period during which they conform to the expectations of the group joined without yet being fully convinced by the community's message.[33] Both paradigms conceive conversion as a transformation of the self, but disagree as to whether such transformation is something visited upon the self or achieved by the self.

In the newer paradigm of the active convert, one of the main arenas in which the activity of the convert can be discerned is the conversion account or narrative. The convert does not simply provide a transparent account of his or her experiences that grants the researcher direct access to 'what really happened'. Instead converts engage in biographical reconstruction such that their past lives are re-interpreted in light of the present. The expectations of the communities of which they are now part, and the roles to which they are now committed, influence the ways in which converts tell their stories. As we have seen with Paul, there is thus raised the issue of reliability. To what extent can conversion narratives be trusted? Is it true that, 'the conversion account is both apologetic and anachronistic ... the conversion account, never disinterested, is a condensed, or disguised, description of the convert's *present*, which he legitimates through his retrospective creation of a past and a self'?[34] In this form, such questioning implicitly seems to doubt the integrity of the individuals concerned, but, in its sharpest form, it can embody a claim about the nature of language. The claims of converts about their experiences 'have ultimately to do with the possibility that a particular language may bring about self-transformation. ... It is through the use of language in the conversion narrative that the processes of increased commitment and self-transformation take place.'[35] In giving an account of their experience, converts offer samples of the language that is itself the key factor that brought about, and sustains, conversion. On this view, researchers should abandon the attempt to penetrate behind the language of the narrative to the conversion experience itself, for the narrative constitutes the

---

[33] Ibid., pp. 166–72.

[34] Fredriksen, 'Paul and Augustine', p. 33 (her emphasis).

[35] P.G. Stromberg, *A Study of the Christian Conversion Narrative* (Cambridge: Cambridge University Press, 1993), p. xi.

experience. Conversion accounts are inherently unreliable not because of a lack of integrity on the part of individual converts, but because they claim to refer to an experience not constituted solely by their own language.

Whichever form is taken by such doubts about the reliability of conversion accounts, the fact that they are raised points the study of conversion in a particular direction. Conversion is understood not as an experience but as a social construct based on the norms of religious communities.[36] Rather than recounting a past experience that provides the basis and explanation of the convert's present, conversion accounts reshape and explain the past in ways consistent with present commitments. In relation to Paul, we have already questioned whether such a pessimistic view is warranted. The inescapable reality that all accounts of the past are simultaneously interpretations of the past does not in itself necessarily lead to unreliability. Further, precisely because conversions take place to, or within, particular religious traditions, converts do not enter upon the experience of conversion entirely devoid of expectations as to what conversion might involve. Far from rendering experience inaccessible, religious communities and the vocabularies they authorise may enable experience. Later accounts that conform to the expectations of a tradition as to what conversion ought to be like may reflect the actual experience quite closely because such expectations were already a factor at the time of conversion. Those who regard conversion as a social construct could suggest that rather than enabling experience, this is simply another kind of construction, anticipatory rather than retrospective.[37] However, if this were the case, the nature of accounts of the experience of conversion would not evolve over time. The

---

[36] For an excellent introduction to social constructionist accounts of conversion, see U. Popp-Baier, 'Conversion as Social Construction', in C.A.M. Hermans et al. (eds.), *Social Constructionism and Theology* (Leiden: E.J. Brill, 2002), pp. 41–61.

[37] E.V. Gallacher, *Expectation and Experience: Explaining Religious Conversion* (Atlanta: Scholar's Press, 1990), p. 138 quotes W. Proudfoot, *Religious Experience* (Berkeley: University of California Press, 1985), who argues that 'Beliefs and attitudes are formative of, rather than consequent upon, the experience. They define in advance what experiences are possible.'

existence of authorised interpretations of conversion within religious traditions would be a dead hand, whereas, in reality, the traditional materials provided by authorised interpretations need not always be deployed in entirely traditional ways. New religious traditions with new accounts of religious experience in general, and conversion in particular, do emerge. The possibility of originality in the interpretation of one's own conversion still exists, and Paul himself may be one of the most significant examples of this. As Luke Johnson puts it:

> The fact that symbols *change* in meaning, sometimes slowly, sometimes with amazing speed, is the surest indication that something more than human linguistic patterns are at work and that the term *experience* points to something real in the world that is not completely captured by our pre-set explanations and interpretations. The traffic, in short, moves both ways. Our language shapes our experience, but our experience also stretches, reshapes, and sometimes even shatters our language.[38]

If this is the case, then conversion accounts can indeed be studied for what they tell us about conversion experiences. However, this does not mean that the conversion experience can be distilled from the account and viewed in isolation from the other factors involved in its interpretation by the convert. Complex relationships exist between conversion experiences and interpretations of them authorised by religious communities, between such interpretations and the conversion accounts offered by individuals, and between conversion experiences and conversion accounts. Students of conversion need to direct their attention to these relationships, in which the weight of the different elements will vary from individual to individual and from context to context. For Paul himself, the recognition that he is actively engaged as he moves through life in an ongoing process of reflection on his conversion experience does not mean that we are compelled to view his conversion simply as his own construction. While our reflections on Paul's biographical statements about his conversion lend partial

---

[38] L.T. Johnson, *Religious Experience in Earliest Christianity: A Missing Dimension in New Testament Studies* (Minneapolis: Augsburg Fortress, 1998), p. 50 (his emphasis).

support to the new paradigm of the active convert, and confirm that he engaged in biographical reconstruction, his conviction that his conversion was an expression of divine grace (Gal. 1:15; 1 Cor. 15:10) and not his own decision bears witness that such activity takes place in the context of the sometimes revolutionary impact of experience.

Paul and the Conversion of Others

All the questions that we have discussed so far reflect the relationship between Paul's own conversion experience, its interpretation, and methodological issues in the study of conversion today. However, Paul was a convert who spent his life making converts of others. Another significant issue is therefore that of the connection, as Paul understood it, between his own conversion and that of others. Did he conceive his own conversion as normative, expecting that of others to conform to its pattern, or did he expect there to be significant differences? What is the relationship between Paul's own conversion and the interpretations of conversion that he implicitly 'authorised' as a figure of authority for the churches that he founded?

Paul's perspective on Jewish and Gentile conversion

When considering Paul's perspective on the conversion of others we should remember that, as apostle to the Gentiles, he was an advocate of conversion whose ability to control the process was limited. Converts bring their existing cultural resources to the task of interpreting their new faith. Their perspectives on their own conversion may not conform entirely to that of its advocate. Paul can tell the Corinthians that 'you are the seal of my apostleship in the Lord' (1 Cor. 9:2), but his correspondence with them reveals considerable frustration that they do not see everything about their new faith in the way that he would wish. It is also the case that Paul's understanding of conversion was controversial in his relations with other Jewish Christians. Paul's conviction that justification is by faith and not by works of the law, and his insistence that law observance is not necessary for Gentile Christians, are usually discussed as issues in his theology or soteriology.

However, they also gave him a particular attitude towards conversion, where soteriology is expressed in action.

Yet, despite these situations of tension or conflict, as we explore Paul's attitude towards conversion we discover indications of diversity. Although his understanding of conversion contains a stable theological core in which the death and resurrection of Christ bring freedom from the guilt and power of sin for those who believe the gospel, Paul does not expect this core always to be expressed in thought or action in exactly the same way. We may begin in the linguistic sphere where Paul rarely uses what might be thought the obvious terms with which to describe conversion. The English word 'conversion' is derived from the Latin verb to turn round (*convertere*), and the possible Greek equivalents such as turn? (ἐπιστρέφω) or repent ?(μετανοέω) appear only infrequently in Paul.[39] Further, Paul tends not to use terms descriptive of Christian identity solely to refer back to the start of the Christian life. Some terms he can apply to past, present and future; others belong predominantly to one of these phases of the Christian life, but not exclusively so.[40] He does not describe conversion in a single way, nor does he have a technical vocabulary that refers only to conversion. The cognate words groups containing the verbs call? (καλέω), justify? (δικαιόω), and believe ?(πιστεύω), are major ones, but many others appear also. For example, when referring to the conversion of the Corinthians, Paul tells them in 1 Corinthians 6:11 not only that they were justified but also that they were washed (ἀπολούω) and sanctified (ἁγιάζω). Paul is prepared to use a wide range of linguistic resources to express what happens when a person begins the Christian life.

When we turn to consider the plight from which conversion to Christ rescues men and women, Paul insists that Jew and Greek alike are under the power of sin (Rom. 3:9). All without

---

[39] The former is used only at 1 Thess. 1:9–10 and 2 Cor. 3:15–16 to describe someone coming to be in Christ, the latter not at all.

[40] Thus, for example, of twenty five occurrences of the verb δικαιόω (justify) only twelve are in the aorist tense. Paul uses it to refer back to conversion, but not only that, and the verb σῴζω (save) is used twenty times but only twice in the aorist tense (Rom. 8:24, 1 Cor. 1:21). Paul characteristically uses it to refer to the present or future rather than to conversion.

distinction need the salvation that comes to those who have faith (Rom. 1:16), and all are one through union with Christ Jesus (Gal. 3: 27–8). However, the patterns of enslavement to, and liberation from, sin's power are subtly different for Jewish and Gentile converts. Some texts are particularly useful for illustrating the conversion of Gentiles. In 1 Corinthians 14:24–25, Paul imagines the impact of prophecy on an outsider who enters the worship meeting of the church. The secrets of the heart of the outsider are laid bare (φανερόω), who is convicted (ἐλέγχω) by all and examined (ἀνακρίνω) by all. The result is a confession that God is truly present in the community. The use made of similar vocabulary elsewhere, especially in 1 Corinthians 4:1–5, leaves little doubt that the secrets of the heart laid bare concern sin. The outsider is thus convicted by a revelation of sin that was previously hidden, not in the sense that things have been done without knowing it, but rather that they have not previously been recognised as sinful. Through prophecy, the conscience of the outsider is sensitised to previously unrecognised sin and conversion achieved by the impact of this on a previously untroubled mind.

The importance of unrecognised sin can also be seen in the rather different context of 1 Corinthians 6:9–11. Here Paul concludes his criticism of the Corinthians' quarrels and their court cases against one another by reminding them of their conversion. They no longer number among the sinners catalogued in the vice list of 6:9–10, conversion having transformed their identity. They must behave in accordance with who they now are. What is striking about the vice list is that it includes some specific sins one doubts were applicable to the past lives of many, if any, of the Corinthian Christians. For example, the term often translated 'robbers' (ἅρπαγες) seems to imply theft with violence. Similarly, how many Corinthians had been truly greedy, or drunkards, or slanderers? Yet the list begins with sexual immorality and idolatry. Given the negative Jewish evaluation of Graeco-Roman norms for sexual behaviour, and of all Graeco-Roman religion as idolatrous, it is difficult to see that many, if any, of the Gentile Corinthian Christians could have avoided these sins in their previous lives. The list serves to place these aspects of their former lives in the category of sin alongside conduct that they probably would already have regarded as wrong before their conversion. Paul invites them to recognise as sin behaviour previously regarded as acceptable. It thus seems that Paul understands the conversion of Gentiles to involve a radical redefinition of moral identity.

When we turn to Paul's own conversion, we find that his understanding of the changes in his own life as a Jewish convert reflect his core convictions that all are under the power of sin and that all must be united with Christ, and yet that there is a different pattern from Gentile converts. Paul's brief accounts of his life as a Pharisaic Jew (Gal. 1:13–14; Phil. 3:4–6) suggest little dissatisfaction with his own performance. Instead he excels, and his persecution of the church stems from his zealous enthusiasm for that which is right. The revolution is, of course, that writing now as the apostle of Christ, Paul knows his persecuting activity as a sin. What his conscience then approved, it now condemns. Paul's fundamental plight was thus the same as that of his Gentile converts; the power of sin was such that he could not recognise his own sin for what it was. Only in Christ has he gained a true perspective. The difference is that he can still refer to himself and Peter as 'not Gentile sinners' (Gal. 2:15). His general characterisation of Judaism remains positive, and there is nothing to suggest the kind of radical redefinition of ethical identity that texts like 1 Corinthians 6:11 require for Gentile converts.

To believe in a crucified Messiah, or no longer to define the boundaries of God's people by Torah observance, are massive shifts for Paul, but of a rather different kind.[41] As he looks back on his former life, Paul could scarcely characterise it by means of a vice list. He thinks of it rather as the concrete embodiment of all that is good in human piety and achievement, something that makes all the more horrific the emergence from his commitment to

---

[41] To characterise these shifts, particularly the second, as not belonging to the realm of ethical identity itself reflects a rather Christian sense of what constitutes ethics. This characterisation is used here simply to highlight the different kind of changes involved for Paul in the conversion of Jews and Gentiles and is not intended to deny that from a Jewish perspective no longer to define the boundaries of God's people by Torah observance involves ethical changes of great magnitude. S.J. Gathercole, 'Review of S.J. Chester, *Conversion at Corinth*,' in *Journal for the Study of the New Testament* 26.2 (2003), pp. 246–48 offers appropriate criticism at this point (246).

it of Paul's persecution of the church. It is indicative of the depth of human enslavement to the power of sin that evil emerges even from that which is good, and it is this which necessitates the renouncement of everything else as loss for the sake of knowing Christ (Phil. 3:8). For Jew and Gentile alike, Paul considers that conversion involves liberation from the power of sin through Christ, and this liberation involves the recognition of previously unrecognised sin. Nevertheless, Paul urges a Christian moral identity continuous in many ways with Jewish moral identity and discontinuous with a typical Gentile moral identity precisely at the points, such as idolatry and sexual immorality, that Judaism took issue with it. Paul thought of the plight from which conversion delivered those who believed in Christ as a universal human one, but this did not dictate simple uniformity. For Jews and Gentiles, conversion involved different changes. Paul did not expect the conversion of all to conform in every way to his own.

Paul as a paradigm for the conversion of others

These elements of diversity in Paul's understanding of conversion are fascinating in relation to subsequent church history, where Paul's status as the archetypal convert has been influential, especially within Protestantism. For as we have noted previously, religious communities often develop normative definitions of conversion. It is one of the reasons that researchers do not find in conversion a single, easily identifiable universal phenomenon. Communities may be specific in detailing what is expected for a conversion to be regarded as legitimate within their own tradition. For several centuries, different Protestant communities have faced the question of whether a genuine conversion experience ought to conform to the pattern of Paul's own.[42] The conclusion of some communities, whether explicit or implicit, that there should be such conformity mirrors in religious experience and theological discourse what has often been the case in research and secular discourse. Other conversions are assessed by what is understood as the pattern of Paul's own. In recent years, some North American

---

[42] See the discussion in B. Corley, 'Interpreting Paul's Conversion – Then and Now' in R. Longenecker (ed.), *The Road from Damascus: The Impact of Paul's Conversion on His Life, Thought and Ministry* (Grand Rapids: Eerdmans, 1997), pp. 1–17 (9–13).

scholars have tackled this issue, calling for more diversity in Protestant understandings of what constitutes Christian conversion. However, whereas our discussion of diversity in Paul's understanding of conversion focussed on different processes of redefinition of moral identity for Jews and Gentiles, the debate here has been more concerned with the dramatic and sudden nature of Paul's conversion.

Richard Peace argues that Mark's Gospel describes 'the unfolding conversion of the twelve'.[43] This describes an experience with quite different contours from that of Paul, but with very similar content: 'The experience of Paul and the experience of the Twelve are different to be sure. The turning of Paul is rapid; the turning of the Twelve is slow. But the core characteristics that define each of these turnings are the same.'[44] Scot McKnight doubts that the core characteristics of the conversion of Paul and conversion in the Gospels can be identified together so closely. His study of the latter finds a compatibility with the stage model offered by Rambo that cannot be discerned in Paul. He argues 'that those who understand conversion through the lens of Paul's experience move the conversion experience away from the norm to the dramatic ... Instead what we find is that a sociological approach to the Gospel evidence reveals that Peter's conversion illustrates most completely the normal pattern.'[45] Nevertheless, by normal McKnight does not mean normative. He does not intend to replace insistence on a Pauline pattern with insistence on a Petrine one. The burden of both studies is that Protestant communities should expect and accept greater diversity in patterns of conversion. To take Paul as the archetypal convert to whose pattern subsequent converts should conform is to neglect other evidence from the New Testament itself.

The example of Paul therefore once again alerts us to some of the complexities involved in the study of conversion. It is not only that the definitions of conversion employed are vital, and not only is there a variable relationship between conversion experiences, conversion accounts and the interpretations of conversion

---

[43] Peace, *Conversion in the New Testament*, p. 4.

[44] Ibid., p. 280.

[45] S. McKnight, *Turning to Jesus: The Sociology of Conversion in the Gospels* (Louisville & London: WJKP, 2002), p. 176.

authorised by religious communities. It is also that particular definitions and authorised interpretations of conversion may themselves be more or less uniform, more or less flexible. In Paul's case, we see a strong insistence on certain core elements of conversion as he defines it that are necessary for everyone, but also the implicit recognition that in other ways conversion to Christ may be different for Jews and Gentiles. In the arguments presented by Peace and McKnight about Paul we find theological rationales presented for the adjustment in a more flexible direction of the definitions and authorised interpretations of conversion operative within particular religious communities. Paul's conversion as usually interpreted should not be normative for others. If these arguments are successful in achieving their goals then experiences that might previously not have been regarded as conversion within particular traditions will come to be accepted as such. Within communities that value conversion highly this would be a significant change. Here is yet another confirmation of the historical nature of conversion itself. Even within particular religious traditions it will not stand still, but evolves over time.[46]

Conclusions and Implications

Paul's status as both archetypal and disputed convert means that to study him in relation to conversion yields not only conclusions about him, but also about the study of conversion. In particular, we have seen the following.

The arguments advanced by Stendahl to support the view that Paul was called rather than converted do not stand up to scrutiny. Paul's own use of the vocabulary of calling militates against construing it and conversion as opposite categories. The adequacy of Stendahl's definition of conversion is thus brought into question, and this highlights the significant part played by definitions of

---

[46] A. Kreider, in his *The Change of Conversion and the Origin of Christendom* (Harrisburg, PA.: Trinity Press International, 1999), studies the development of conversion during the first six centuries of Christianity. He focuses on the differences between conversion in the second and sixth centuries but still discerns sufficient continuity to discuss becoming a Christian in both contexts as 'conversion'. The category develops across without thereby necessarily becoming incoherent.

conversion in its study. We may appropriately term Paul a convert, and his experience of coming to Christ a conversion, so long as we are clear about how we are using the term and so long as it is clear from whose perspective conversion is so defined. Students of conversion should be aware of common elements in conversion across space and time, and therefore of likely lines of investigation, but also they should be keenly aware that such elements may be combined in very different ways within conversion according to historical and cultural context.

The attempt to suggest that Paul's conversion is not significant for his theology is unconvincing, but raises profound questions about the relationship between later concerns and interests and the accounts offered by converts of their experiences. To say that Paul's experience shaped his theology is not necessarily to say that this theology emerged complete in the immediate aftermath of his conversion. It could be that his conversion experience shaped his reaction to subsequent issues in his career as a missionary, and that these episodes prompted further reflection on the significance of his conversion experience. To acknowledge this is not to identify development in conversion accounts with distortion, or to reach the view that conversion is simply a social construct in which the convert is complicit. Experience may itself exert influence, and not only be shaped by other factors. It is, however, to recognise the existence of a complex web of relationships between conversion experiences, conversion accounts and the interpretations of conversion authorised by particular communities as part of their social identity. Students of conversion need to be aware of these relationships and to explore them, avoiding the assumption that influence flows between these elements in only one direction. The relative importance of each may vary from case to case and context to context.

Paul's understanding of conversion does have a stable theological core, but he makes flexible use of a diverse vocabulary in order to describe it and does not expect conversion to be an identical process for Jew and Gentile. In particular, he expects a different and more radical reformulation of moral identity for Gentiles than for Jews. Paul himself shows that particular definitions of conversion do not necessarily insist on uniformity in conversion. There may be some flexibility within them. Students of conversion should carefully assess definitions in this regard, probing carefully for features that are regarded as essential and those that are allowed to be variable. Paul's own limited flexibility in his understanding of conversion contrasts with the insistence within some strands of Protestantism on their interpretation of Paul's conversion as normative for all experiences of conversion. Recent attempts within Protestant scholarship to challenge this insistence highlights the way in which authorised definitions of conversion change and develop within traditions. Students of conversion need to be aware of this and not assume that the same words and concepts mean precisely the same thing at one historical moment as another, even within the same tradition.

Contained in all three of these conclusions is the recognition that the term 'conversion' describes not a single universal phenomenon but rather a cluster of related phenomena strung out across space and time. When we study conversion in various historical and cultural contexts, there is no reason to deny ourselves the use of contemporary definitions from the social sciences and other disciplines so long as we remain fully aware of the implications. In the case of those who apply to themselves the concept of conversion, we need to be aware that their understanding of it may not precisely match the contemporary definition that we are using to help us to analyse them. For those who do not apply the concept to themselves, but whose experience nevertheless seems to belong within the cluster of related phenomena now termed conversion, we need to remember that they are being discussed as converts *in relation to* our interests as researchers. Paul himself stands on the cusp between these two categories. The pervasive influence of his vocabulary, and of interpretations of his Damascus Road experience, on the understandings subsequently packed into the term 'conversion' reflect his position as archetypal convert,[47] but his failure to make much use of the possible Greek equivalents to the

---

[47] Along with the language already discussed, one might point as influential his images of transformation such as new creation?(καινὴ κτίσις, Gal. 6:15; 2 Cor. 5:17), being conformed to Christ (σύμμορφος, Rom. 8:29; Phil. 3:10, 21), being transformed into his likeness (μεταμορφόομαι, μετασχηματίζω, Rom. 12:2; 2 Cor. 3:18; Phil. 3:21), being joined to him (κολλάω, Rom. 12:9; 1 Cor. 6:17), and being united with him (σύμφυτος, Rom. 6:5).

Latin verb *convertere* remind us that he is also a disputed convert. The view that Paul may appropriately be described as a convert has been defended in this essay, but the winning of that argument is only truly helpful if it is allied to a concern to explore Paul's very significant place in the historical development of conversion.

The fact that he occupies such a significant place in its history of course builds some circularity into such study of Paul and conversion. The definitions of conversion found in contemporary social science and other branches of study, which one might use as analytical tools to probe the New Testament data, are partially shaped by the Pauline materials. There is thus a danger that answers to questions about Paul and conversion are partially determined by Paul without that fact being recognised by the researcher. This is not dissimilar to the problem attendant upon attempts to employ the typology of sects in the study of early Christianity. Bengt Holmberg points out that Troeltsch developed this typology as a result of his reflections upon medieval Christian history. We must reckon with 'the circular reasoning involved in using Christian sects of later ages to analyse and explain that very movement that they all wanted to imitate to the best of their capacity: New Testament Christianity'![48] Despite the cloak of a later, largely secular, discourse, the specifically Christian conceptual roots of much Western social scientific theory remain plain.[49]

Yet for certain purposes, the inherent likelihood of a close fit between the analytical tools selected and the subject of study may be an advantage. If we wish to compare Paul's understanding of conversion with others, contemporary scholarly definitions of conversion may be helpful as sensitising devices. When well chosen, they provide us with recognition of dimensions of conversion widespread in later contexts, to the possible presence of

---

[48] B. Holmberg, *Sociology and the New Testament* (Minneapolis: Augsburg Fortress, 1990), pp. 11–12.

[49] For a recent influential discussion of this relationship, see J. Milbank, *Theology and Social Theory: Beyond Secular Reason* (Oxford: Blackwell, 1990).

[50] Conscious of previous studies that tended to emphasise the individual and cognitive dimensions of conversion at the expense of the communal and moral or vice versa, in my study of conversion in Pauline Christianity I adopted as a sensitising device the suggestion of B. Jules-Rosette that

which we ought to be alert in the Pauline evidence.[50] They enable us to formulate preliminary questions about changes in experience and belief, community and morality, and the rituals that mark them. Such questions may be revised or discarded as unhelpful in the light of research. The aim is to be sensitive to the available evidence not to force it into pre-determined shapes. The Pauline inheritance of contemporary definitions of conversion does, however, mean that they may be less useful for purposes that are not comparative. One may be appreciative, for example, of Segal's use of contemporary sociological resources in his study of Paul, and of McKnight's use of Rambo's process model in his study of conversion in the Gospels, without accepting their claims that their fruitful use of such resources demonstrates something objective about Paul or Jesus in relation to the nature of conversion perceived as a universal and essentially unchanging category.[51] Such claims overlook the problem of the Pauline inheritance, which means that contemporary definitions of conversion have only limited explanatory power, both in relation to Paul, and in relation to the study of later instances of conversion where Paul has also been influential on the individuals and communities involved. To apply, or to refuse to do so, the terms conversion and convert in relation to particular experiences and people does not tell us very much about historical reality unless the definitions in relation to which such decisions are made are clearly described.

---

conversion is 'an experience rooted in both self and society. It involves a personally acknowledged transformation of self and a socially recognised display of change'. See Chester, *Conversion at Corinth*, pp. 12–15 and B. Jules-Rosette, 'The Conversion Experience: The Apostles of John Maranke', *Journal of Religion in Africa* 7 (1976), pp. 132–64 (132).

[51] McKnight comments that 'the claim of L.R. Rambo is that the consensus model he presents fits the evidence to conversion for all religious conversions. Granted his modern evidence, we are led to think that all conversions, both modern and ancient, fit the same pattern. Our study confirms the model for conversion to Jesus' (*Turning to Jesus*, p. 176). This conclusion overlooks the potential influence of the New Testament on Rambo in formulating his model of conversion.

9

Conversion to Christianity

The Colonisation of the Mind?*

Brian Stanley

Missionary activity always holds an implicit psychological violence, however discretely it is conducted. It is aimed at turning the minds and hearts of people away from their native religion to one that is generally unsympathetic and hostile to it ... Missionary activity and conversion, therefore, is not about freedom of religion. It is about the attempt of one religion to exterminate all others. Such an exclusive attitude cannot promote tolerance or understanding or resolve communal tensions. The missionary wants to put an end to pluralism, choice and freedom of religion. He wants one religion, his own, for everyone and will sacrifice his life to that cause. True freedom of religion should involve freedom from conversion. The missionary is like a salesman targeting people in their homes or like an invader seeking to conquer. Such disruptive activity is not a right and it cannot promote social harmony ... the conversion mentality is inherently intolerant ... conversion is inherently an unethical practice and inevitably breeds unethical results.[1]

* This paper is republished with kind permission of the World Council of Churches from *International Review of Mission*, Vol. XCII, No. 366 (July 2003): pp. 315–31.
[1] David Frawley, 'The Missionary Position', BJP: News Reports, www.bjp.org/news/feb1799.htm (last accessed December 19, 2002). For helpful comments on earlier drafts of this article, I am indebted to David Burnett, Robert E. Frykenberg, John Lonsdale, and Steve Walton.

Those statements are extracted from an article, cheekily entitled 'The Missionary Position', which has been displayed for over two years on the website of the Bharatiya Janata Party, the governing party of India. The author is David Frawley, or Vamadeva Shastri, an American who, it should be noted, is himself a convert – from Catholicism to Hinduism. Frawley's statements are characteristic of Hindu attempts to brand missionary religions, and Christianity in particular, as intrinsically intolerant, and conversely to claim for a Hindu monistic perspective on religious truth a monopoly of the virtue of tolerance. In the name of 'pluralism, choice and freedom of religion' he is implicitly supporting the right and duty of the Indian government to take legislative action to curb Christian evangelistic activity in India.[2]

By way of comment on these claims by a Hinduised American, we may refer to a native of India who is now a professor of English and Comparative Literature at Columbia University in New York. In her provocative book, *Outside the Fold: Conversion, Modernity, and Belief*, Gauri Viswanathan has argued that religious conversion is profoundly threatening to dominant communities, for it possesses the potential to destabilise the equilibrium between majority and minority. In such contexts of disparity, she points out,

> dominant communities prefer to use the term 'proselytism' rather than 'conversion' to indicate the forcible nature of religious change. The term also carries with it a baggage of associations that identify religious change as an effect of manipulation, propagandistic activity, loss of individual self-control and will power, and sustained political mobilization. The use of the term 'proselytism' further denies subjectivity, agency, or choice to the subject and replaces individuals with masses as the unit of analysis.[3]

---

[2] For an authoritative recent survey of debates over Christian conversion in modern India, see Sebastian Kim, *In Search of Identity: Debates on Religious Conversion in India* (New Delhi: Oxford University Press, 2002).

[3] Gauri Viswanathan, *Outside the Fold: Conversion, Modernity, and Belief* (Princeton, NJ: Princeton University Press, 1998), p. 87. For an argument that the very notion of a Hindu 'majority' in India is a myth created in the interests of fundamentalist elites see R.E. Frykenberg 'The Concept of 'Majority' as a Devilish Force in the Politics of Modern India', *Journal of Commonwealth and Comparative Politics* 25 (1987), pp. 267–74.

Viswanathan's observations can be given a broader application. It can be said that Frawley's identification of a commitment to conversion with the proselytism that denies religious freedom and toleration is representative of majority opinion in Western pluralistic societies, whether in intellectual circles or at the level of generally received wisdom. Beneath the placid surface of the current pluralist orthodoxy in religious studies are flowing currents of an essentially illiberal kind: it is assumed that for the sake of ethnic harmony and mutual human understanding religious affiliation should, *even* must, remain confined within the traditional territorial boundaries of particular communities of faith. Missionary or conversionist religions that refuse to acknowledge those boundaries as sacrosanct are deemed guilty of the sins of 'proselytism' and 'intolerance'.

The main thrust of the secular academic case against Christian missions is no longer that missions have been besmirched historically by the extent of their complicity with the expansionist or exploitative designs of Western colonial governments. Although the damage done to Christian mission by the extent of its historical compromises with the colonial project is self-evident to Christians, there is now discernible in secular scholarship what one historian has termed 'a gathering swell of reaction against binary models which assume that Christianity was little more than a tool of imperialism, and that it is best analysed within the context of colonial imposition or capitalist machination'.[4] This realignment reflects the weakening hold of classical Marxism on historians, who are now less inclined to locate the heart of the imperial impulse in the grand designs of colonial governments or their subservience to capitalist interests. Rather, the focus of attention has shifted from politics and economy to culture, mentality and language. This reorientation has led analyses of Christian missions in two potentially divergent directions.

On the one hand, following the example of Edward Said's massively influential *Orientalism*,[5] historians and postcolonial

---

[4] Leon De Kock, *Civilising Barbarians: Missionary Narrative and African Textual Response in Nineteenth-Century South Africa* (Johannesburg: Witwatersrand University Press and Lovedale Press, 1996), p. 14.

[5] Edward Said, *Orientalism* (London: Routledge & Kegan Paul, 1978).

theorists are now more concerned to expose the intellectual and discursive structures of representation and mentality that under-pinned assumptions of European superiority over the oriental or pagan 'other' in the colonial past, and continue to do so in more subtle form in the postcolonial present. The colonisation of the mind through the inculcation of Western education, literature and religion is now seen to be logically prior to, and ultimately more destructive than, the colonisation of material resources and the territory that contains them. From this perspective, conversion to Christianity has invited attention as the alleged symbolic moment of capitulation to the cultural and ideological power of the West.

The Congolese philosopher V.Y. Mudimbe presents a stark example of this approach. Mudimbe has made the sweeping claim that 'missionary speech is always pre-determined, pre-regulated, let us say *colonised*'.[6] It should be noticed that any understanding of evangelisation merely as the transmission of a fixed body of propositional truth will tend to reinforce the conviction of oppo-nents of Christian mission that it is *intrinsically* about the colonis-ation of consciousness. Mudimbe concludes:

> A person whose ideas and mission come from and are sustained by God is rightly entitled to the use of all possible means, even violence, to achieve his objectives. Consequently, 'African conversion' rather than being a positive outcome of a dialogue – unthinkable per se – came to be the sole position the African could take in order to survive as a human being.[7]

The possibility of a genuine dialogue between missionary and hearer leading to the outcome of conversion is thus dismissed as 'unthinkable'. In Mudimbe's indignation against the missionary program of 'domestication', he deprives Africans of any independ-ent will or agency except the inclination to collaborate in their own domestication through acceptance of the 'social engineering'

---

[6] V.Y. Mudimbe, *The Invention of Africa: Gnosis, Philosophy, and the Order of Knowledge* (Bloomington & Indianapolis, IN: Indiana Univer-sity Press, 1988), p. 47.

[7] Ibid., p. 48. See the comments of J.D.Y. Peel, *Religious Encounter and the Making of the Yoruba* (Bloomington, IN: Indiana University Press, 2000), pp. 4–6.

of training an indigenous priesthood. The climax of the conversion process is thus assimilation to an alien identity:

> the phase where the convert, individually a 'child', assumes the identity of a style imposed upon him or her to the point of displaying it as his or her nature; the conversion has then worked perfectly: the 'child' is now a candidate for assimilation, insofar as he or she lives already as an entity made for reflecting both a Christian essence and, say, a Domincan [*sic*] or a Franciscan or a Jesuit style.[8]

For Mudimbe, as for many other commentators today, to be confident that one has God on one's side legitimates coercion or violence in the pursuit of one's divinely sanctioned aims: in his view, as also in Frawley's, the illusory certainty of faith leads inevitably to the unethical outcome of psychological domination.

It is doubtful, however, whether such monochromatic interpretations as Mudimbe's represent the majority view, at least among scholars who take historical evidence seriously. The growing emphasis on the cultural and linguistic fabric of imperialism has promoted the study of missions as inter-cultural encounters, and hence has stimulated the asking of questions about the perceptions and aspirations of those to whom missions were directed. From this standpoint, the phenomenon of conversion to Christianity or Islam in modern Africa or other primal societies has demanded investigation as an instance of unusually sharp cultural discontinuity – as a 'great transformation' in which individuals or, more commonly, groups reformulate their identity in response to major changes in the scale and contours of their social environment.[9] Such a line of inquiry invites the scholar to seek to inhabit the mental framework of the indigenous receptor. As such, it tends to undermine interpretations of conversion as the colonisation of the mind, for, once an indigenous standpoint has been adopted,

---

[8] V.Y. Mudimbe, *The Idea of Africa* (London: James Currey; Bloomington & Indianapolis, IN: Indiana University Press, 1994), p. 109.

[9] See Robin Horton, 'African Conversion', *Africa* 41 (1971), pp. 85–108 and 'On the Rationality of Conversion', *Africa* 45 (1975), pp. 219–35, 373–99; Robert W. Hefner (ed.), *Conversion to Christianity: Historical and Anthropological Perspectives on a Great Transformation* (Berkeley, CA, and Oxford: University of California Press, 1993), ch. 1.

what is no longer politically correct (and quite rightly so) is to deny any independent agency to indigenous actors. Thus Gauri Viswanathan, once a research student of none other than Edward Said, began her academic quest to investigate the literary and cultural underpinning of British rule in India out of a conviction, inspired by the theories of the Italian Marxist Antonio Gramsci that 'cultural domination works by consent and can (and often does) precede conquest by force'.[10] Yet, as we have seen, her most recent book, as a result of taking seriously the dislocation and civil exclusion experienced by converts to Christianity under the British Raj, concludes that conversion to Christianity ran clean across the logic of British colonialism – a conclusion that is ultimately opposed to her initial premise.[11]

Despite such a notable example of the adoption of the convert's perspective leading to the collapse of a view of conversion as capitulation to Western domination, other scholars, while attempting to take the two-way nature of missionary encounters seriously, still baulk at the unpalatable conclusion that those non-Western people who became Christians did so because they found Christianity to be intrinsically attractive. This conclusion is then avoided by arguing that the missionary-indigenous encounter, although a two-way one, was rigged or skewed by the fundamental inequalities of the colonial context.

The most notable example of this interpretation of conversion is provided by the American anthropologists Jean and John Comaroff, the most influential and hotly debated secular scholars currently writing in the field of mission studies. In the first of their promised three volumes analysing the nineteenth-century London Missionary Society mission among the southern Tswana peoples of South Africa, they write that 'the missionary encounter must be regarded as a *two*-sided historical process; as a dialectic that takes into account the social and cultural endowments of, and the consequences for, *all* the actors –

---

[10] Gauri Viswanathan, *Masks of Conquest: Literary Study and British Rule in India* (London: Faber & Faber, 1990): pp. ix–x, 1. Viswanathan draws on Quintin Hoare and Geoffrey Nowell Smith (eds.), *Selections from the Prison Notebooks of Antonio Gramsci* (London: Lawrence & Wishart, 1971), p. 57.

[11] Viswanathan, *Outside the Fold*, pp. 88, 93, 110–11.

missionaries no less than Africans'.[12] However, this splendidly
sensible statement is, in practice, undermined by the way in
which the Comaroffs actually treat the subject of 'conversion
and conversation' in Chapter 6 of their first volume. There they
discuss the process whereby the LMS missionaries – 'these
gentle soldiers of God's Kingdom' – became, in the long run
'every bit as effective, in making subjects, as were the
stormtroops of colonialism'.[13] For the Comaroffs, the colonisation of consciousness took place, not because dialogue was
absent, but rather because it was *stage-managed*. Missionaries
reformed the African 'by engaging him in an argument whose
terms they regulated, and whose structures bore the hegemonic
forms, the taken-for-granted tropes, of the colonising culture'.[14] If this is still dialogue, it sounds like the dialogue of the
deaf. However, in their second volume, partly in response to
their numerous critics, the Comaroffs place greater emphasis
on the fact that the Batswana, as well as the missionaries, possessed agency, and that this agency led in diverse directions, to
both resistance and acceptance, and to a host of hybridising
selective appropriations in between.[15] Nevertheless, even in
volume II, the consistent premise of the argument is that 'the
point of colonial evangelism, after all, *was* to erase what was
indigenously African and to replace it with something

---

[12] Jean and John Comaroff, *Of Revelation and Revolution: Christianity,
Colonialism, and Consciousness in South Africa* Vol. 1 (3 vols.; Chicago,
IL, and London: University of Chicago Press, 1991), p. 54. See also the
second volume in the trilogy: *Of Revelation and Revolution: The Dialec-
tics of Modernity on a South African Frontier* (Chicago, IL, and London:
University of Chicago Press, 1997).

[13] Comaroffs, *Of Revelation and Revolution*, Vol. I, p. 200.

[14] Ibid., p. 199.

[15] Comaroffs, *Of Revelation and Revolution*, Vol. II, pp. 47–53, 117.
See the comments by Charles Piot and Mark Auslander, and the
responses by the Comaroffs, in *Interventions: International Journal of
Postcolonial Studies* 3 (2001), pp. 3, 87, 113–16. This is a special issue of
the journal devoted wholly to engagement with the Comaroffs, especially
Of Revelation and Revolution, Vol. II; it reproduces papers delivered at
the December 1998 meetings of the American Anthropological
Association.

different'.[16] Such a statement may make Christians today uneasy, but it is hard to deny that this is what most nineteenth-century missionaries thought they were doing.

More dubious is the contention of volume I that missionaries so dominated the terms of the conversation that even the raw material of the conversation, the language itself, became colonised. According to the Comaroffs, the Setstwana language was reduced from 'primitive disorder' to 'literate order' – that is, classified according to Western linguistic and ethnic models, expressed in clear grammatical form, and rendered an appropriately submissive vehicle for rendering the word of God in writing. Everyday Setstwana terms, such as *modumedi* ('one who agrees') were 'commandeered' and given new Christian meaning, in this case 'believer' or 'convert'. For the Comaroffs, 'linguistic classification and translation were metonyms of an embracing process of "conversion": the process of making difference into similarity, of reducing the lower order diversities of the non-European world to the universalistic categories of the West.'[17] When all is said and done, therefore, their model of Christian conversion remains that of proselytism: the goal of the missionary enterprise, and to some degree its effect also, was religious standardisation, imprinting the image of Western evangelical Christianity on the rest of the world.

The relocation of academic interest away from studies of the formal interactions between missionary societies and colonial governments towards the dynamics of conversion to Christianity is a welcome development, although the outcome of such reorientation is not necessarily in every case to undermine simplistic views of conversion as capitulation to colonial domination. However, before proceeding with our analysis of the dynamics of conversion to Christianity in modern missionary history, it is necessary to divert our attention from the interpretation of Christian conversion in a modern mission context to conversion as it is understood in the New Testament.

Conversion itself as a noun (*epistrophē*) appears only once in the New Testament, in Acts 15:3, where Paul and Barnabas report to the Jewish believers in Phoenicia and Samaria 'the conversion of

---

[16] Comaroffs, *Of Revelation and Revolution*, Vol. II, p. 117.
[17] Comaroffs, *Of Revelation and Revolution*, Vol. I, pp. 218, 221.

the Gentiles',[18] a usage which indicates that the concept of conversion to Christianity was already something that made sense to Luke's readers. But the verb *epistrepho* (to turn, return, turn around) appears thirty-six times, in eighteen of which the meaning is a theological one, expressing the idea of turning in repentance from sin and towards God.[19] It has this meaning particularly in the book of Acts with reference to the first missionary endeavours of the early church, whether addressed to Jews or Gentiles. In Acts 'conversion' involves repentance from sin (3:19; 26:20); a turning from darkness to light, from the power of Satan to Jesus as Lord (11:21; 26:18). There is also the concept of the new birth or birth from above which is central to the vocabulary of the Johannine literature, the First Letter of Peter, and is arguably present also in the Pauline corpus in modified form as the idea of being raised, or made alive, with Christ.

The point to be stressed is that, whether the image employed is that of conversion, new birth, or spiritual resurrection, the actors involved are not simply the evangelist and the new believer or believers in Christ. All three images imply the presence and activity of the Holy Spirit. Luke's account of the first Gentile conversions in Acts stresses the initiative of the Spirit rather than human agency. It is the 'angel of the Lord' who drives Philip into the wilderness to meet the solitary Ethiopian eunuch and the Spirit who then compels him to approach his chariot (Acts 8:26, 29). It is the sudden outpouring of the Spirit on Cornelius and his household that convinces Peter and the Jerusalem church that Gentiles are to be included in the household of God (10:44–7; 11:17–18). Paul and Barnabas report to the Antioch church at the end of their first missionary journey that *God* 'had opened a door of faith for the Gentiles' (14:27). James convinces the Council of Jerusalem that the turning of the Gentiles to God but not to Judaism is to be welcomed by citing the prophets to the effect that the ingathering of all the peoples is intrinsic to the eternal purpose of God (15:13–21). The Johannine, Petrine and Pauline images lead to a similar

---

[18] All Bible quotations in this chapter are taken from the New Revised Standard Version.

[19] Colin Brown, (ed.), *New International Dictionary of New Testament Theology* Vol. I (3 vols.; Grand Rapids, MI/Exeter: Zondervan/Paternoster, 1975), p. 355.

conclusion: the rebirth or spiritual resurrection of the new believer cannot be engineered, either by him- or herself or by anyone else: more than human agency is required. Hence, whatever validity social scientific analyses of conversion may possess in relation to the general phenomenon of conversion from one religion to another, Christian theology cannot rest content with any understanding of conversion to Christ as purely a matter of human agency, whether on the part of the evangelist or the convert. The New Testament compels Christians to insist that conversion *to Christ* is an act in which the agency of the Spirit of God is primary, and that of the evangelist and the convert merely secondary.

With this foundational theological principle in mind, we can now return to the examination of the contentions made by those who see conversion to Christianity as a form of colonisation of the mind. The essence of their case is the representation of the act of evangelisation, either (as claimed by Frawley and Mudimbe) as a one-way process, in which the missionary endeavors to implant within the mind of the hearer a normative set of beliefs, a new 'religion' that replaces the previous one, or (as argued by the Comaroffs) as a lop-sided conversation in which the linguistic terms are controlled by the evangelist.

In response to Frawley and Mudimbe, we may draw upon Andrew Walls' insistence that conversion (or equally, new birth or resurrection) in the New Testament is not primarily about replacement but about the transformation and reorientation of humanity towards God.[20] The predominant emphasis is rather on the convert turning in repentance away from sin towards an acknowledgement of Jesus as Lord and Christ. This is the case whether it is Jews or Gentiles who are doing the turning. The idea of conversion as a substitution of one 'religion' for another is not uppermost. It can hardly be so in the case of Jews, since the assumption in Acts is that Jews who turn to Jesus as the Christ will continue to be Jews, worshipping Yahweh in temple or synagogue. What conversion to Jesus as Lord means for Gentiles is a crucial issue that emerges in the course of Acts, and finds its initial resolution at the Council of Jerusalem. For Gentiles the 'religious' implications of believing in

---

[20] See Andrew F. Walls, *The Missionary Movement in Christian History: Studies in the Transmission of Faith* (Maryknoll, NY/Edinburgh: Orbis Books/T&T Clark, 1996), p. 28.

Jesus were much more stark than they were for Jews, since belief in Jesus as Lord and continued adherence to the gods of the Greek pantheon was incompatible. Nevertheless, even in the Gentile case, the primary emphasis is on the direction in which peoples and their cultures turn – *to* Christ – and not on a cultural background they must leave behind. Jewish society was familiar with the person of the proselyte: a pagan who had come to believe in the God of Israel and therefore turned his or her back on their own nation and affiliated himself or herself to the nation of Israel. Circumcision was the normal requirement for male proselytes in first-century Judaism.[21] It would have been conceivable for the first Jewish Christians to insist that this pattern should be followed by the first Gentile believers. That is precisely what the Judaizing party as recorded in Acts 15 and Galatians 2 wanted. But Paul, Barnabas and (after initial hesitation) Peter carried the day in the opposite direction. The principle was established that Gentile Christians were to live as Gentiles, and not as Jews. As Walls reminds us, they were not to be proselytes – carbon copies of Jewish believers – but converts, expressing allegiance to Christ within their own cultures.[22]

Contrary to the almost universal assumption today, therefore, seeking converts to Christ is not, or *ought* not to be, a matter of engaging in proselytism, of trying to persuade others to be, think and behave exactly like us. This implies that there is a fundamental legitimacy to the quest of all those who have sought to express their allegiance to Christ as Lord within the categories of their own cultural and indeed religious background. Hence to be a Hindu Christian or even a Muslim Christian ought not to strike us as being any more problematic than the concept of a Gentile Christian was for the first Jerusalem church. This is not to deny that for a Hindu or a Muslim to be converted to Christ poses some extremely sensitive questions of which beliefs and practices have

---

[21] J. Nolland, 'Uncircumcised Proselytes?' *Journal for the Study of Judaism in the Persian, Hellenistic and Roman Period* 12/2 (1981), pp. 173–94.

[22] Walls, *Missionary Movement*, pp. 51–52; and his *The Cross-Cultural Process in Christian History: Studies in the Transmission and Appropriation of Faith* (Maryknoll, NY/Edinburgh: Orbis Books/T&T Clark, 2002), pp. 67–68.

to be abandoned, and which may be retained, just as it did for the first Gentile believers. The essential issue, however, is the same, and Western Christians, the spiritual descendants of those Gentile converts, ought to permit Hindu or Muslim seekers after Christ no less flexibility than the Council of Jerusalem permitted to the first Gentile converts.

It remains the case that for Christians there is a message to be transmitted, a Christocentric gospel that has been revealed and has to be defended against all distortions and competitors (Gal. 1:6–9). Yet in the very act of proclaiming that gospel across a cultural frontier, it is not simply the outer packaging of the message that needs to be adapted: the process of translating the message into a new cultural medium will result in a message that carries accents and tones which it did not carry before, even though there must be sufficient continuity with previous formulations of the message for it to be recognisably the same message.[23] The gospel proclaimed to Gentiles in Athens or Corinth was neither discontinuous with nor identical to that proclaimed to Jews in Jerusalem or Antioch. Moreover, the evangelists involved in such proclamation found themselves and their theological perceptions to be quite fundamentally changed in the process. Peter was never the same again after his experience in Caesarea, and his understanding of the purpose of God in Christ was immeasurably broadened. Similarly, it could be argued that Paul's evangelistic encounters with a Greek culture that placed pre-eminent value on wisdom led him to a deeper comprehension of the cross as the revelation of the 'foolish' wisdom of God (1 Cor. 1), even though it is clear that he continued to draw as a Jew on his own religious tradition of the divine wisdom.

In congruence with this New Testament pattern, scholars of modern Christian missions are beginning to write about the 'conversion of missionaries', about the quite fundamental and transformative effect of immersion in alien cultures on the mental and theological frameworks of many missionaries. In some instances, such as the religious pilgrimages travelled on Chinese soil by the Welsh Baptist Timothy Richard or, still more controversially by the American Presbyterian Pearl S. Buck, these 'reverse conversions' could lead missionaries to theological positions that

---

[23] See Walls, *Cross-Cultural Process*, p. 80.

were apparently subversive of orthodoxy.[24] But it would be misleading to isolate such contentious examples and in so doing to
imply that the vast majority of missionaries remained unaffected
by their experience, obstinately committed to rehearsing the
precise formulae and methods they had imbibed in seminary or
Bible school (though it goes without saying that this was, and is,
true of some). Evangelical Christians, because of their proper
concern to preserve the good deposit of the faith, have tended to be
particularly hesitant about admitting the dynamically interactive
and two-way nature of all true missionary encounters. They have
sometimes been slow to realise that a primary focus on the
substitutionary death of Christ for the penalty of human sin may
not be a wholly intelligible or even theologically adequate interpretation of the gospel for some peoples from a primal religious
background.[25]

One evangelical who came more rapidly to this conclusion was
J.H. Lorrain, a Baptist missionary in the Lushai Hills (now
Mizoram) in North-East India in the early twentieth century.
Within ten years of arriving in the territory, Lorrain could report
in 1912:

> Our first message as soon as we could speak the language, was of a
> Saviour from sin. But the people had no sense of sin and felt no need
> for such a Saviour. Then we found a point of contact. We proclaimed
> Jesus as the vanquisher of the Devil – as the One who had bound the
> 'strong man' and taken away from him 'all his armour wherein he
> trusted', and so had made it possible for his slaves to be free. This, to

---

[24] Ibid., pp. 236–58; Xi Lian, *The Conversion of Missionaries: Liberalism in American Protestant Missions in China, 1907–1932* (University
Park, PA: Pennsylvania University Press, 1997), pp. 95–128. See also
Lewis Rambo, *Understanding Religious Conversion* (New Haven, CT,
and London: Yale University Press, 1993), pp. 97–99, 194; and Steven
Kaplan, 'The Africanization of Missionary Christianity: History and
Typology', *Journal of Religion in Africa* 16 (1986), pp. 166–86, especially pp. 180–82.
[25] However, in some primal contexts, e.g. the Orang Olu of Sarawak, an
emphasis on penal substitutionary atonement has fitted primal religious
categories extremely well because of the prominence of sacrifice and
notions of the grave consequences of the infringement of taboos in such
societies. I owe this point to my research student Rev. Tan Jin Huat.

the Lushais, was 'Good News' indeed and exactly met their great need.[26]

Some seventy years before, a decidedly anti-charismatic American missionary in Bolivia named Peter Wagner arrived at much the same conclusion, with consequences that are now well-known; Lorrain's exposure to the reality of cross-cultural communication had led him to the perception that the formulation of the gospel customary in Western evangelicalism was neither as effective nor as authentically biblical as he had formerly supposed.[27] Today Mizoram is one of the most highly Christianised regions of the world. Missionary speech may indeed appear to be 'pre-regulated', to use Mudimbe's term, but conversion on a significant scale has usually taken place only when the pre-regulation has been abandoned and missionaries have been prepared to allow their encounters with indigenous peoples to change both them and the formulation of their message.

We turn, second, to the claim of Jean and John Comaroff, that the act of translation of Christian vocabulary into vernacular languages necessarily commits the indigenous convert to the acceptance of an alien conceptual framework.

This is a questionable representation of what is involved in the process of language learning and translation. To learn a language as a stranger in a host culture involves vulnerability and openness. Those who attempt to dictate the linguistic terms of the encounter will be very poor language learners. Doubtless some missionaries were that, but on the whole missionaries stand out from the surrounding assortment of colonial representatives by their absorbing commitment to acquire genuine fluency and understanding in the vernacular. Similarly, as Andrew Walls and Lamin Sanneh have emphasised, the process of biblical translation impels the translator (even if unconsciously or unwillingly) towards an acceptance of the fundamental equality of all cultures in the sight of God: it involves a search for dynamic equivalences, and hence

---

[26] *Baptist Missionary Society Annual Report*, 1913, p. 2, cited in C.L. Hminga, *The Life and Witness of the Churches in Mizoram* (Serkawn, Mizoram: Baptist Church of Mizoram, 1987), p. 57.
[27] See C. Peter Wagner, 'My Pilgrimage in Mission', *International Bulletin of Missionary Research* 23.4 (1999), p. 166.

the necessity of exploring cultures on their own terms.[28] Further questions arise about the Comaroffs' argument if we view the dynamics of translation from the perspective of the indigenous converts. Let us consider first evangelisation in New Testament times.

Luke tells us that the Gentile converts in Caesarea and Antioch heard a message about Jesus which proclaimed that he was Lord of all (*pantōn kyrios*; Acts 10:36) or Lord (*kyrios*; Acts 11:20). Despite the recent argument of Andrew Walls that the proclamation of Jesus in Antioch as *kyrios* rather than as *christos* – Messiah – represented a bold innovation, transposing the gospel into Hellenistic thought-forms,[29] New Testament scholars now inform us that the term *kyrios* was well rooted in Palestinian Jewish culture and that lordship had been ascribed to Jesus as early as the very first Aramaic-speaking Jerusalem church.[30] Nevertheless, Walls' argument can perhaps be recast as follows. Whatever meaning of *kyrios* may have been uppermost in the minds of Peter and the Jewish believers from Cyprus and Cyrene who preached Jesus to the Gentiles in Antioch, it is clear that what those Gentiles in Caesarea and Antioch *heard* to such signal effect was indeed a startling claim about the status of Jesus of Nazareth as one to whom could be applied in a unique and exclusive sense the term currently employed to refer to cult divinities, and, by extension through the imperial cult, to the Roman emperor. The first Jewish Christians acknowledged Jesus as *kyrios*; how far and at what

---

[28] Walls, *Missionary Movement*, pp. 26-42; Sanneh, Lamin, *Translating the Message: The Missionary Impact on Culture* (Maryknoll, NY, Orbis, 1989), pp. 192–209; *idem*, *Encountering the West: Christianity and the Global Cultural Process: The African Dimension* (London, Marshall Pickering, 1993), pp. 73–116.

[29] Walls, *Missionary Movement*, pp. 52-53; and Walls, *Cross-Cultural Process*, pp. 79–80.

[30] William Horbury, *Jewish Messianism and the Cult of Christ* (London: SCM, 1998), pp. 112–19; and Larry W. Hurtado, *One God, One Lord: Early Christian Devotion and Ancient Jewish Monotheism* (2nd edn.; Edinburgh: T&T Clark, 1998). Walls' interpretation appears to reflect an older and now largely discredited tradition of scholarship deriving from W. Bousset, *Kyrios Christos* [1913], new edition, (Nashville, TN: Abingdon Press, 1970).

stage that title began to imply ascription of divinity rather than simply the status of a messianic king is debatable; but when received into the Hellenistic world, the proclamation of Jesus as *kyrios* or, still more, as *pantōn kyrios*, acquired new and portentous layers of meaning.[31] A similar argument has been advanced in relation to the apostle Paul's inclusion in the letter to the Philippians (2:9–11 and 3:20) of exalted imperial language about Jesus which invited Gentiles to regard him as infinitely superior to the emperor.[32] First-century Jewish Christians were not afraid to apply to Jesus titles which, though well rooted in the scriptural traditions of Israel, to a Gentile audience carried distinct resonances determined by the context of the Roman Empire.

In these seminal instances drawn from the history of earliest Christianity, therefore, we find a paradigm, not of Christian evangelists dominating the terms of missionary encounters by the imposition of alien meanings on indigenous terms, but rather a preparedness to use language about Jesus which invited interpretation by the indigenous hearers in ways that led to a less ambiguous ascription of divine status to him, and hence to the clarification and enrichment of Christian doctrine.

These foundational New Testament examples are concerned with translation, not in the narrow sense of translating from one language into another, but in the broader sense of the communication of a central theological concept from one cultural medium to another. However, a similar principle can be found at work in modern missionary contexts, where translation in the narrow linguistic sense has provided the conceptual environment within which conversion to Christ has taken place.

---

[31] For a discussion of the origins of the ascription of Lordship to Jesus in relation to the Lukan writings, see J.A. Fitzmyer, *The Gospel According to Luke I-IX* (The Anchor Bible, Vol. 28; New York, NY: Doubleday, 1981), pp. 200–204. Fitzmyer tends to discount the role of missionary encounters and to posit the transfer by the first Palestinian Christians of the title *kyrios* from Yahweh to Jesus. He notes, however, that such a transfer 'is not yet to be regarded as an expression of divinity' (p. 203), an admission that leaves the door open to the formative role of the missionary context.

[32] See Peter Oakes, *Philippians: From People to Letter* (SNTS Monograph Series 110; Cambridge: Cambridge University Press, 2001), pp. 129–74.

Historians of modern Africa are now noting with some frequency the liberative potential of vernacular biblical narrative, especially the story of ancient Israel, for African peoples oppressed by slave-traders, colonial authorities, or white settlers. Many of the first converts in nineteenth-century Africa were saddled with Western names in what looks like a vindication of the Comaroff thesis of conversion as a capitulation via linguistic engineering to an alien identity. Thus the former Yoruba slave, Ajayi, freed by the British navy from a Portuguese slave ship and resettled in the recaptives' colony of Sierra Leone in 1822, was given on his baptism the name Samuel Crowther in honour of a member of the home committee of the Church Missionary Society, the Rev. Samuel Crowther of Christ Church, Newgate, in London. The fact that the Yoruba Samuel Crowther appeared before Queen Victoria and Prince Albert in 1851 resplendent in clerical black frock-coat as a trophy of the missionary enterprise before being consecrated in 1864 as the first African Anglican bishop might appear to lend further credence to the Comaroffs' case.[33] Yet by becoming 'Samuel' the young Ajayi joined his own story of literal and spiritual redemption with that of the Samuel who was the child of promise and the architect of a godly kingdom. When Crowther led the CMS mission party to his native Yorubaland and rediscovered his own mother, Afala, she was baptised in 1848 as Hannah. The anthropologist J.D.Y. Peel comments:

> As Afala bore Ajayi in the flesh, now Samuel reaffiliated himself to Hannah in the spirit. He was no longer just *any* Samuel, a Samuel named for an obscure London vicar or the bearer of a name without intrinsic meaning, but Samuel, son of Hannah. He thus fashioned a new narrative for himself, which is the more powerful because it is also an old narrative.[34]

For many individual Africans and African peoples as collectivities, as also for members of the scheduled castes of modern India, part

---

[33] See Walls, *Missionary Movement*, p. 104. For the original Samuel Crowther (1769–1829) see Donald M. Lewis (ed.), *The Blackwell Dictionary of Evangelical Biography 1730–1860* Vol. I (2 vols.; Oxford: Blackwell, 1995), p. 277.

[34] J.D.Y. Peel, 'For Who Hath Despised The Day of Small Things? Missionary Narratives and Historical Anthropology', *Comparative Studies in Society and History* 37/3 (1995), p. 597.

of the attraction of Christianity has been its foundation upon a universal scriptural narrative that held up a mirror and promise of redemption to their own local experience of marginality or oppression. It was a narrative which, in a way that could never be the case with the non-vernacular Qu'ran, invited the hearer or reader to step right into its pages, drawing the spheres of biblical and contemporary history together. As John Lonsdale puts it, 'the Bible, telling of a small tribe at the centre of history', could inspire Africans 'to counter-attack, to project on the world's stage the modern normality of their own particular ethnicity'.[35] In a similar way, Andrew Wingate's study of group conversion to Christianity of Dalits in late twentieth–century Vellore draws attention to the importance of both Old and New Testament narratives for the victims of caste oppression. In a Hindu context where human inequality is a fundamental premise of social organisation, the portrait of Jesus in the Gospels as the friend, protector and healer of the poor had a vivid immediacy.[36]

What is emerging from a number of recent studies is an emphasis on translation as a broader and more populist process than the technical business of producing authorised vernacular versions of the Bible, crucially important though that endeavour is. Most Christian converts in modern Africa heard the gospel from other Africans, many of them young people who were themselves young in the faith: historians are now describing the first African churches of the colonial era, whether Catholic or Protestant, as a youth movement.[37] These young evangelists characteristically presented the gospel through story, based on their own loose

[35] John Lonsdale, 'Jomo Kenyatta, God and the Modern World', in Jan-Georg Deutsch, Heike Schmidt, and Peter Probst (eds.), *African Modernities: Entangled Meanings in Current Debate* (Oxford: James Currey, 2002), p. 45. For an important exposition of the significance of the vernacular Bible for the formation of national identities, see Adrian Hastings, *The Construction of Nationhood: Ethnicity, Religion and Nationalism* (Cambridge: Cambridge University Press, 1997).

[36] Andrew Wingate, *The Church and Conversion: A Study of Recent Conversions to and from Christianity in the Tamil Area of South India* (Delhi: ISPCK, 1997), p. 85.

[37] Bengt Sundkler, and Christopher Steed, *A History of the Church in Africa* (Cambridge: Cambridge University Press), pp. 88–89; and John

rendering of official translations. Thus a Presbyterian missionary in Kikuyuland in 1918 doubted whether missionaries needed to translate evangelistic storybooks into Kikuyu, since Kikuyu evangelists were making their own translations of stories from the Swahili Bible and were so 'skilled in giving the gospel narratives in their own words, fitted to the understanding of the villagers'.[38]

In such hands, the translated message was very far from conforming to the Comaroffs' stereotype of the infusion of alien meanings into indigenous terms. On the contrary, the gospel proclaimed by the young Kikuyu converts (or 'readers' as they were known) was an indigenous rhetoric. Its meaning or application was the subject of intense argument between Kikuyu Christians, leading to quite diverse Christianities that continue to mark the Kenyan Christian landscape today.[39] It was also a language of debate that could be used to challenge the traditional preferences of wealthy elders. The early Kikuyu converts called the gospel *Uhoro wa Ngai* – the Word of God. But whereas European missionaries thought of *uhoro* in conceptual terms as the *Logos*, the eternal Word of God, in Kikuyu *uhoro* meant equally 'language', 'case', 'story', 'message', or 'verdict'. The gospel as *uhoro wa Ngai* was thus a polemic or argument. Converts who acceded to this argument were deemed to have 'believed'. But, like many other languages, Kikuyu did not express the variety of abstract, existential 'belief' demanded by post-Enlightenment Christianity. The Kikuyu word translated as 'believe' was *îtîkia*, 'to give assent to'. It connoted the approving sounds of collective endorsement made by a group of village elders persuaded by a convincing argument – murmuring 'Eeeh'. To 'believe in the gospel', *kuîtîkia Uhoro wa*

Lonsdale, 'Mission Christianity and Settler Colonialism in East Africa', in Holger Bernt Hansen and Michael Twaddle (eds.), *Christian Missionaries and the State in the Third World* (Oxford: James Currey, 2002), p. 199.

[38] Derek Peterson, 'The Rhetoric of the Word: Bible Translation and Mau Mau in Central Kenya', in Brian Stanley (ed.), *Missions, Nationalism, and the End of Empire* (Grand Rapids, MI: Eerdmans, 2003).

[39] John Lonsdale, 'Kikuyu Christianities: A History of Intimate Diversity', in David Maxwell and Ingrid Lawrie (eds.), *Christianity and the African Imagination: Essays in Honour of Adrian Hastings* (Leiden: Brill, 2002), pp. 157–97.

Ngai, thus meant more than the inward act of personal faith of Western Protestantism: it meant acceding to a public argument, converting to a set of premises laid out to form 'a reason that convinces', a new path of wisdom for the community.[40]

The end result of such a process of lay translation of the Christian message was not simply a form of Christianity which had high potential for indigeneity but also an understanding of what faith in Christ means that may have been closer to biblical norms than the individualised and conceptualised understanding held by the European missionaries. This discussion of the dynamics of popular communication of the gospel has a further implication that bears upon our earlier emphasis on the agency of the Holy Spirit in conversion. The final section of this article offers some tentative reflections on ways in which such interpretations by contemporary historians of conversion to Christianity from the converts' perspective might be reconciled with the insistence of theology that conversion to Christ requires the agency of the Spirit.

I have argued that the process of conversion to Christianity was less tightly regulated by the missionary than many critics suppose and indeed many missionaries desired. Evangelisation conducted by indigenous agents in a vernacular medium defies control by those who initiate the mission process in any particular region. From the very beginnings of Christian expansion in New Testament times, the message of the gospel has been heard, received, or rejected within the intellectual categories embodied in the language of the host culture. Converts have read their own stories into the pages of scripture and applied biblical narratives to their own situations. All this implies a degree of open-endedness and unpredictability in Christian missionary encounters that is both creative and dangerous. Converts have the potential to enrich or correct Christian doctrine by redressing the imbalances intrinsic to the missionary's culturally conditioned understanding of the faith. Equally, however, they have the potential to distort orthodoxy by filtering out emphases that have less resonance with their own cultural environment. Converts have responded to what they have

---

[40] This paragraph draws heavily on Peterson, 'The Rhetoric of the Word'.

seen in the gospel and not necessarily to what missionaries thought they ought to see in it. These observations suggest several conclusions.

First, it is necessary to reiterate the simple point that not all conversions to Christianity represent conversions to Christ. The visible church and the eternal body of Christ are not identical, though evangelical Christians in particular have been anxious to make the two correspond as closely as possible. Academic commentators have noted how obsessively concerned missionaries have been with the two inter-related issues of how to discern the genuineness of conversion and how to avert the threat of 'backsliding', often erecting all sorts of educational and baptismal hurdles in the path of converts in an attempt to weed out the bogus runners.[41] Christian, and especially Protestant, evangelisation in primal societies has often proceeded symbiotically with the acquisition of literacy, as is symbolised by the nomenclature of 'readers' for the first converts in East Africa. But evangelical missionaries, even as they have been eager to encourage the capacity to read the scriptures, have been wary of skin-deep converts who have been more interested in the medium than the message, more keen to become literate than to accept for themselves the truth enshrined in the biblical text. The literary scholar Vanessa Smith has described how early nineteenth-century evangelical missionaries to Polynesia, reacting to a situation in which their treasured gift of literacy was being eagerly espoused as the white man's occult power, found it necessary to erect a distinction between false and true readers. The false readers were those who did not progress beyond memorisation and mimicry of the text, whilst the true readers or converts displayed a capacity to interpret and appropriate the text for themselves. Smith observes that 'It is appropriation, paradoxically, which demonstrates a grasp of essential meaning ... Where the false converts held to the letter of the printed word, the true convert recontextualises the biblical Word.'[42] She notes that by such a distinction between

---

[41] Lonsdale, 'Mission Christianity and Settler Colonialism', p. 199.
[42] Vanessa Smith, *Literary Culture and the Pacific: Nineteenth-Century Textual Encounters* (Cambridge: Cambridge University Press, 1998), pp. 2–3.

mere repetition and true literacy missionaries had, somewhat unwillingly, surrendered the prerogative of interpretation to the convert.[43]

Smith's astute observations point towards our second concluding reflection. The true readers in her analysis were those whom the missionaries judged to have been truly converted, born again of the Spirit. They were identified by their capacity to apply the scriptures to their own situation; for them, unlike the false readers, the scripture had become a living word, personal, contemporary, and contextually specific in its thrust. Such an emphasis is, of course, congruent with the classic Reformed understanding of the relationship of word and Spirit in drawing people to faith in Christ. Faith, insisted Calvin, is no mere intellectual assent to the doctrines of Christ, but rather 'a firm and certain knowledge of God's benevolence toward us, founded upon the truth of the freely given promise in Christ, both revealed to our minds and sealed upon our hearts through the Holy Spirit'.[44] Without the breath of the Spirit, the proclaimed word of the gospel has no power to convict or save. But when the Spirit breathes upon the word, hearts and minds are turned towards Christ, and, either individually or corporately, there is the deep acceptance that the word of the gospel is indeed for us, here and now in our particular context, that eloquent 'Eeeh' of the Kikuyu elders as they become persuaded of the rhetoric of Christ. Smith's argument, though itself wholly secular, thus carries for the Christian mind the theological implication that genuine conversion to Christ, as distinct from mere conversion to Christianity as an exotic implanted religion, will be marked in some measure by inculturation, for authentic inculturation is no more nor less than a preparedness to hear, receive and interpret the word of Christ in scripture as it addresses us in our particular context and in the distinctive cadences of our own language.

---

[43] Ibid., p. 5.

[44] John Calvin, *Institutes of the Christian Religion*, edited by John T. McNeill, 2 vols. (London, SCM, 1961), Vol. I, Book III, ii.7, p. 551. In Book III, ii.8 Calvin refutes the notion of the schoolmen that there is a mere intellectual assent to the truth of Scripture that may be termed 'unformed faith'; for Calvin, all faith depends on the witness of the Spirit.

Our third summative observation may appear problematic. Any understanding of conversion to Christ as an event that requires the intervention of the Spirit of God immediately raises the dilemma of why that intervention does not invariably, or at least with uniform frequency, accompany the proclamation of the word of Christ. Thus we can suggest plausible cultural and socio-logical answers to the question of why primal religionists in the north-eastern states of India have responded eagerly to the gospel whereas the vast majority of Hindus in the remainder of India so far have not, but can we supply a wholly satisfying theological answer? I fear we cannot, and Christian academics attempting to eke out a living from the stony terrain of mission studies generally confine themselves to the more straightforward task of tilling the cultural and sociological soil, while leaving the big issue of Chris-tian theodicy to the theologians (though increasingly they too seek to avoid it by denying the soteriological necessity of conversion).

It is not difficult to perceive why there is not an invariably effi-cacious bestowal of the Spirit whenever the gospel is proclaimed. If such were to be the case, church growth would, admittedly, be a simple matter. Conversion would be guaranteed so long as the evangelist got the message right. In practice, therefore, the agency of the Spirit would disappear, for it would be an assumed and wholly forgettable part of the equation. All would depend upon the theological accuracy and homiletical competence of the evan-gelist. Any potential convert who came within the faithful evange-list's line of fire would succumb. There would be little or no scope for that convert in his or her turn to make the message authenti-cally their own, for that could imperil the automatic relationship of word and Spirit and bring the steamroller of Christian expan-sion juddering to a halt. Conversion to Christ would indeed have become the colonisation of the mind, and the New Testament vision of a richly diverse new creation united in Christ would be greatly impoverished.

What is much more problematic is how Christians can make theological sense of the seemingly unavoidable reality that God has permitted conversion to Christ to be in some measure contin-gent upon social and cultural context. Drawing the distinction between conversion to Christ and conversion to Christianity may soften the dilemma, but it does not remove it altogether, unless we are to follow modern Asian theologians such as the late Stanley Samartha, who was prepared to say that conversion to God in Christ in settings such as India need not imply conversion to Christianity.[45] We are therefore forced to construct a theology that places the structures of economy, culture and society – and even of 'religion' – within the cosmic arena of spiritual contestation in which the principalities and powers are at work. Those principalities and powers are already subject to the authority of the exalted Christ, and yet are still, for a time, active in their opposition to the gracious purposes of God for his world (Eph. 1:21–22; 3:8–10; 6:12). The perils of such a theology of spiritual warfare are manifest: all too easily in the past and even today it has led Christians into forms of crass and implicitly racist territorialism, in which particular regions of the map are branded as being peculiarly subject to satanic dominion. Such dangers are inherent in the language employed, for example, in the article on the '10/40 Window' in a recent evangelical dictionary of mission: 'From a careful analysis of the 10/40 Window, it appears that Satan and his forces have established a unique territorial stronghold that has restrained the advance of the gospel into this part of the world.'[46] No theology of the powers that explicitly or implicitly divides the world into supposed territories of darkness and supposed territories of light is acceptable. Nevertheless, some kind of integration of a theology of the role of the Spirit in conversion with the reality of the uneven spread of Christianity has to be attempted. If Christians decline that challenge, the alternatives open to them are either to abandon the global evangelistic commission as an anachronistic relic of the colonial era or to reduce Christian conversion to the colonisation of the mind by human persuasion.

Perhaps it is sufficient to conclude this article with the reminder that the sovereign unpredictability of the wind of the Spirit is

---

[45] See E. Klootwijk, *Commitment and Openness: The Interreligious Dialogue and Theology of Religions in the Work of Stanley J. Samartha* (Zoetermeer: Uitgeverij Boekencentrum, 1992), pp. 308–10.

[46] Article on '10/40 Window' in A. Scott Moreau (ed.), *Evangelical Dictionary of World Missions* (Grand Rapids, MI/Carlisle: Baker Book House/Paternoster, 2000), p. 938. The '10/40 Window' refers to the window between 10 and 40 degrees north of the equator spanning the globe from West Africa to Asia.

integral to the biblical witness (John 3:8). It is also borne out by the witness of history. The real breakthrough of Christianity to the Gentile world was provoked, apparently fortuitously, by the scattering of the Jerusalem church following the death of Stephen (Acts 11:19). In the early years of the fourth century, nobody would have predicted that the heartland of Christianity for the next millennium would lie on and even beyond the northern and western frontiers of the Roman Empire, amongst peoples then still barbarian and uncivilised, a far cry from the cultured and urban(e) Christianity of the Mediterranean world. In 1910, when representatives of Western Protestant missions gathered at the World Missionary Conference in Edinburgh to coordinate their strategy for the evangelisation of the world in their generation, they expected the greatest triumphs of Christian conversion to come from the ancient civilisations of India, Japan, and China, and not from the supposedly primitive and sparsely populated continent of Africa. What further surprises the Spirit has in store for the church cannot, by definition, be predicted. We can be confident, however, that the Christianity of the future is going to look decreasingly like the product of colonisation by the Western mind.

10

Changing Your Mother?

Hindu Responses to Conversion

Robin Thomson

Changing your religion is the greatest sin on earth. It is like changing your mother.
– *A listener phoning in to a Radio Leicester program on conversion*

The singular objective of all churchmen in India is conversion, or to use their term, the harvesting of souls for Jesus.
– *Arun Shourie*

Christianity ... did not systematically convert, but its presence acted as an irritant to existing religious belief and provoked self-questioning, reformist reactions.
– *Sunil Khilnani*

Hindu leaders throughout the twentieth century have spoken out against religious conversion: from Vivekananda to Mahatma Gandhi to the leaders of Rashtriya Swayam Sevak Sangh (RSS) and Vishwa Hindu Parishad (VHP) today. At the beginning of the twenty-first century the issue of conversion continues to provoke strong feelings and heightened social tension, in India and beyond. A series of violent incidents in India from around 1998 showed the depth of feeling – attacks on Roman Catholic priests and nuns, attacks on Protestant missionaries, burning of churches and schools. Christians responded with vigorous protest. These were

preceded by the publication in 1994 of Missionaries in India, a
scathing critique of Christian efforts at conversion by the influential journalist Arun Shourie.[1] Other Hindu leaders spoke out or
wrote against conversion, notably those who supported the movement for 'Hindutva' or 'Hinduness', the concept that India's distinctive identity was Hindu and that minorities in India must
conform in some way to this identity. The rise to power at the
Centre of the Bharatiya Janatha Party (BJP) gave political and
administrative weight to such views. The gruesome murder of the
Australian missionary Graham Staines, with his two sons, in
Orissa in January 1999, sent shock waves throughout India and
was almost universally condemned by Hindus. It seemed to signal
an end to extreme violence but not to the issues. Prime Minister AB
Vajpayee called for a 'national debate on conversion'. The visit to
India of Pope John Paul II in November 1999 continued to
sharpen the debate.

What happens in India has its effects throughout the South
Asian 'diaspora' – the nearly 20 million scattered round the world.
A group of Hindus and Christians in Britain began meeting in
1999 to tackle the tensions spilling over from the debate. The first
meeting saw heated questions, accusations and misperceptions
from both sides. Feelings were strong but the group agreed to meet
again and has continued to do so. In 2002, anti-conversion legislation was passed in the states of Tamil Nadu and Gujarat, while at
the same time Hindu charities in the UK were accused of misusing
funds for the 're-conversion' of tribal people in Gujarat. An attack
on a Hindu temple in London, in November 2003, by so-called
Christian activists, was not directly connected with conversion,
but did nothing to improve understanding. In February 2004, the
Delhi-based campaigning weekly *Tehelka* chose for its re-launch
cover story: 'George Bush has a big conversion agenda for India'.[2]

Why does conversion arouse such strong feelings? The incidents quoted above are recent, but the issues they illustrate are not
new. In his masterly survey, *In Search of Identity: Debates on Religious Conversion in India*, Sebastian Kim demonstrates the con-
sistency of the issues between Hindus and Christians since the

---

[1] Arun Shourie, *Missionaries in India* (New Delhi: ASA Publications,
1994; New Delhi: Rupa, 2001).

[2] *Tehelka* (7 February 2004), p. 1.

beginnings of the Protestant missionary movement in India, over 200 years ago.[3] They include: the perceived threat to family, community and culture, the social and political implications, the colonial past, and the sense of religious exclusiveness (two sides of the same coin?).

Forced Conversions?

There has always been a perception that conversions are 'forced or fraudulent'. This is the abuse that the 'Freedom of Religion' bills were designed to check. When the British Hindu-Christian group in Britain began meeting, this was the basic allegation. However, over time it became clear that neither side actually wanted to defend forced conversions. Somewhat to the group's surprise, they agreed on a statement which affirmed 'the importance for both our communities of religious freedom – to worship, to teach, to share, to change one's faith, or to be left alone not to change'. The group unanimously repudiated 'strategies for conversion which are coercive or manipulative' and condemned all attacks on places of worship.

'Forced' conversions are a distraction from more basic questions: What is actually happening in conversion? What are the issues that cause division? What are the substantial points of difference, in belief and practice, between people of different faiths? Even without the distractions, these questions are very difficult to deal with. The reality is that any conversion can be unsettling and disruptive. There can be a variety of motives, factors for choice, and further implications, for individuals and communities. Almost all allegations of 'forced' conversion spring either from misunderstanding of these complex issues, from feelings of hurt and betrayal, or from a sense of threat to vested interests.

The Problem with Conversion

For most Hindus, the very idea of conversion seems unnecessary and irrelevant, though many do not oppose it. For others, it is

---

[3] Sebastian Kim, *In Search of Identity: Debates on Religious Conversion in India* (New Delhi: Oxford University Press, 2003), pp. 12, 14, 145.

positively distasteful, and they oppose it actively. Why? There are four principal reasons.

Conversion is seen as a threat to family, community and culture

It is natural to hope that your children and relatives will follow the beliefs that have guided you in your life, and to be upset when they do not. This is all the more so when you believe that religion cannot be separated from family and community. Hindus, like Sikhs or Jews, believe that you are born into your religious community. For Hindus, the family and caste community you are born into are determined by your karma. They are part of your destiny. To be a Hindu is a way of life, with an elaborate social structure and rituals to maintain it. Changing your 'religion' is not a matter of discarding certain beliefs and adopting others. You actually have a lot of freedom to do that within Hinduism. Changing your religion means rejecting your family and community. It is like 'changing your mother'.

Christians have often changed the customs of those who were converted. In southern Gujarat, for example, tribals who have become Christians no longer contribute to the expenses of the religious festivals which they used to celebrate with the rest of the tribe. This has caused tension and was one of the factors in the spate of attacks on churches there at the end of 1998.

Conversion is the product of social and political forces

The disruption of community and culture is linked to another question that troubles many thoughtful observers. There may be 'genuine' cases where people are making free and thoughtful choices (as much as any changes can be free in today's world). But are not the vast majority of so-called 'religious' conversions actually influenced by social and political forces, and motivated by the desire for economic and social advancement?

This question became urgent in the late-nineteenth and early-twentieth centuries, when large numbers of those from the 'Depressed Classes' became Christians. It was further sharpened when the colonial administration proposed separate electorates based on religion and community and the 'politics of numbers' became intense. The question is asked whenever Christians in India work with poor or disadvantaged people. It is raised in connection with tribal peoples, especially where there are separatist movements seeking greater autonomy or independence. The commonly held view is that the independence movements of North East India have been instigated and fuelled by Christianity, and the same suspicions have been directed towards other tribal movements, like the Jharkhand movement in Madhya Pradesh and Bihar. When 200 families converted to Islam in the South Indian village of Meenakshipuram in 1981, Hindu, Muslim and Christian observers agreed that the main cause was the social inequality and discrimination which they experienced as Dalits (the majority were Hindu but a few Christian families from other villages were also converted). Moreover, as Christian theologians, both Catholic and Protestant, have wrestled with the issues of conversion, several have reinterpreted it almost entirely in terms of social and political liberation, thus strengthening this perspective.[4]

Conversion is seen in the light of the colonial past

The spread of Christianity in the last 400 years in South America, Asia and Africa was intertwined with the colonial and economic expansion of the European powers. The relationship was complex and certainly not as simple and one-sided as some believe. Whatever the actual relationship, the links (real or supposed) have left many with the suspicion that the spread of Christianity is part of the spread of Western domination, whether colonial in the past or economic and cultural today. The Portuguese intervention in Goa appeared to be inextricably connected with the spread of the Catholic faith there and further south. In the later British period many people identified Christianity with the colonial rulers. So there could be advantages in being linked to the Christian faith. The *Tehelka* story connecting George Bush with a 'conversion agenda for India' was far-fetched and based on the flimsiest connections. But behind it lies the perception that religious conversions are still somehow linked to plans for political and territorial domination – whether of the USA or the Vatican.

---

[4] Ibid., pp. 96–98, 121–31.

An unfortunate legacy of the colonial period in India was the linking of personal laws with religious communities, which tended to polarise differences. The British colonial administration maintained separate personal laws for different faith communities, covering areas such as marriage, divorce, adoption and inheritance. As a result, they dealt with converts only on the basis of the legal community to which they were supposed to belong, without taking into account their inner, personal and spiritual experience.

The Indian Succession Act of 1865 created personal laws for Indian Christians. This gave them legal rights but it also meant that being a 'Christian' was defined as being part of a different legal community, rather than as a spiritual and religious choice. So the division between communities hardened and it became impossible to continue as part of both. You had to choose. The change of legal status was often followed by other changes including name, diet and clothes worn. Conversion was seen very much in these external changes, rather than as a personal and spiritual experience.

Conversion is seen as religious exclusiveness

Those religions that actively encourage others to change their beliefs are seen as exclusive and arrogant. To claim that you have the truth implies that others are wrong and in some way inferior. This is the central charge against conversion, shared by the vast majority of Hindus, however friendly and appreciative of Christian values and practice, and of Christ himself. In fact, the more they appreciate the teaching and example of Christ, the more they might feel it unnecessary to talk about conversion. This was the view of Rammohun Roy in Calcutta of the 1820s: 'there was no need to abandon his previous identity or change his religious context. He believed he had found a way to experience the fullness of Christ without conversion to Christianity.'[5] Others argue that Hinduism is superior to Christianity and other religions that believe in conversion, because it can accommodate the whole range of religious belief, practice and experience without narrow limitations that force choice. Swami Dayananda Saraswati argues that those who insist on conversion are aggressive. Their

---

[5] Ibid., p. 18.

aggression hurts those who do not believe as they do. So it is 'violence ... against humanity, against cultures, against religions ... My dharma is not violence. It does not allow conversion. And that dharma has to be protected.'[6]

Reflections

These issues are interlinked. The first two, and to some extent the third, are closely connected to the relationship between the inner and outer aspects of conversion. They are also connected to the question of motives in conversion.

The relationship between the inner and outer aspects of conversion

Conversion is an inner experience that has outward effects. Both aspects are important, and neglecting either leads to distortion. The colonial authorities looked only on the outer aspects, at the converts' legal status and community membership, resulting in rigid categories. Mahatma Gandhi believed that conversion, if it had any validity at all, could only be an inner, spiritual change of an individual. It need not – and should not – involve change of religious community. He was completely opposed to 'mass movements' to Christianity, particularly among the Scheduled Castes/Harijans. They must be motivated, he argued, by social and economic considerations.

Conversion involves inner change. For example, the good news of Jesus centres around grace, forgiveness and acceptance of persons as they are. For villagers, tribals, or slum people, Christ may be seen as one who liberates by giving acceptance and dignity. This leads to inner spiritual change. But these inner changes have outer effects in ethical, cultural, social and political aspects of life. These changes may be very positive; certainly the converts hope they will be. But we cannot ignore the potential for the 'socially

---

[6] Swami Dayananda Saraswati 1999 at a seminar on 'Violence to Hindu Heritage' convened by the Citizens' Committee For Dharma Rakshana Sammelan, Chennai, 1999. From the website www.christianaggression.org/item_display.php?id=1068320923&type=articles (accessed December 2005).

alienating quality of conversion'.[7] For example, when people living in slums no longer pay bribes to the slum landlord, or low caste people in the village no longer bow down in abject fear and submission to higher caste people, or tribal people no longer join in festivals.

Motives in conversion

Once again we need to hold together the inner and outer aspects of conversion. We also need to distinguish the perspectives of two different people: the convert, or seeker, and the agent of conversion – the preacher, missionary, or other religious figure.

Converts and seekers

There is often an assumption that those converted, especially where the numbers are large, are passive participants in the process, and gullible as well. The 'Freedom of Religion' bills assumed that people such as Dalits, tribals, or women, needed special protection on this account. Ram Puniyani comments: 'The conversions are projected to be a purely passive process in which the poor Adivasis [tribals] are converted by inducement and allurement. This gives the image that those converted are mere passive beings bereft of intelligence just because they are poor and so susceptible to the anti-national activities of the missionaries.'[8] This is why some find it hard to believe that conversions can be anything but forced. Those who are changing must somehow be enticed by the promise of rewards, whether material or spiritual, or forced by some pressure. Gauri Viswanathan argues that conversion was a response to change and to the 'realignment between state, religion, culture and empire' in both Britain and India. In both places conversion was a disturbing affirmation of the right to freedom of belief and practice. 'Conversion is a subversion of secular power.' These changes were threatening to many, because 'conversion unsettles the boundaries by which selfhood,

---

[7] Gauri Viswanathan, *Outside the Fold: Conversion, Modernity and Belief* (Princeton, NJ: Princeton University Press, 1998).

[8] Ram Puniyani, 'Issues in Secular Politics', in IMC-Editorial (email discussion forum), October 2002. See www.pluralindia.com or www.boloji.com/voices/index.htm or ram.puniyani@gmail.com.

citizenship, nationhood and community are defined, exposing them as permeable borders'.[9] Where this happens:

> dominant communities prefer to use the term 'proselytism' rather than 'conversion' to indicate the forcible nature of religious change. The term also carries with it a baggage of associations that identify religious change as an effect of manipulation, propagandistic activity, loss of individual self-control and will power, and sustained political mobilization. The use of the term 'proselytism' further denies subjectivity, agency, or choice to the subject and replaces individuals with masses as the unit of analysis.[10]

On 4 November 2001, 40,000 Dalits converted to Buddhism on the same day in New Delhi. A year later several other groups were talking about doing the same, some of them numbering millions. They apparently had not decided which way to move – to Buddhism, Islam, Christianity, or their own religious identity. A poster in Nagpur railway station invited a number of groups from the 'Other Backward Communities' to join in solidarity at a rally in Pune. It proclaimed in large letters 'We Are Not Vedic Hindus.' Whatever their motivation, it would be naive at best, and patronising at worst, to assume that the groups involved are passive and gullible. We could say that the initial motive for any conversion is the desire for change. That is very broad. It could include social, economic, spiritual, cultural, emotional, or psychological change. Each of these could be a motive, separately or combined. One may lead to another. Some may begin with concern for well-being in this life and then realise the possibilities in the next life; others might seek eternal salvation and then discover the implications for life in the here-and-now.

'Missionaries'
If the motives of the one seeking conversion are complex and hard to disentangle, what is the role of the 'missionary', the person who is seeking to share their beliefs with others? There has been a lot of discussion about the 'right to convert' (i.e. the right to 'make converts'), assuming that the 'missionary' is the dominant figure, who

---

[9] Viswanathan, *Outside the Fold*, p. 16.
[10] Ibid., p. 87.

does something to 'convert' the other. As a result there are frequent questions about the time and effort spent in social services, that is, caring for people's material, this-worldly needs. Is this a distraction? Or is it, as often alleged, simply a cover, a 'sweetener', an inducement, exploitation ...? India's Constitution (Article 25.1) balances the right to religious freedom with the need not to infringe others' rights, nor to harm society: 'Subject to public order, morality and health and to the other provisions of this Part, all persons are equally entitled to freedom of conscience and the right freely to profess, practise and propagate religion.' Does this include the 'right to convert'? In 1977 the Supreme Court argued that it did not. The judgment was controversial. It seemed to be based on the perception that any attempt to persuade or influence another person necessarily violates their freedom of conscience, or that the act of 'converting' is one-sided, with no freedom of will for the convert. In 2003 the Allahabad High Court dismissed a petition, based on the same premise, to stop religious meetings called 'Yesu Darbar'. Its judgement, upheld by the Supreme Court, implied that people are free to make their own response to religious proclamations or appeals, as long as these do not use wrong methods. In other words, they are seen as responsible agents.

It is important to clarify the relationship of inner and outer aspects of conversion, the complexity of motives, and the balance between those looking for change and those seeking to change others. But that still leaves the fundamental question: is religious conversion itself a valid action?

Conversion as religious exclusiveness

For Hindus this is still the fundamental issue. From the nineteenth-century Pandits in Calcutta to Mahatma Gandhi to Dayananda Saraswati, all agree that the desire to convert is fundamentally wrong. Francois Gautier, a journalist who has lived for thirty years in India, sums it up: 'Conversion belongs to the times of colonialism. We have entered the era of unity, of coming together, of tolerance and accepting each other as we are – not of converting in the name of the one elusive "true" God.'[11] This perspective is based on the Hindu idea of tolerance. If all ways are equally valid

---

[11] Francois Gautier, in *Asian Voice* (30 March 2002), p. 6.

paths to God and manifestations of the divine, then why urge only one way? Surely the Hindu perspective is better? In discussion some insist 'there are no differences ... All faiths are equal.' This sounds friendly and open, but can actually inhibit discussion and exploration.

Alongside the claim to tolerance and breadth, many Hindus feel that their faith is undervalued. They actively desire to promote Hindu spirituality, Hindu practices like yoga, or Hindu beliefs in the Religious Education curriculum. They want to see a much greater awareness of 'India's greatest gift to the world: the Hindu religion, culture and philosophy.'[12] There is an ambivalence here: on the one hand, the insistence that all religions are essentially equal and the same; on the other hand, the conviction that the Hindu way is actually the best – perhaps because it is felt to be the broadest and most accommodating of all?

There is a similar ambivalence in the efforts by some Hindus, like the Arya Samaj in the nineteenth century, and the Vishwa Hindu Parishad today, to 're-convert' those who have left the Hindu fold. This is sometimes through a shuddhi (purification) ceremony. At other times it is called a 'homecoming', clearly with the idea that it is better to be at home, where you really belong. Sebastian Kim points out that while Christians argue for freedom of religion on the basis of 'rights', Hindus argue against conversion on the basis of 'tolerance'. Neither basis is adequate by itself. 'Rights', he feels, have not adequately recognised the rights of those of other faiths, while Hindu 'tolerance' is actually calling others to conform to a particular view of truth.[13] At the heart of this debate are issues of truth.

Two Different Ways of Looking at Truth

According to one view, you are born into your religion. Religion, culture, community and country are all closely linked. Mahatma Gandhi felt that 'Every *nation* considers its own faith to be as good as that of any other ... the great faiths held by *the people of India* are adequate for her people.' (Notice the words I have italicised).

---

[12] Editorial in *Asian Voice* (23 October 2004), p. 3.
[13] Kim, *In Search of Identity*, pp. 85–86, 185–86.

Different parts of the world will follow different religious paths, which are most suitable to them. So the West is 'Christian' while South Asia is Hindu, Sikh, or Muslim, the Middle East is Muslim, and so on. Underlying this is the deeply held conviction that the different manifestations of belief and practice are only that – they are simply outward expressions of an underlying universal spiritual reality. It may be called by different names, but it is the ultimate source of all spiritual energy. Each region, culture, or group has its own way to God, and they are all valid. They all lead to the 'eternal religion behind all religions, this sanatana dharma, the timeless tradition ... Our historical religions have to transform themselves into the universal faith or they will fade away.'[14] There is no point in fighting over apparent differences. And it is wrong to change from the religion into which you were born; this only creates tension and disloyalty.

This is a geographical, cultural, community approach to religion. Truth depends on where you are and who you are. On this understanding, there is clearly no valid place for conversion. The Hindi word for conversion is dharmantaran, which means literally 'change of religion'. If this is what conversion means, then clearly it is offensive to this point of view.

Another view is that expressed by Paul, the first-century Christian preacher, to the elders of Athens, the cultural capital of the Mediterranean world (Acts 17:22–34). It is true, he said, that people have been seeking God in their different ways and places. Their images and ideas represent their yearning for God. And God has revealed himself, to some extent, to everybody. Everybody knows God as Creator and the Source of our being, though he is much greater than our imagining. But at a certain point in history, God intervened and actually became part of our world, as a human being. That became the decisive turning point. It was not just us seeking God, but God seeking us. And it provided the standard by which all can judge how far our efforts to seek God have been authentic. While Paul did not mention Jesus by name, he clearly identified him by referring to his resurrection.

To evaluate whether Jesus' coming was decisive, we need to understand the problem. The Bible describes all humanity as

---

[14] S. Radhakrishnan, *Eastern Religions and Western Thought* (London: Oxford University Press, 1939), pp. 80–81.

separated from God by sin and evil. We need a mediator – some-body to represent both God and humanity – to overcome this, to offer forgiveness; to overcome death. Only Jesus offers this, through his life, death and resurrection. He invites us to a loving, personal relationship in which we are accepted by God. That is why he is the universal saviour, not because one 'religion' is better than another.

This view is radically different. It distinguishes spiritual reality from culture, community and geography. On this understanding, all need conversion – not from one 'religion' to another but from sin and self toward God. 'Conversion is not primarily to a religion or tradition, it is to God the source of all. In Jesus Christ, we see fully the sacrificial love of the One who creates us and is working to redeem us.'[15]

The Future of Dialogue Between Christians and Hindus Around Conversion

Can these two views of truth be reconciled? Once their radical dif-ference is recognised, we need to re-examine some of the issues that obstruct our understanding and cause tensions between com-munities. In order to support communities and families facing issues of conversion and individuals coping with the realities of conversion, in dialogue with Hindus, Christians need to address the underlying assumptions and implications.

Christians need to avoid insensitive pressure to change cultural practices or community customs. Hindus need to realise that a change of faith does not have to mean rejection of family or com-munity. Both need to realise that these are very closely connected. As a result, some feel themselves forced (for various reasons) to leave their family and community to follow a new faith. They feel great pain and loss and often experience continuing tension. They may have been pulled by attraction to their new faith and its culture. Or they may have felt pushed and become critical of their old faith culture. Either way, whatever their original motivation,

---

[15] Bishop Michael Nazir Ali, in a message to a conference on *Conversion and the Church of England: Some Asian Perspectives*, organised by the Committee for Minority Ethnic Anglican Concerns in September 1999.

they may find themselves in a position of criticism both ways; wanting to reform their old faith and culture, but equally aware of shortcomings in the new.

Being in between can be stimulating, but it is usually uncomfortable. Dr. B.R. Ambedkar, the architect of India's constitution, announced his intention to leave Hinduism over twenty years before he actually did so. During that time he was moving back and forth between the Hindu culture of which he was so critical and the various possibilities for change that lay ahead. In the end his choice was Buddhism.

Christians involved in mission need to acknowledge both the inner and outer aspects of conversion. It is an inner change with outer effects. These may be closely linked. People's motives for change may be mixed. Sometimes they may seek the outer effects first and only later realise their inner basis. Or they are not prepared for the implications of their choices. When Christians or Hindus focus on only one aspect, they distort the complex nature of the changes that are taking place and sometimes they exploit them.

Christians also need to be clear in their understanding of conversion and particularly how we describe the process of conversion. Who is converted? By whom? Often we hear of somebody 'converting' others or of a person who 'converted' to Islam or Christianity. Christians believe that true conversion is the work of God, who produces an inward, spiritual change and choose, therefore, to speak of a person 'being converted' (by God). Of course, no change takes place in a vacuum, as we have seen, and there is a role for the representatives of the new faith in the process of conversion, for example in baptising. So there are human factors which cannot always be separated.

The idea of 'Christendom' is unhelpful in this context. Christian faith is not linked to any particular part of the world. As we have noted, 'Conversion is not primarily to a religion or tradition', it is to a relationship with God the source of all, through Jesus Christ. His followers may belong to every people and language and culture. And they should not be tied to any particular political system or power bloc. In today's world some find it hard to make this separation. They argue that cultures, or 'civilizations', are ultimately religion-based and shaped. While there is truth in this –

because our faith is fundamental to our worldview – it is even more true that faith in Jesus Christ can and should be expressed in every culture.

If the assumed link between Christianity and a particular culture is challenged in this way, this has implications for the view that to share Christian faith with others is a mark of 'Western arrogance'. Christian faith is not Western, and the majority of Christians no longer live in the West. Christians of all backgrounds must seek to convey this break with colonial history. Allied to this point is the experience that religious language is easily misunderstood. Christian use of the language of spiritual warfare and conquest can be misinterpreted as a coded desire for domination, by the church that is viewed as the instrument of Western imperialism.

To conclude, the relations between Christians and Hindus are concerned with a wider range of issues than conversion alone, and in these wider concerns lies great potential for greater understanding. It is particularly important that Christians find areas of common concern with people of different faiths. Key areas of mutual concern include family life, education and opposition to discrimination. These are matters which can bring us together, rather than divide us. Perhaps then we will be able to face each other with respect, and truly evaluate the challenges of our beliefs.

11

Conversion and Apostasy

The Case of Islam[1]

Peter Cotterell

Muslim *da'wa*

Not all religions are inherently proselytising: Judaism is only marginally so, and Sikhism and the 'Traditional Religions' are essentially ethnic. But both Islam and Christianity are proselytising. As Dr. Zaki Badawi has said 'Islam is a proselytising religion ... it is more or less a duty of a Muslim to proclaim his religion and to see if other people would be attracted to it.'[2]

This duty of the Muslim is *da'wa*, 'calling', and corresponds to the concept of Christian mission. However, Islam categorises the conversion of a Muslim away from Islam and to some other

---

[1] The discussion of conversion and apostasy as presented here has been based on a somewhat rigid application of the quadrilateral, Qur'an, Abrogation, Hadith and Shari'a, with the recognition that while the result probably represents the majority view within Islam, other patterns using different criteria or making different judgments (on the role of abrogation and istihsan, for example) could emerge. And finally it must be noted that while Shari'a Law lays down the hudd punishment for apostasy, it is only a Muslim Majority State that can authoritatively introduce Shari'a Law and with it the apostasy law.

[2] In an interview reported in *Third Way*, 19/4 (May 1996), p. 18.

system of belief as *ridda*, 'apostasy,' for which the Shari'a Law punishment is death. The regularly quoted Muslim axiom 'There is no compulsion in religion' (Qur'an 2:256), appears to misrepresent the situation with respect to the conversion of a Muslim, who is required to remain within the Muslim religion. In some parts of the Muslim world the situation is formalised. Thus in Malaysia the Federal Constitution forbids non-Muslims attempting to convert Muslims, but sanctions the reverse process, Muslims attempting to convert non-Muslims.[3]

In his consideration of the apparent conflict between Qur'an 2:256 and the Traditions requiring that the apostate be executed, the Muslim scholar Mawdudi (1903–79) offers a means of reconciling the two:

> Qur'an 2:256 obviously forbids compulsion in religion. The Hadith obviously state that the apostate from Islam should be executed. Since the Qur'an also states that Muslims are to obey the Prophet as well as the Book, Qur'an 2:256 can have application only for non-Muslims. Muslims must be compelled to remain Muslims.[4]

While Mawdudi's views are extremely influential in contemporary Muslim thinking, he was a radical founder of *Jama'at-i-Islami*, fervent advocate of the understanding that the Muslim community should be governed by Shari'a Law. His massive commentary on the Qur'an, *Tafhim al-Qur'an*, and other writings reflect such views.

2. The Qur'an and Conversion

The Qur'an does not present a complete and holistic systematic theology. In fact, orthodoxy might be said to rest on a quadrilateral consisting of Qur'an; the principle of abrogation, *naskh*, to decide between apparently conflicting passages of the Qur'an;[5]

---

[3] US Department of State; www.state.gov/g/drl/rls/irf/2001/5604.html, (last accessed on 25/05/02).

[4] Syed Sila Husain and Ernest Hahn (trans.), *The Punishment of the Apostate According to Islamic Law* (Lahore: Islamic Publications, 1994), p. 102.

[5] See Mohammad Hashim Kamali, *Principles of Islamic Jurisprudence* (2nd edn. Kuala Lumpur: Ilmiah, 1998), ch. 7.

Hadith ('Traditions'), and specifically the *sahih*, 'reliable' Traditions; and Shari'a Law.[6] But even this quadrilateral allows for the construction of a multiplicity of more-or-less orthodox holistic theologies: there is not one single Law School, but four, and there is no certainty about the dating of individual suras, still less of individual verses within the suras. In the following I have attempted conscientiously to employ the quadrilateral with some rigidity, insofar as it relates to the issue of apostasy. But this serves to highlight the genuine interpretive dilemma that Muslims face when attempting to produce a systematic and holistic theology. In practice, many Muslims would wish to see the Shari'a Law modified at some points, perhaps not least in the matter of the punishment for apostasy.

The very early Meccan sura *Al-Kafirun* (sura 109, 'The Unbelievers'),[7] sets out Muhammad's pacific view of other religionists at the beginning of his ministry:

> Say: O ye that reject faith!
> I worship not that which ye worship,
> Nor will ye worship that which I worship.
> And I will not worship that which ye have been wont to worship,
> Nor will ye worship that which I worship.
> To you be your way and to me mine.

As Yusuf Ali comments in his introduction to the sura, it teaches that 'in matters of truth we can make no compromise, but there is no need to persecute or abuse anyone for his faith or belief'.[8] However, this approach to other religions appears to be abrogated by later suras.

Thus, sura 47 is dated by Yusuf Ali to the first year of the *hijra*, and its contents are relevant to that period of Muslim history, poised between the rejection of Muhammad's message at Mecca

---

[6] It is interesting that the Libyan leader Mu'ammar al'Qaddafi has suggested reducing the quadrilateral to a duality, Qur'an and abrogation. Of course, he is not the only Muslim to make such a suggestion. See Peter Riddell and Peter Cotterell, *Islam in Context* (Grand Rapids, MI: Baker, 2003) pp. 211–16.

[7] Yusuf Ali, *The Meaning of the Holy Qur'an* (Beltsville: Amana, 1989), p. 1707. Ali describes it as 'another early Makkan Surah'.

[8] Ibid.

and the ultimate triumph of the message in much of Arabia. At this point the future is uncertain, and in uncertainty there were those who turned back from their commitment to Islam. The response is unequivocal:

> Those who turn back as apostates after guidance was clearly shown to them – the Evil One has instigated them and buoyed them up with false hopes ... But how will it be when the angels take their souls at death, and smite their faces and their backs? (Qur'an 47:25–27)

Here the punishment of the apostate is reserved to Allah, a post-mortem judgement. The same is true of Qur'an 16:106–109:

> Anyone who, after accepting faith in Allah, utters unbelief – except under compulsion, his heart remaining firm in faith – but such as open their breast to unbelief – on them is wrath from Allah, and theirs will be a dreadful penalty ... Without doubt, in the hereafter they will perish.

However, in the later third sura[9] there is at least an indication that apostasy carries with it temporal as well as eternal consequences:

> How shall Allah guide those who reject faith after they accepted it, and bore witness that the messenger was true and that clear signs had come to them? ... of such the reward is that on them (rests) the curse of Allah, of his angels and of all mankind (Qur'an 3:86–87).

The concern appears to be with those who turn from an original faith in Muhammad's message to unbelief, from *iman* to *kufr*, rather than with the nature of that *kufr*, whether it is not-belief in Allah or commitment to another religion. Zwemer draws a distinction between *ridda*, the move from Islam to *kufr* unbelief, and *irtidad*, movement from Islam to commitment to another religion.[10] Doi, however, in his consideration of *ridda*, makes no such

---

[9] See Bell's comments on the dating of this part of Sura 3 in C. Bosworth and M. Richardson (eds.), *A Commentary on the Qur'an* Vol. I (Manchester: University of Manchester, 1991), p. 82. See also Bell's *The Qur'an Translated* Vol. I (Edinburgh: T&T Clark, 1937), p. 53; he dates these verses to year 3 of the Muslim calendar.

[10] S. Zwemer, *The Law of Apostasy in Islam* (London: Marshall, 1924), p. 33.

distinction: failure to observe the Ramadan fast or to make the pilgrimage are 'acts of Irtidad'.[11] According to Doi, *ridda* involves 'rejection of the religion of Islam in favour of any other religion either through an action or through words of mouth'.[12]

Qur'an 5:33 suggests drastic punishment for those who oppose Muhammad and, by implication, Allah:

> The punishment of those who wage war against Allah and his messenger, and strive with might and main for mischief through the land is: execution, or crucifixion, or the cutting off of hands and feet from opposite sides, or exile from the land.

The enemies in mind are apostates, heretics, or political opponents, defined loosely as those who 'strive for mischief in the land'. In his comment on this verse Yusuf Ali writes: 'For the double crime of treason against the State, combined with treason against Allah, as shown by overt crimes, four alternative punishments are mentioned ...'[13] Muhammad Ali, in his translation of the Qur'an, connects this verse to the case of men from the Uraina tribe (see below, 'The Traditions') who were clearly apostates, murderers, and thieves.

The origins of the bizarre set of punishments is obscure, but it is significant that a similar set of punishments is put into the mouth of Pharaoh in the Qur'anic account of Pharaoh's confrontation with the Israelites and Moses, in Qur'an 26:49.

The Traditions, *Hadith*

Bukhari and Muslim[14] both record a tradition from Anas bin Malik concerning men from the Ukl or Uraina tribe (the relevant traditions name both tribes), who joined Muhammad at Medina but found the climate problematic.[15] Muhammad gave them leave

---

[11] A.I. Doi, *Shari'ah: the Islamic Law* (London: Ta Ha, 1984), p. 265.
[12] Ibid.
[13] Ali, *Meaning of the Holy Qur'an*, n. 738.
[14] The collections of Traditions attributed to Bukhari and Muslim are recognised by Islam as *sahih*, 'reliable'.
[15] Bukhari 8: LXXII, 797, p. 522; *Sahih Muslim* (Lahore: Ashraf, 1980), III, DCLXIX, pp. 4130–37.

to drink milk from his camels: a kindness to which they responded by killing the watchmen and stealing the camels. Caught and brought back to Muhammad they were condemned to have hands and feet cut off, eyes put out, and to be left in the desert without water, to die. Bukhari concludes with an explanation that 'Those were the people who committed theft and murder *and reverted to disbelief after being believers.*'

Bukhari also records the Traditions lying behind those Qur'anic passages which leave the punishment of the apostate to the afterlife,[16] but adds a Tradition requiring that the apostate be killed:

> Some Zanadiqa[17] (atheists) were brought to Ali and he burnt them. The news of this reached Abbas who said, 'If I had been in his place, I would not have burnt them, as Allah's apostle forbade it saying "Do not punish anybody with Allah's punishment (fire)." I would have killed them according to the statement of Allah's apostle, "Whoever changed his Islamic religion, then kill him." (Bukhari 9, LXXXIV, 57)

4. The Law Schools

The four principal Sunni schools of law developed in the four great centres of Islam: in Arabia, the Maliki school and the Shaf'i school, which was later centred on Cairo; in Iraq, at Kufa, the followers of Abu Hanifa (d. 767); and in Baghdad, the Hanbali school, later expounded by Ibn Taymiyya (d.1283).

These four Sunni Law Schools agree that the penalty for *ridda* is death: 'The punishment by death in the case of apostasy has been unanimously agreed upon by all the four schools of Islamic Jurisprudence.'[18] The punishment is mandatory. There is provision within Shari'a Law for discretionary punishments, *ta'zir*, but this provision applies only to these offences for which there is no specific punishment laid down in Shari'a Law, and only then for

---

[16] Bukhari 9: LXXXIV, pp. 42–44.

[17] According to H.A.R. Gibb and J.H. Kramers (eds.), *Shorter Encyclopaedia of Islam* (Leiden: Brill, 1974): art. 'Zindik', the Zindik was not so much an atheist as a heretic. Indeed, in that age and in that society it is difficult to conceive of there being such a thing as an atheist.

[18] Doi, *Shari'ah*, p. 266.

minor offences.[19] An exception is made in the case of those who are forcibly converted or are forcibly made to renounce their faith. The principle of *Istihsan* or equity may also apply to individual cases: '*Istihsan* in Islamic law and equity in Western law, are both inspired by the principle of fairness and conscience, and both authorise departure from a rule of positive law when its enforcement leads to unfair results.'[20]

In all cases of supposed heresy or apostasy a period of three days is to be granted to the accused so that they may explain their reasons and receive explanations in the hope that they might return to Islam. Malik records the story of a man who came to Umar and reported the fate of a *kafir*.

> Umar asked, 'What have you done with him?' He said, 'We let him approach and struck off his head.' Umar said, didn't you imprison him for three days and feed him a loaf of bread every day and call on him to tawba [repentance] that he might turn in tawba and return to the command of Allah?'[21]

The Maliki Law School also deals with the punishment of the apostate who conceals his apostasy:

> Yahya related to me from Malik from Zayd ibn Aslam that the Messenger of Allah ... said, 'If someone changes his deen ['religion'] strike his neck!'
> The meaning of the statement of the Prophet ... in our opinion ... is that 'if some one changes his deen, strike his neck!' refers to those who leave Islam for other than it ... They are killed without being called to tawba ['repentance'] because their tawba is not recognised. They were hiding their kufr ['apostasy'] and publishing their Islam, so I do not think that one calls such people to tawba, and one does not accept their word.[22]

In Malaysia in 2002 a bill (Syariah Criminal Offences [Hudud and Qisas] Bill) was introduced to establish Shari'a Law in Terengganu

---

[19] See art. 'Ta'zir' in P.J. Bearman et al., *The Encyclopaedia of Islam* (Leiden: Brill, 2000).
[20] Kamali, *Principles*, p. 245.
[21] Idris Mears (ed.), *The Al-Muwatta of Malik bin Anas* (Norfolk: Diwan Press, 1982), pp. 36.18, 343.
[22] Ibid.

State. Its provision for apostasy (apparently distinguishing between *irtidad* and *ridda*) states that the offender 'is given three days to repent, failing which the punishment is death and his properties confiscated'.[23] The bill was approved by the State Legislature. However, this legislation runs contrary to the Malaysian Federal Constitution, and consequently had no authority in law. The central government has been subject to continuous pressure from the *Parti Islam SeMalaysia* (PAS), which had a majority in Terengganu State and in Kelantan State, to make Malaysia a fully Muslim nation and to bring in Shari'a Law. However, in the general elections held in 2004 the PAS suffered a major defeat: the moderate governing alliance gained 198 of the 219 seats in parliament, and the PAS lost control of Terengganu State.

Ridda in Practice

Assassination of *opponents of Muhammad* was authorised by him, and an example is recorded by Ibn Ishaq. Sallam b. Abu'l Huqayq had brought together a small coalition of lesser tribes to oppose Muhammad, but with no success. The Khazraj tribe then asked Muhammad's permission to kill him. Receiving that permission they travelled to Khaybar, where Salam was living, and killed him while he was in bed.[24]

Following the occupation of Mecca and later following the death of Muhammad, some of the Arab tribes that had embraced Islam abandoned both their allegiance to Muhammad and their adherence to Islam. Muhammad is said to have sent Zaid against the b. Fazara, and Umm Qirfa was captured. According to Mawdudi[25] she had become a Muslim but had then become an apostate, a *kafir*: 'She was a very old woman ... Zayd ordered Qays b.al-Musahhar to kill Umm Qirfa, and he killed her cruelly [*Tabari*] by putting a rope to her two legs and to two camels and driving them until they rent her in two.'[26]

---

[23] *Utusan Online*, www.utusan.com.my/utusan/content.asp?y (last accessed 8 July 2002).

[24] A. Guillaume, *The Life of Muhammad* (Oxford: Oxford University Press, 1955), pp. 482–83.

[25] Husain and Hahn (trans.), *The Punishment of the Apostate*, p. 22.

[26] A. Guillaume, *The Life of Muhammad*, p. 665.

Mawdudi, a Pakistani Muslim scholar (1903–1979), records the case of a group of Christians and their double change of heart. Ali b. Abu Talib, the Sunni fourth Rightly Guided Caliph, was told of a group of Christians who had become Muslims and then become Christians again. When brought before Ali they responded: 'We were Christians. Then we were offered the choice of remaining Christians or becoming Muslims. We chose Islam. But now it is our opinion that no religion is more excellent than our first religion. Therefore we have become Christians now. Hearing this, Ali ordered these people to be executed and their children enslaved.'[27]

Salman Rushdie gained unwelcome fame with the publication of *The Satanic Verses* in 1988.[28] The story is ultimately the story of the conflict between Gibreel (Gabriel) and Saladin (Satan), the two revolving around the central character Mahound (Muhammad). The book's title refers to the incident in which, while reciting the words of 'The Star' (sura 53), he is supposed to have compromised his doctrine of *tawhid*, the unqualified one-ness of God, by giving credence to the principal deities of Mecca: 'Have ye seen Lat, and Uzza, and another, the third (goddess), Manat ...' To which Rushdie added the words believed to have been spoken by Muhammad, but later retracted by him: 'They are the exalted birds, and their intercession is desired indeed.'[29] Yusuf Ali makes no comment on these words (the 'Satanic Verses'), although the Ahmadi translation of the Qur'an[30] has an extended footnote, initially dismissing the event as a mere invention, but then suggesting that the offending words were called out by someone in the crowd and wrongly attributed to Muhammad.

The event was, of course, problematic for Islam in that it suggests that Muhammad himself temporarily compromised this fundamental doctrine of *tawhid*. Salman Rushdie brought the event out of obscurity, not merely making mention of it in his book, but naming his book after the event, a book, moreover, by a Booker

---

[27] Husain and Hahn (trans.), *The Punishment of the Apostate According to Islamic Law*, p. 24.
[28] Salman Rushdie, *The Satanic Verses* (London: Penguin-Viking, 1988).
[29] Rushdie, *The Satanic Verses*, p. 114.
[30] *The Holy Qur'an with English Translation and Commentary* (Pakistan: Beltsville Md, Amana, 1996.). See n. 2882, p. 1138. See also Tabari's comment in Guillaume's *Life of Muhammad*, pp. 165–66.

Prize winner. The Muslim world was furious, and a *fatwa*, 'judgment, opinion,' was pronounced by the then spiritual leader of Iran, Ayatollah Khomeini, identifying Rushdie as an apostate subject to death ('whose blood must be shed') at the hands of any Muslim, promising that 'whoever is killed in this path will be regarded as a martyr'.[31]

Rushdie subsequently spent many years under special police protection, unable to live openly for fear of someone attempting to fulfil the *fatwa* and so gain the reward being offered of one million dollars. The *fatwa* was repeated by Ali Khamanei, the successor to Khomeini following his death in 1989.

In 2003 Ibn Warraq (a pseudonym) edited a book containing more than fifty, mostly anonymous, accounts of contemporary apostasy.[32] The fact that the majority of testimonies are anonymous is itself a stark commentary on the whole issue of conversion from Islam. On Muslims converting to Christianity Ibn Warraq comments:

> Many are attracted by the figure of Jesus, others find the Christian dogma of forgiveness of sins comforting, and still others are impressed by the charitable behaviour of individual Christians around them .But if there is a common thread running through these conversion testimonies it is that Christianity preaches the love of Christ and God, whereas Islam is forever threatening hellfire for disobeying, and obsessively holds up the wrath of God in front of the believerm[33]

This assessment is well illustrated by the anonymous testimony of a woman who lived 'in the West,' brought up as a nominal Christian, who converted to Islam following her marriage to a Muslim. Knowing little about Islam, she took to reading not only the Qur'an (in translation) but also the Traditions, found on the Internet. It was this intellectual study of Islam that led her to abandon Islam and become what she calls 'a closet Christian'.[34]

---

[31] Malise Ruthven, *Islam in the World* (London: Penguin Books, 2000), pp. 376–79.

[32] Ibn Warraq, *Leaving Islam: Apostates Speak Out* (New York: Prometheus, 2003).

[33] Ibid., p. 92.

[34] Ibid., pp. 123–26.

Steven Masood was born into an Ahmadi community near to Peshawar in northern Pakistan. Disheartened by the orthodox Muslim designation of the Ahmadis as unbelievers, *kafir*, he determined to become a true Muslim, to follow the path of the prophet's *sunna*. His study of the Qur'an led him to the study of the Bible, facilitated by the gift of a copy of John's Gospel in Urdu, and he began the arduous task of reconciling the comments of the Qur'an regarding the *injeel*, the gospel, and what he was now reading. And this eventually led to him leaving Islam for Christianity: in his own words to himself, 'You can't keep two swords in one scabbard.'[35]

It was not without cost. Born Masood Ahmad Khan, his parents disowned him and denied to him his family name: he became Steven Masood. Faced with persecution from Ahmadis and orthodox Muslims alike, he moved to England. But here, too, he encountered frequent opposition, on one occasion having acid thrown at him. As he comments: 'Islam does not allow its adherents to abandon faith that easily … they become targets of all sorts of persecution, which then persuades some of them to abandon what they have found. Others remain faithful, but restart a new life, but a quiet one, somewhere else.'[36]

Apostasy and Freedom of Religion

The United Nations Declaration of Human Rights sets out in its preamble the hope that

> Every individual and every organ of society, keeping this Declaration constantly in mind, shall strive by teaching and education to promote respect for these rights and freedoms and by progressive measures, national and international, to secure their universal and effective recognition and observance, both among the peoples of Member States themselves and among the peoples of territories under their jurisdiction.

The right to freedom of religion is enshrined and loosely defined in Article 18: 'Everyone has the right to freedom of thought,

---

[35]   Steven Masood, *Into the Light* (Carlisle: Authentic, 1986), p. 143.

[36]   Centre for Islamic Studies, *Newsletter* (2004), p. 9.

conscience and religion; this right includes freedom to change his religion or belief, and freedom, either alone or in community with others and in public or private, to manifest his religion or belief in teaching, practice, worship and observance.' Article 18 is repeated in the European Convention on Human Rights, in Article 9.1.[37]

Islam's apostasy laws are in clear breach of the Declaration: Muslims do not have freedom to change their religion. But further, non-Muslim minorities, the *dhimmi*, have only a limited freedom to worship, precisely not in public.

Malaysia provides a relevant case study. Its Constitution appears to guarantee through Article 11(1) the right of individuals to profess their choice of religion. However, this apparent right is not, in fact, an absolute right. A report in the *New Straits Times*, 14 November 2003, refers to the existence of two law systems in Malaysia, the civil law system and the 'Syariah', *Shari'a* Law, and suggests that matters relating to a Muslim wishing to change religion is a matter for the Shari'a law courts rather than the civil courts. In the Shari'a courts, the Muslim law on apostasy would hold, contrary to the apparent Constitutional position. The report related to the assertion by Daud Mamat, Kamariah Ali and Mad Yacob Ismail that since they had converted to Christianity some five years previously the Shari'a courts could no longer have any jurisdiction over them, and could not try them for apostasy.

Malaysia is, in fact, only 59 per cent Muslim and 8% Christian, but Islam is the official religion of the country. This explains the decision of a High Court judge in the case of a Malay woman who had become a Christian and applied to have the term 'Islam' removed from her identity card. The judge ruled: 'An ethnic Malay is defined by the Federal Constitution as "a person who professes the religion of Islam".'[38]

Since it is internationally recognised that while individuals may change their religion they may not change their ethnicity, this

[37] Saudi Arabia was the only Muslim nation that did not ratify the Declaration, objecting specifically to article 18: D.P. O'Sullivan, 'Al-Islam: An Alternative Approach to the Universal Protection of Human Rights', *The Islamic Quarterly* XLI, 2, (1997), pp. 134–36.

[38] US State Department, *Malaysia: International Religious Freedom Report* at www.state.gov/g/drl/rls/1rf/2001/5604.htm (last accessed on 26 October 2001).

ruling would appear to constitute all ethnic Malays immutable Muslims.

Egypt has an ancient Christian tradition going back to Athanasius, and although Egypt's population is predominantly Muslim the country does not practice Shari'a Law. However, one judge, Supreme Court Justice Said al-Ashmawi, is reported as saying 'I hold that Egyptian law is actually Islamic law.'[39] This attitude is reflected in the 2003 arrests of a total of twenty-two Christians, mostly converts from Islam, charged with falsifying their identity documents. The charge arises from the fact that while the courts will readily change the 'religion' entry from a non-Muslim religion to Islam, it is all but impossible to have the change from Muslim to a non-Muslim religion.[40]

In 1981 the Secretary General of the Islamic Council,[41] Salem Azzam, published the Council's 'Universal Islamic Declaration of Human Rights',[42] expanding on the 'Universal Islamic Declaration' published in the previous year.

The interpretation of the Declaration is governed by the opening statement of the Foreword, and by the first of the 'Explanatory Notes' appended to the document. The Foreword states that 'Islam gave to mankind an ideal code of human rights fourteen centuries ago.' The Declaration is based on the Qur'an. The Explanatory Note 1(b) says that 'the term "Law" denotes the Shari'ah, i.e. the totality of ordinances derived from the Qur'an and the Sunnah and any other laws that are deduced from these two sources by methods considered valid in Islamic jurisprudence.' There are thirty-one references to 'law' in the Declaration, of which thirty refer to Shari'a Law.

---

[39] Barnabas Fund: www.barnabasfund.org/Apostasy.htm (last accessed October 2003). Egypt's Constitution has been amended by the National Assembly so that Islam is 'the religion of state' and Shari'a Law is 'the principal source of legislation'. (Simon Qadri (ed.), *Persecution of Christians in Egypt* [New Malden, Surrey: Christian Solidarity International, 1998], p. 5).

[40] Qadri (ed.), *Persecution of Christians in Egypt*, p. 5.

[41] Based in Grosvenor Crescent, London; the *Declaration* was first issued in Paris.

[42] www.alhewar.com/ISLAMDECL.html (last accessed November 2003.).

The Declaration separates the right to freedom of belief, thought, and speech from the right to freedom of religion. Article XIII, 'Right to Freedom of Religion,' states only that 'every person has the right to freedom of conscience and worship in accordance with his religious beliefs'. This may be compared with the fuller statement of Article XVIII of the United Nations Declaration. The Islamic Statement is superficially satisfactory, but is notable first for what it does not say, and secondly for the heavy qualification by the Explanatory Note of what it does say. What is not said is that freedom of religion includes both private and public expressions of religion as an individual or a community, and the right to *manifest his religion or belief in teaching, practice, worship and observance*. More significantly, there is no reference to the right to change religion. The Explanatory Note on the role of Shari'a Law means that Muslims may change religion only on pain of death[43] as prescribed by all four Schools of Law.

It must at once be said that while governments in general may recognise the right to freedom of belief and freedom of religion, the right to the *exercise* of religious belief is always subject to the condition that it does not involve any practice that is contrary to law. Muslims and Mormons in the United Kingdom or in the USA may believe in polygamy, but may not practice it.[44] Obviously this does not exclude the possibility of a man cohabiting with several women, but only one of the women would be recognised by the state as a 'wife'.

The problem of human rights, then, lies not so much in the Islamic Statement as in the quadrilateral: Shari'a Law, the *Hadith*, the provisions of the Qur'an and the attendant principle of abrogation, which necessarily inform and restrict the Statement.

And so the issue of conversion and the concept of apostasy come back to the issue of the quadrilateral: the interpretation of

---

[43] And presumably the right to freedom of worship for the non-Muslim is subject to the limitations imposed by the so-called 'Covenant of Umar'. See N. Calder, J. Mojaddedi, A. Rippin (eds.), *Classical Islam: A Sourcebook of Religious Literature* (London: Routledge, 2003), pp. 90–93.

[44] See the interesting discussion of this point by Mohamed Berween, 'Al-Wathiqa: The First Islamic State Constitution', *Journal of Muslim Minority Affairs*, 23/1 (April 2003), pp. 110–12.

Qur'an and Hadith and the understanding of their role in formulating Islamic Law. In a radical attempt to deal with the problem of
the apparent incompatibility of Shari'a Law and contemporary
human rights perceived by some Muslims. Abdullahi Ahmed An-
Naim has suggested that Shari'a Law should be drawn from the
early Meccan Suras alone. The Medinan Suras are taken to relate
specifically and exclusively to the situation then faced by Muhammad in Medina.[45]

This proposal certainly has merit, and would resolve the issues
of polygamy and the amputation provisions of *hudud* law. But it
would presumably also deal with the problem of *ridda*, apostasy,
since the law was produced only in the second and third centuries
of Muslim development and was influenced by recent history.[46]

The above discussion clearly reflects the prevailing view of the
so-called democracies regarding the obvious conflict between the
United Nations Declaration and the Islamic Declaration, and the
assumption that it is the former that is, or should be, universally
normative. However, these rights have been ignored in varying
measure by China, Singapore, Sudan, Myanmar, India, Iran,
Saudi Arabia, Indonesia, Algeria and Cuba (among many others),
and not only the Islamic world but also the wider Asian community has challenged the assumptions of the United Nations Declaration. The global economic and political context, which enabled
the Western democracies to dominate the United Nations and
dictate the Declaration, has altered radically, and alternative and
pragmatic approaches to human rights are being asserted.[47]

Nor can it be assumed that the United Nations Declaration is
an essentially Christian Declaration. On the contrary it is a secular
expression of post-Enlightenment sentiment, and has no specific
moral authority as its foundation. As its title asserts, it is a declaration of *rights*, but has nothing to say about *responsibilities* and, of
course, nothing to say about duty owed to God. This is no mere

---

[45] See Katerina Dalacoura, *Islam, Liberalism and Human Rights*
(London and New York: I.B. Tauris, 2003), pp. 61–62; and A.A. An-
Naim and F.M. Deng (eds.), *Towards an Islamic Reformation* (New
York, NY: Syracuse University Press, 1990).
[46] Dalacoura *Islam, Liberalism and Human Rights*, p. 62.
[47] See Samuel Huntington, *The Clash of Civilizations* (London: Simon
and Schuster, Free Press, 1997), pp. 192–98.

debating point: without any such sanction a Declaration must always be subject to challenge.[48] To quote Archbishop William Temple, 'There can be no Rights of Man except on the basis of faith in God.'[49] And indeed this is what Islam has done in its Declaration, offering an alternative view on human rights, but a view which, unlike the United Nations Declaration, can claim an authoritative base, a divine sanction. As Bernard Lewis has expressed it, no movements from within Islam 'ever questioned the three sacrosanct distinctions establishing the subordinate status of the slave, the woman, and the unbeliever'.[50] And, we may add, neither do such movements challenge the Muslim concept of *ridda*, apostasy, whatever Muslim individuals might think.

Mawdudi carefully considered the problem posed by the radical and uncompromising *ridda* laws, on the one hand because they appear to contradict the Qur'anic principle that there is no compulsion in religion, and on the other, seeing the laws as promoting hypocritical and insincere professions of conversion to Islam. The laws are, however, justified because of Islam's status as a holistic religion, not merely a religion within a secular society. Abandoning Islam is then seen as opposing the stability of society.[51]

---

[48] See Dalacoura, *Islam, Liberalism and Human Rights*, ch. 1, 'Human Rights and Authenticity', for a discussion of this important question, usually blandly ignored by liberal sociologists.

[49] William Temple, *Citizen and Churchman* (London: Eyre and Spottiswoode, 1941), p. 74.

[50] Bernard Lewis, *What Went Wrong?* (New York, NY, and London: Weidenfeld and Nicolson, 2002), p. 83.

[51] Husain and Hahn (trans.), *The Punishment of the Apostate*, pp. 44–53.

12

The Emerging Debate on Apostasy in Britain

A Bradford Perspective

Philip Lewis

On 5 February 2005, *The Times* carried a story under the headline: 'Muslim Apostates cast out and at risk from faith and family'. The article went on to speculate that some 15 per cent of Muslims in the West had lost their faith, amongst whom a proportion converted to Christianity. While noting that in some Muslim countries 'including Saudi Arabia, Pakistan, Egypt and Yemen' such people 'face execution or imprisonment', the focus of the article was on the fate of converts in Britain. Women, in particular, featured prominently in the article. Yasmin, from the North of England, who had been baptised in her thirties, had set up a series of support groups across England with some seventy people on its list. Support was necessary because the convert was judged to have brought shame on the family and dishonoured Islam. To avoid potentially fatal reprisals converts invariably have to flee their Muslim community. Another female convert clarified the situation: 'If someone converts, it is a must for family honour to bring them back to Islam, if not, to kill them. Imams in Britain sometimes call on the apostates to be killed if they criticise their former religion.'

The only family profiled in the article were the Husseins from Bradford. Brought up in Pakistani Muslim homes, Nissar and his wife Kubra claim that they and their family have been the victims of violence and religious hatred for three years following their adoption of Christianity. The Catholic weekly *The Tablet* reported that:

> Police in Bradford have confirmed that a Muslim family who had converted to Christianity has suffered a campaign of intimidation by Muslim youths. The Hussein family have been taunted in the street, had their car rammed and set alight and had bricks thrown through a living-room window. West Yorkshire Police ... over the last three years ... had investigated 11 crimes against the Husseins. They said five of these had been classed as hate crimes. (*The Tablet*, 5 March 2003)

BBC Radio 4's *Sunday* program, in the context of discussing the Hussein family and the case of another female convert, canvassed wider opinion on this issue. Patrick Sookdheo, spokesman of The Barnabas Trust, a charity which highlights the persecution of Christians around the world, commented that:

> Islamic law specifies certain treatments for those who leave Islam. At the most extreme end, it sanctions the death penalty for any convert who leaves Islam, for say, Christianity. As long as you have a religion with a legal code that calls for death, and if not death, various degrees of punishment and that that is being taught in mosques, through their literature, books etc. that creates a very real problem in the community. Islam is a religion which is very conservative and although many people within it may be decent, to go against the wishes of a few ... that can be very difficult ... so they tend to be much more compliant with these kinds of abuses.[1]

---

[1] Imam Dr. Abdul Jalil Sajid from Brighton, who chairs the Mosques and Community Affairs of the Muslim Council of Britain (MCB), with whom I spoke subsequently, clarified several points: while it is true that pre-modern classical Islamic law did specify that in an Islamic state a Muslim should not be free to change his religion, of the fifty or more Muslim states today, only Iran and Saudi Arabia enact this as codified law! Undoubtedly, the Prophet, when he entered Mecca, did order the execution of some 'apostates' as a threat to the fledgling Muslim community – for what today we would call high treason. The distinguished

The reporter covering the story for *Sunday*, Shazia Khan, continued:

> Although many Muslim scholars and the Islamic Shariah law have specified death as a punishment for apostasy, the Qur'an itself does not actually say this. Dr Zaki Badawi, Principal of the Muslim College [in London] and chair of the Muslim Shariah Council, says the Islamic position is clear: 'The Qur'an mentions apostasy but does not specify punishment for it in this day ... in this here and now. In fact, it says, these people will be questioned by God in the Day of Judgement. So their punishment, if any, will be in the Day of Judgement ... and God's own judgement, wish, his own decree, will be the determining factor.'[2]

Shazia Khan went on to paraphrase Dr. Zaki Badawi to the effect that: 'He says that in Islam, there is "no compulsion in faith"

---

[1] Pakistani scholar S.A. Rahman, a Chief Justice of Pakistan, in his monograph *Punishment of Apostasy in Islam* (Lahore, Pakistan: Institute of Islamic Culture, 1972) had drawn the distinction between simple apostasy, which was simply an offence between the individual and God, and compound apostasy, which involved active sedition against a Muslim state, which properly carried draconian punishments. In Britain, apostasy laws are void, and the Qur'anic teaching that there is 'no compulsion in religion' takes priority. Indeed, British Muslims enjoy greater religious freedom in Britain than in many Muslim countries.

[2] Anne Elizabeth Mayer, in her celebrated study, *Islam and Human Rights: Tradition and Politics* (Boulder, CO: Westview Press Inc., 1995), notes that 'no verse in the Qur'an ... stipulates any earthly penalty for apostasy', p. 146. Classical rules for the death penalty were extrapolated from incidents in the Prophet's life and from events after his death. Such could admit of quite different interpretations. Dr. Hassan Al-Turabi, the Sudanese Islamist theorist, in a controversial article 'Opinion on Apostasy stirs a heated debate in Islamic juristic circles' excoriates Muslims for abstracting Prophetic sayings from their historic context and generalising them so as to negate the freedom of religion. 'Freedom of faith is one of the primary principles of religion. However, Muslims have ceased to deal directly with the main sources of their faith ... [but] are content with memorising quotations which ... represent the interpretations of previous generations ... The state of dependence on the achievements of their ancestors reflects the symptoms of decadence and ignorance of the Muslims [today]', *The Diplomat* (June 1996).

[Qur'an 2:256] and that the Islamic Shariah law should be changed to reflect this.'[3] She pertinently went on to observe: 'But what Islam says and what people actually understand Islam to say are two different things. I spoke to a twenty-eight-year-old woman who was born into a Muslim family in the North of England. We will call her Hannah. At sixteen she converted to Christianity and moved out of her parents' home. When she was baptised four years later, her family were outraged and she has been on the run ever since.' She reported Hannah as saying:

> My dad turned up at my house with fifty other Muslim guys banging on the door. I was just praying that they would not get in ... and I really believed that God protected me. They were shouting death threats: 'You are a traitor, we are going to kill you ... You have betrayed your whole community, your whole family ... You have brought shame on us.' I had to move out straightaway after that.
> (*Sunday*, 20 February 2005)

In the days following the article in *The Times*, the local Bradford daily newspaper, the *Telegraph and Argus*, carried two further stories about the Hussein family. The first expanded on the family's plight, which was described as 'both outrageous and shaming' and reported that the Bishop of Bradford had invited Muslim leaders to discuss how to combat religious intolerance (8 February 2005). Nissar Hussein's plea formed the headline for the second: 'Leave us alone to practise our faith in peace.' The journalist reporting the story asked: 'Are the public institutions of multi-faith Bradford doing enough to support the victims of such practices?' (18 February 2005).

What is the reality behind the headlines? Does it amount to a concerted and coordinated attempt by local Muslims to punish an apostate from Islam? Are Christians and Muslims able to go

---

[3] See Patricia Crone, *Medieval Islamic Political Thought* (Edinburgh: Edinburgh University Press, 2004). This book has an illuminating section entitled 'the moral status of coercion' where she shows how the obvious meaning of Qur'an 2.256 was qualified: '[It] was commonly held to prohibit forced conversion of *dhimmis* ['protected' People of the Book, Jews, and Christians] not the warfare whereby *dhimmi* status was imposed on them, and some said that both this and other verses enjoining tolerance had been abrogated when holy war was prescribed in Medina' (p. 373).

beyond the formulaic pleasantries of interfaith relations and engage in a substantive dialogue about the critical issue of religious freedom and tolerance? Are we any nearer to understanding the different histories and theologies which have generated distinct attitudes amongst Christians and Muslims to the question of leaving an inherited faith? The following description of two recent meetings in Bradford suggests provisional answers to these questions.

Drawing on the trust which has been built up over a quarter of a century, the Bishop of Bradford called a meeting for Christians and members of the Bradford Council for Mosques (BCM) to talk about this case. The Council has been working for twenty years to ensure that it can speak for as many mosque communities as possible in the city of some 80,000 Muslims. Meetings with successive Bishops, drawing together an ecumenical spread of Christian interfaith workers, have become part of a dense network of relationships which bridge religious and ethnic divides in Bradford.

Before meeting the Bishop, leading Muslims had shown, publicly in local press and radio, both courage and clarity in unequivocally condemning the intimidation and harassment of the Hussein family. Mr. Ishtiaq Ahmed, the information officer of BCM, pointed out that: 'As a minority in this country we ask for protection from abuse and persecution. We should be doing that for others too. We cannot have double standards' (*Telegraph and Argus*, 8 February 2005). He expanded his comments on the *Sunday* program:

> As a minority faith in this country, we are asking for changes in legislation to give us protection against religious intimidation, harassment and discrimination. And if we are asking that for ourselves, we cannot as a community afford to have double standards. Equality, the right to belong to any faith, the right to live with dignity and respect, is the right of every individual. If we are seeking that for ourselves, we must be able to give that to others as well.

Mr. Ayub Laher, chairman of Bradford Council for Mosques' Interfaith Committee and Northern representative of the Muslim Council of Britain, added:

We abhor violence because there is no compulsion in religion. We want people to follow their faith but if they leave it's their personal decision ... [However,] each Muslim community had its own cultural traditions and sometimes these took precedence over the religious requirements.[4] This is our adopted country and our home and the laws must be kept ... We keep emphasizing that. But there are always youngsters ... who are hard to control.

(*Telegraph and Argus*, 8 February 2005)

When the Muslim leaders met the Bishop, they reiterated these sentiments. They also remarked that they could not unilaterally police disaffected young men outside the orbit of the mosques. However, the president of the BCM had already given pledges to the Hussein family that they would make available members of the community to keep an eye on the church when they attended worship. Further, he pointed out that Manningham, where the church and mosque are located, has a local drug problem. Young men also steal shoes and mobile phones from Muslims at prayer, as well as occasionally trying to disrupt their mosque service.

Two important developments emerged from this conversation. The first was to arrange a meeting with the police and youth service to see whether we can develop localised inter-agency strategies which might both offer practical support to the Hussein family and engage disaffected young men, an increasing and worrying problem for *all* communities. The second, a suggestion

---

[4] Mr. Laher was here probably hinting at notions of extended family/ clan honour which apostasy was seen as compromising. This was the burden of Dr. Shabbir Akhtar's remarks fifteen years earlier with relation to the Rushdie affair: 'Although many contemporary learned authorities reject the view that apostasy is a capital offence ... the law of Islam rarely needs to be applied in such cases since the apostate's family will take the law into their own hands and kill the apostate on account of the stigma thought to attach to the rest of the family. Particularly in Indian sub-continental contexts, a man's *izzat* (roughly speaking, honour) is thought to be at sake if a family member converts to another faith. There is immense social pressure to disown the apostate if not to kill him or her. In Birmingham recently a Bengali father murdered his own daughter because she left to become a Jehovah's Witness.' See Dr. Shabbir Akhtar, *Be Careful with Muhammad!* (London: Bellew Publishing Co Ltd, 1989), p. 74.

which came from the BCM leaders, was to provide a platform for some respected religious scholars in the city. Their opinions drawing on Islamic jurisprudence would add weight to the public pronouncements of the BCM. Such scholars, after all, preach to the faithful week in and week out from the mosque pulpits. Further, the world of traditional Islam has been slow to rethink venerable teachings embedded in revered ancient texts. For example, Islamic seminaries in Indo-Pakistan and Britain continue to study the famous twelfth-century Hanafi legal text, *Hidaya* ('guidance'), compiled by Al-Marghinani, which rehearses classical Islamic teaching on apostasy.[5]

So it was that Anglican and Catholic interfaith advisers sat together with members of the BCM and a number of Muslim religious teachers, including Syeed Irfan Shah Mashadi, a much respected traditional scholar with a considerable following in Pakistan and Britain. Syeed Mashadi, who is learning English, preaches at the beautiful new central mosque in the city. The details of the Bishop's meeting were communicated to him in Urdu, particularly the abuse and attacks on the Hussein family. He was at pains to point out to us the commonalities between 'People of the Book' and Muslims, cousins in the 'Abrahamic community'. He repeated episodes from the Prophet's life which reflected his respect for Christians. The fact that we both believe in One God and are bearers of 'heavenly books' provides a secure foundation for coming together to solve problems. He made a plea that there be a regular pattern to such meetings. We agreed that too often Islam and the West perpetuate mutual misconceptions. Contentious subjects like 'jihad' are rarely traced back into the spiritual

---

[5] This text has been much criticised by some of Indo-Pakistan's most famous modernist scholars, Iqbal (d.1938) and Fazlur Rahman (d. 1988). See. P. Lewis, *Islamic Britain: Religion, Politics and Identity Among British Muslims* (London: Tauris, 2002), pp. 132–39. In a recent study on apostasy, Al-Marghani is painted as a rigorist with regard to whether it is mandatory or merely desirable for an apostate to have an opportunity of repentance. 'He maintains that the repentance option is desirable rather than mandatory ... [he] also thinks that an apostate who does not use the repentance option promptly should be killed at once ...'. See Y. Friedmann, *Toleration and Coercion in Islam* (Cambridge: Cambridge University Press, 2003), pp. 127–28.

heart of Islam and their true meaning elaborated. The notion in common currency that Muslims are dedicated to violence and fighting is painful for Muslims.

Much common ground emerged: Christians and Muslims alike have responsibilities to educate their own communities in the religious and ethical norms of their traditions. Sadly, what goes on at street level often bears little relationship to either tradition. Syeed Mashadi, a dignified religious leader, had himself fallen foul of racist and anti-Islamic taunts in Britain. He was at pains to point out that he did not confuse such actions with authentic Christianity. Nor should we confuse the actions of angry and disaffected young men abusing the Husseins with Islamic norms. He insisted that in the UK Muslims could not, indeed should not, build walls around their communities in a misguided attempt to prevent leakage out or across traditions. Most importantly, those who leave should be free from abuse and persecution. He stressed that even in a Muslim majority society, it is public authorities that deal with 'apostates' not individuals taking the law into their own hands. Anyone breaking the law in Britain by abusing and attacking those who left Islam could not look to Islam to justify such inexcusable behaviour.

He clarified his position so that there would be no suggestion that Christians and Muslims welcomed people leaving their faith. It causes pain for both communities. In reply to our prompting, he reiterated that if a young Muslim were, hypothetically, to come to him and seek advice and confessed he had been involved in persecuting an 'apostate' in Britain – where Islamic law did not obtain – he would not hesitate to point out that such actions were quite unacceptable according to Islamic law. If another religious scholar had advised him differently, that person would be the more culpable.

Such clarifications of the situation facing an 'apostate' in Britain were welcome. The meeting, after all, had been called to clarify what light Islamic law, as understood by a respected traditional scholar, could shed on the situation facing those who had left Islam and joined another faith in the UK. However, what also emerged was the need to explain how and why Christians have come to value 'religious freedom'. Too often we can, unwittingly, give the impression that such a position suggests an *indifference* to religious truth. This, hopefully, will be the subject of a follow-up meeting. It would be good to have an opportunity to clarify both the teachings of the Declaration on Religious Freedom of the Second Vatican Council and the rationale for the Catholic Church's shift from condemnation to endorsement of religious freedom. Such a development was hardly the result of religious indifferentism or expediency, but rather the fruit of a principled engagement of Catholic tradition and complex contemporary realities.

Islamic tradition, too, is complex and multi-layered. Historically, the four main Sunni legal schools have generated a great deal of internal debate and diversity. A distinguished, contemporary, traditional scholar from Pakistan, also influential in Britain, Muhammad Taqi 'Uthmani, the vice president of a celebrated Karachi 'seminary', has commented that had Western science and philosophy come to the notice of Muslim scholars while still under Muslim rule in nineteenth-century India, they could have incorporated much from these new disciplines. Instead, they found themselves in defensive mode, seeking to respond to the assaults on their social and intellectual world from colonialism, which led them to a rejectionist stance with regard to such disciplines.[6] The situation is Britain today is more promising and there are signs of an emerging debate and openness to Western knowledge from within the world of traditional Islamic seminaries.[7]

The ordeal of the Hussein family, while inexcusable, will nonetheless have served a useful purpose if more *'ulama* and leaders of Muslim organisations develop the confidence and exhibit the courage to challenge unthinking and oppressive family solidarities by repeating the points forcibly made by Syeed Mashadi. We may yet arrive at a point where more and more British Muslims agree with the position developed some fifteen years earlier by a Bradford philosopher and member of the BCM:

---

[6] See Muhammad Qasim Zaman, *The Ulama in Contemporary Islam: Custodians of Change* (Princeton, NJ: Princeton University Press, 2002), p. 82.

[7] See J. Birt and P. Lewis, 'The establishment of Islamic seminaries in Britain: Between sectarianism and engagement with wider society', in Martin van Bruinessen and S. Allievi (eds.), *Producing Islamic Knowledge: Transmission and Dissemination in Western Europe* (forthcoming).

The potential risks inherent in the offer of religious freedom are worth taking. Why? Well, if there is a God, I would argue, it can be expected *a priori* that he wants a voluntary response born of genuine gratitude and humility themselves rooted in reflection and morally responsible choice. Seen in this light, heresy and even apostasy are morally more acceptable than any hypocritical attachment to orthodox opinion out of the fear of public sanctions. Fortunately, for us we have the evidence of the Koran itself in favour of this view: 'there is no compulsion in religion' (Qur'an 2:256).[8]

---

[8] Shabbir Akhtar, *A Faith For All Seasons: Islam and Western Modernity* (London: Bellew Publishing Co Ltd, 1990), p. 21. This position is increasingly finding favour with a range of Muslim scholars: see M.H. Kamali, *Freedom of Expression in Islam* (Cambridge: The Islamic Texts Society, 1994); Abdulaziz Sachedina, *The Islamic Roots of Democratic Pluralism* (New York, NY: Oxford University Press, 2001); and Tariq Ramadan, *Western Muslims and The Future of Islam* (New York, NY: Oxford University Press, 2004).

13

Conversion from Hinduism and Sikhism to Christianity in India

Theodore Gabriel

The principal foci of this essay will be the political issues relating to conversion from Hinduism and Sikhism to Christianity, rather than the theological or theoretical aspects, though such considerations are not totally avoidable and will be referred to here and there.

Hinduism and Religious Conversion

One of the distinctive characteristics of conversion from Hinduism to Christianity is that it is so much easier than, say, conversion from Islam, or indeed Sikhism, to Christianity or vice versa. This is because Hinduism has such a broad view of religion and religious beliefs. Hinduism, unlike many other religions does not have a specific set of creeds or beliefs or rituals. It is very diverse, it is tolerant of divergent opinions, and it gives abundant latitude for differing beliefs and practice from the mainstream to its adherents. The word 'heresy' is absent in Hinduism. There was even an atheistic strand in Hinduism propagated by scholars such as Charvaka, who promoted a kind of epicurean philosophy of the world. The *nastikas* such as Charvaka were allowed to have their say in the tolerant religious climate of India. In a way, the religion of Hinduism is itself a creation of Western scholars or 'orientalists' who systematised the diverse collection of beliefs and religious practices in the Indian subcontinent and thus made the idea of a religion called Hinduism possible. However, the term and the religious identity of Hinduism are now acceptable to the vast majority of Indians.

Hinduism is also ready and willing to absorb ideas, tenets and practices from other religions. The Hindu intellectual V.R. Krishna Iyer, a Brahmin and former Chief Justice of India, states the following: 'If acceptance of the law of dharma given by Jesus is conversion, then I am already a Christian and there is no doubt whatsoever.'[1] Sri Narayana Guru, the famous savant of Kerala told a Christian missionary who was trying to convert him, 'I was a Christian long before you were born.'[2] Iyer even makes the claim 'Jesus Christ is of the East so we Indians can better understand Jesus and his dharma than the people of the West.'[3] Radhakrishnan in his work *Eastern Religions and Western Thought* finds many parallels between Hindu concepts of God and salvation and the thought of early Christian theologians such as Origen.[4] Elsewhere, he argued that Jesus 'attached no importance to professions of allegiance. There is nothing in common between the simple truths taught by Jesus and the Church militant with its hierarchic constitution and external tests of membership.'[5] Radhakrishnan thus seeks to equate the broad universality and pluralism of Hinduism and the teachings of Jesus.

Religious Experience in Hinduism

For Hinduism, experience is more important than creeds, doctrines and systematic theology. *Anubhava* (religious experience,

[1] V.R. Krishna Iyer, 'Human Rights and Religious Conversion in the Light of the Constitution of India', in P. Thomas (ed.), *Human Rights and Religious Conversion* (Delhi: Media House, 2002), p. 25.
[2] C.R.K. Vaidyar, *Sri Narayana Guru Swantam Vacanannalilute* (Sri Narayana Guru Through His Own Words; Kottayam: DC Books, 1990), p. 59.
[3] Iyer, 'Human Rights and Religious Conversion', p. 23.
[4] S. Radhakrishnan, *Eastern Religions and Western Thought* (Oxford: Oxford University Press, 1940).
[5] S. Radhakrishnan, *East and West in Religion* (London: George Allen & Unwin, 1967), p. 58.

the experiencing of God) is above all other considerations. If a Hindu can experience God by perusing the gospel or by witnessing the lives of Christians, he will empathise with and feel that he can experience God within the Christian faith. Mahatma Gandhi is an outstanding example of such empathy. The non-violence, the self-sacrifice, compassion for the poor and sick, and obedience to God testified in Jesus' life and death was a great influence on him, though he withdrew from the brink of converting to Christianity, since he felt that the religion of Hinduism also had great models for such virtues. (Nevertheless, it has often been argued that Gandhi, in his ideology and practice was more Christian – in the sense of being closer to Christ's ethical teachings – than many creedal Christians.)

This characteristic of a broad perspective on religion and a pluralistic and tolerant view of religions have the implication for Hindus that conversion to Christianity is not a matter of a great leap of faith. For Christian missionaries, on the other hand, this poses two problems. First, most Hindus might feel that there is no need to convert to Christianity, in spite of their admiration and attraction for the gospel message, because they think that Hinduism already encompasses all the virtues and even the teachings of Christianity. Secondly, the missionary is never quite sure whether the convert really subscribes to the idea of 'one faith, one church, and one baptism' (i.e. the exclusivity that Christianity often enjoins and demands). They may feel that the convert might compromise the exclusive truth claims that Christianity makes. To the Hindu, owing to the still highly Western cultural character of Christian ritual, the conversion might imply a cultural rather than a religious or spiritual conversion. Moreover, it is worth noting that Hindu fundamentalist organisations, such as the Sangh Parivar, have expressed concern, because the tolerance and doctrinal flexibility of Hinduism might lead to easy conversions, in that a Hindu will not feel the conversion process to be such an uprooting and traumatic one.

The Debate on Conversion from Hinduism

The political controversies surrounding conversion of Hindus to Christianity is not, as is commonly believed, of recent origin.

Nineteenth-century India under the British Raj witnessed great religious ferment and debate. The debates between Raja Ram Mohan Roy and Joshua Marshmann, a Baptist missionary, are well known. Gandhi, in spite of his general non-aggressive and tolerant approach to matters of faith, was also severely opposed to the proselytising activities of Christian missionaries. He went to the extent of saying, 'If I had power and could legislate I should certainly stop them from proselytising.'[6] This statement foreshadows legislation regarding conversion later in Orissa, Madhya Pradesh, Arunachal Pradesh and recently in Tamilnadu.

Curiously, Nehru, a self-professed agnostic, was opposed to legislating on religious conversion. He opposed the Indian Converts Bill (regulation and registration), mooted in the Lok Sabha (House of Commons) by Jethalal Joshi in 1954, on the grounds that legislation against religious conversion would cause harassment to a large number of people. Nehru's words have indeed proved to be prophetic because of the possibility of abuse of the powers granted to local authorities in such legislation. Such laws are liable to a wide variety of interpretation and could be used to intimidate those who wished to change their religion for genuine reasons and thus impinge badly on their fundamental rights. However, it is evident that the Nehru administration was concerned by the increasing activities of foreign missionaries in India, and sought to restrict their tenure in India and limit their work to humanitarian activities rather than proselytising. The Niyogi Commission instituted by the Madhya Pradesh Government in 1954 was the result of such concerns. The Niyogi Commission was composed entirely of Hindus, except for one member, S.K. George, a Syrian Christian, who was not considered by Indian Christians to be representative of their community.

The Niyogi report merely articulated popular Hindu fears regarding the conversion of Hindus, and especially tribal people and the untouchables (known as scheduled castes) and was roundly rejected by the Christian community of India.

---

[6] Quoted in Sebastian Kim, *In Search of Identity: Debates on Religious Conversion in India* (New Delhi: Oxford University Press, 2003), p. 73.

Conversion of Untouchables and Tribals

The question of the conversion of tribal people and the untouchables is particularly interesting, as well as ambiguous. The central issue is whether they are Hindus. The untouchables are *avarna* (outcastes) and technically outside the Hindu fold, as are obviously the Christians and the Muslims. Thus their conversion is not in reality from Hinduism to Christianity and could also be construed to be from one non-Hindu category to another non-Hindu category. Since both the untouchable and the Christian are *mlecca* (polluted), such conversions should not really alter their *locus standi* from the Hindu perspective.

The tribal people are now claimed by the Sangh Parivar to be Hindu. However, their religious practices and deities are distinctively different from pan-Hindu practices and the Hindu pantheon. Nevertheless, it must be admitted that many of the untouchable and tribal groups in India are seeking a 'sanskritization' of their religious identity by means of a neo-Vedantin interpretation of their rituals and by identifying their deities with pan-Hindu gods and goddesses, such as Vishnu, Shiva and Kali. A striking example would be the Muttappan duo of deities in northern Kerala who have been in recent times categorised as incarnations of Vishnu and Shiva. The tribal masks worn in their ritual are said to be indicative of the *dashavatara* (ten incarnations) of Vishnu.

Christians, however, could legitimately question the motives of Hindus who in the past have excluded and even oppressed these groups and now suddenly claim them to be within the Hindu fold and express concern at their conversion to Christianity. Indeed, Paul Thomas questions whether the Sangh Parivar have any genuine interest in the liberation and uplift of these people.[7] After all, they were opposed to Mahatma Gandhi who was instrumental in making these provisions for these oppressed people of India.

Allegations Against Christian Proselytisation

The central argument against Christian conversion is that often such conversion is not genuine or spiritual but induced by material

---

[7] P. Thomas (ed.), *Human Rights and Religious Conversion*, p. 12.

considerations. Christian missionaries are alleged to have offered material benefits such as jobs or houses to persuade Hindus and others to convert to Christianity. The term 'Rice Christians' is familiar to us. Most legislation on religious conversion is designed against such material attractions. Hindu leaders often find it disturbing that Christian missionaries can draw on abundant funds from affluent Western nations to finance their proselytising activities. Christian missionary activity is thus categorised as a tool of Western dominance. The Hindus might resent Christian proselytisation as a tool for a neo-colonial attitude, another instance of the alleged reintroduction of Western dominance into liberated European colonies. They equate the Christianisation of India with Westernisation, since Christianity is fallaciously seen as a Western religion. Globalisation in the economic field is a new phenomenon in India, which had so far been the scene of protected indigenous trade and production of goods. Globalisation has brought ventures such as Western fast food outlets and numerous other foreign corporations into competition with Indian industries. Consequently, such companies are resented by many Hindus, especially those which are marked by Western cultural characteristics. There have been demonstrations, boycotts and even attacks on, for example, McDonald's food retailers, Western sponsored beauty competitions, and other obviously Western enterprises by Hindu fundamentalist organisations such as the Rashtriya Swayam Sevak Sangh (RSS) and Vishwa Hindu Parishad (VHP).

The point is that, unfortunately, Christianity, as noted earlier, is viewed as part of this Western takeover. It is understood to be primarily a Western religion, rather than one of a Semitic or Eastern provenance. Therefore, Christian evangelisation, especially since the indigenisation process in Christianity in India, has not advanced far, being viewed as another instance of the intrusion of Western culture, Western attitudes of superiority and Western dominance in Indian affairs. And it is difficult for many Christian organisations to refute such objections, since they are often financed by European or American churches and organisations. Consequently, such evangelisation becomes highly suspect in Hindu eyes as a move to undermine Indian culture and independence from the West. Moreover, many traditional Hindus feel on the defence, in that many of the younger generation of Indians, including those from non-Christian faiths, are greatly attracted to Western culture, in matters of dress, music and food. More specifically, Christian boys and girls are usually thought of, often erroneously, as in the vanguard of these innovations in the attempt to Westernise Indian life.

India and Western Missions

Of course, not all Indians are hostile toward Christianity and the West. As an Indian Christian myself, brought up in Kerala, I certainly feel that the Christians of India owe a debt of gratitude to Western missionaries who first brought the faith to India, and set up educational, medical and even industrial units, most of which were of enormous value to the country. The Christian community was, of course, particularly helped, especially those estranged from their Hindu family as a result of their conversion to the Christian faith. Indeed, many Hindus also have great admiration and respect for the educational and social welfare activities of the Christian missionaries. Christian educational institutions are, even today, highly regarded in India for their high standards, discipline and pastoral care of students. The Madras Christian College and their former Western missionary professors are almost legendary characters in South India. The Protestant missions made it a principle to admit and employ non-Christians in their educational institutions. Medical institutions such as the Christian Medical College and Hospital in Vellore are likewise highly regarded for both their proficiency and also the care they provide, especially to patients from poor backgrounds, both Christian and non-Christian.

It would be wrong, however, to categorise Indian Christians as the champions of colonialism or the pioneers of Western culture in modern India. Though this is a popular perception among Hindus, such a perspective is fallacious and invalid. Indian Christians, barring (possibly) the Anglo-Indian mixed race members, have the same cultural characteristics as their Hindu counterparts. In the matter of food, dress, home décor, etiquette, familial relationships, and so on, they are no different from their Hindu counterparts. It is only in matters of religious belief and observance that they can be distinguished. The Indian Christians of India are well integrated within the mostly Hindu cultural milieu of India.

The British in India

Part of the problem surrounding conversion and Christianity in India has been the attitudes of colonial officers of the former British regime in India ('the Raj'), during which they practiced a kind of social ostracisation of Indians (even the most educated ones) from their social circles. They were willing to meet their Indian colleagues at work, but not for social intercourse, which they limited entirely to their compatriots from the West. During that time, Indian religions were characterised as superstition and their rituals as bizarre and ridiculous. True there were many British and other European and American scholars who had a love for and an authentic understanding of Indian religions and culture, but the majority of British expatriates in India looked down upon Indian beliefs and religious practices. The rise of Hindu nationalism can be seen mainly within this era and, I would argue, was due to European political and cultural superciliousness and hegemony. (The Moguls were, on the other hand, keen to adopt Indian customs and culture and many of them married Hindus.) Indians, however 'civilised' according to the European understanding, were stereotyped by British colonials as unhygienic, unsystematic, disorganised, unmannered, uncouth and given to superstitious practices such as astrology and looking for auspicious signs at the beginning of any new venture or journey. The British author E.M. Forster has given a graphic account of British colonial attitudes in the nineteenth and early twentieth centuries in his novels set in India.[8] Thomas concurs: 'Denigration of Indian culture by British colonials contributed to the idea of a Hindu nation.'[9] Such attitudes, bordering on racism, must have hurt the Hindu psyche badly. Indeed, the hostility and rancour they generated are still there, and have rubbed off, to some extent, on Indian Christians.

---

[8] See particularly Forster's *Passage to India* (San Diego: Harcourt Brace Jovanovich, Inc., 1924).

[9] P. Thomas (ed.), *Human Rights and Religious Conversion*, p. 122.

The point is, however, that, drawing on a particularly biased interpretation of this history, Hindu fundamentalists protest that Christian evangelisation is a tool for the continued Western dominance of India, both in the religious sphere and in the cultural sphere, with consequences also for the economic and the political areas of Indian life.

The British also had a hand in uniting India, with the annexation of many princely states, and the formation of a strong central governmental system. However, in doing this, they unwittingly provided the framework for political power to be vested in the hands of the majority community. This was significant, for political power had slipped through the hands of Hindus for many centuries: 600 years of Muslim rule; 200 years of British rule; and prior to that, because they lacked a common religious identity, the country was fragmented into so many sovereign states. In a nation where authority was founded on the majority principle, the fundamentalists saw the opportunity to place power into the hands of the Hindus over a large and administratively unified nation. This was a totally new situation in India. Such a vast hegemony had only existed in the mythical accounts of King Bharata, and latterly during the Maurya and Gupta empires. Thus the attempt to forge the Hindus into a political force began and continues. Consequently, the issue of Christian conversion is an increasingly contentious one.

Christian Attitudes to Democracy in India

Indian Christians are fully committed to democracy, though they do not have much political influence, being only 4 per cent of the population. Moreover, unlike the Muslim and Sikh minorities and the Dalits, they have not organised themselves into a political party – even though such a move might have augmented their political strength and bargaining power in public fields. If at all they have fielded candidates for elections it has been under the auspices of one of the major political parties of India. There are some Christian Members of Parliament affiliated to the BJP – though one would not normally expect them to ally with a fundamentalist, Hindutva party. In Kerala, where they exist in some strength, they are said to be a major factor in the Kerala Congress Party (not to be confused with the Indian National Congress). It can be seen that the lack of political power has eroded the privileges of Christians in recent times, mainly due to the policies of BJP governments. Tribal people and Dalits who convert to Christianity now lose their special 'scheduled' status. There is more governmental interference in Christian-managed educational institutions. In the Central Government there has been no Christian Prime minister, no President, nor any ministers of cabinet rank. (It is significant that Nehru appointed Rajkumari Amrit Kaur, a Christian, as Health Minister in the first Indian cabinet). The highly regarded former bureaucrat Dr. Alexander, a close and well favored associate of former Prime Ministers Indira and Rajiv Gandhi, was let down by the Congress Party when he put himself forward for the position of President of India.

Some of the fallout from this has taken the form of personal attacks on Sonia Gandhi by the Sangh Parivar outfits. Sonia, though born a Roman Catholic in Italy, is nevertheless now an agnostic, an important member of the Gandhi family and culturally and socially well-integrated within Indian life. She speaks fluent Hindi, gives speeches in Hindi to vast crowds and to party members, and has given up her Italian nationality. However, there are allegations from Hindu fundamentalists that she is essentially a foreigner, a Christian, and a symbol of the continuing Western dominance of Indian politics. Though such a stance has been roundly criticised by the Indian National Congress and most of the Indian intelligentsia, Sonia voluntarily resigned from the post of Prime Minister after the successes of her party in elections, standing down in favour of Manmohan Singh, one of her lieutenants. She did this principally to avoid confrontation with the fundamentalists and possible civil strife in the country – a magnanimous gesture applauded by most of the old political stalwarts and the enlightened sections of Indian society, both Hindu and non-Hindu.

Caste in Christianity

Christianity is in principle an egalitarian faith. The Bible consistently emphasises that God is absolutely just and has no trait of favouritism, either on the basis of wealth, status, or power. Paul states, 'There is neither Jew nor Greek, slave nor free, male nor female, for you are all one in Christ Jesus.'[10] But the fact is that the caste system is often seen as well entrenched within Christianity in India. In South India, for example, caste like groups such as the Vellala, Nadar and Syrian Christian are endogamous and will have separate churches and even cemeteries. Their social interaction with lower castes such as new converts and Dalits are minimal. Dalits are 70 per cent of the Roman Catholic Church in India, yet the key positions are held by the remaining 30 per cent of the church.[11] Dalits (untouchables) suffer the same discrimination in Christianity as they do in other Hinduism. Indeed, by converting to Christianity, they also lose the privileges and exemptions that the Indian constitution guarantees for their upliftment. Thus egalitarianism as a motivation for conversion to Christianity is rather ambiguous and unclear.

Demographic Issues

The attitude of the Sangh Parivar seems to be colored by demographic considerations more than anything else. In a democracy with universal franchise, majority-minority questions are important. Theoretically, no one can convert to Hinduism. The *varshnashrama dharma* doctrine states that one is born into a particular caste by virtue of his deeds in a previous life. It is true that neo-Vedantin organisations such as the Arya Samaj and the Ramakrishna Mission have engaged in conversion of non-Hindus into Hinduism. So also have sects such as the Hare Krishna and the Swami Narayan movement. The Arya Samaj focused mainly on reconversion of Hindus who had joined the Christian or Islamic fold. They had a *shuddi* ('purification') ceremony for affecting this. It is apparent that they subscribed to the theory that Christian and the Muslim are *mlecca*, just as the scheduled castes, and needed to be purified. Thus the Hindus are apprehensive that they are steadily losing members from their ranks while they are unable

---

[10] Gal. 3:27–29.
[11] See 'Cast Identity Within the Church: Twice Alienation': http://www.dalitchristians.com/Html/CasteChurch.htm (accessed December 2005).

to gain members from other faiths since it is not a religion with proselytising fervour; neither are conversions to Hinduism theoretically possible. However, since Hindus are 80 per cent of the vast population of India and the Christians are only 4 per cent, it is difficult to see why the Sangh Parivar should be overly concerned about Christian expansion. Islam, though demographically much larger, is not very active in proselytisation. Thus, Hindu fears that they are a 'dying race' or that they will become a minority in India in the course of time seem not to be based on reality.

In a way, this feeling marks the transition of India from an autocracy, monarchy, or oligarchy to a democratic nation. Democracy is new to India and, as for all fledgling nations, India has teething problems with the new political system. One finds that there is a proliferation of political parties, the genesis of which is mainly due to personal aggrandisement or schisms, based not on political or democratic principles, but questions of personal power and other pragmatic considerations. Thus, the numerical dimension of politics has now become very important in India. As long as the political parties were defined with respect to secular ideologies, such as socialism or Marxism, politics stayed well clear of religion. But, in recent years, the emergence of parties based on religion has vitiated the political scene. In the early decades of independence, with the exit of the only religious political party in India, the Muslim League to Pakistan, political identities in India remained secular for a long time. The Akali Dal emerged in the 1960s with the rise of Sikh nationalism, but is not so prominent nowadays. But there was always the possibility of religiously based politics, with incipient groups in existence, such as the RSS, The Hindu Mahasabha, The Arya Samaj, and such organisations whose remit was, in earlier times, purely religious and social, not political. However, more recently, Hindu fundamentalists have formed their political wing, mainly the Bharatiya Janatha Party (BJP). It has an unashamedly non-secular ideology, based on the superiority of what they term Hindutva ('Hinduness').

Consequently, demographic considerations are now important in the Indian religious context. To some extent, that they have not attempted a coup in India indicates that the Hindus are committed to the democratic principle. India has not been declared a Hindu state, though many of their actions, termed 'saffronization', seem to indicate this is their ultimate objective. As to their appeal, this is not, I would argue, great among educated, middle-class Hindus, but is rather more so among the poorer and less-educated in what is often termed 'the Hindi belt'. That said, there are minority groups subscribing to Hindutva ideology in all regions, and even in such a tolerant society as in Kerala, recently there have been attacks on Christians, especially those seen as having an evangelistic agenda. The Sisters of Charity, founded by Mother Teresa, and evangelists of the Assemblies of God, have also recently been targeted for violence in Kerala. Many would agree with Swami Tattwamayananda: 'If the Christian considers his fundamental duty to convert all non-Christians into his faith, the Hindu has every right to defend his own faith from what he may consider as interference in his religious life.'[12] He adds that many Hindus appreciate and respect the spiritual personality of Jesus but fail to understand why the Christian missionaries expect them to respect their so called 'obligation' to convert all non-Christians into the Christian faith.[13] However, it is doubtful that Christian missionaries have a demographic agenda in India behind their proselytising program. Christians in India have no political organisation equivalent to the BJP or the Muslim League. They seem to have no ambitions of securing political power.

Religious Conversion and the Indian Constitution

The Christian missionary need not have any reservations about propagating his faith in India. The constitution guarantees the right to, not only profess and practice one's faith, but also to propagate it (Art. 25). There were lengthy debates in the Constituent Assembly of India regarding the right to propagate and convert into religions. K.M. Munshi, later on Cabinet Minster for Food and Agriculture, and the founder of the Bharathiya Vidya Bhavan, emphasised the right to protect citizens from coercive and unethical methods of conversion, while B.R. Ambedkar, the chair of the Constituent Assembly, emphasised the fundamental rights of

---

[12] Swami Tattwamayananda, 'Religious Conversion: The Hindu View', in Thomas (ed.), *Human Rights and Religious Conversion*, p. 55.
[13] Ibid., p. 52.

citizens, free speech and the right to 'liberty of conscience and the free exercise of his religion, including the right to profess, preach and to convert within limits compatible with public order and morality'.[14]

Hindu Concerns about Conversion to Christianity

The motivations for religious conversion are very complex.[15] It could be a cognitive, intellectual reasoning process, or affective, emotional and passionate. It could be for pragmatic reasons such as marriage to a member of another faith, in which the motivating factor is the desire to marry a particular individual, not to convert spiritually. It may be the result of a sudden inspiration, the message of a preacher that strikes a chord in the listener's mind, the witnessing of a ritual such as the Hajj or the Kumbh Mela, or a dream or vision as happened to Paul and Sadhu Sundar Singh, to cite two prominent examples. In both their accounts, Christ appeared and spoke to them. Therefore, conversion need not necessarily indicate or imply the inferiority of the original faith of the convert, or any deficiency in its beliefs and practices.

What the Hindus feel is culpable is that the Christian conversion actively targets people who are rather naïve, easily influenced (they might even say easily brainwashed) into accepting the viability and superiority of the Christian faith. Tribals and scheduled castes may be individuals who are not fully conversant with their own religious faith, its beliefs, or the underlying significance of its practices – the rituals may be mechanically enacted. The Christian exposition is simple, appealing and direct. It is a message of love and redemption, not complex theological argument. However, most Christian missionaries do not intimidate others into accepting and adhering to their ideology by threats, by presenting dire eschatological consequences, or by strict control of the member's lives – though many used to do that in earlier times. Most, nowadays, appeal to the liabilities of human existence, unhappiness,

---

[14] Sebastian, *In Search of Identity*, p. 48.

[15] L. Rambo, 'The Psychology of Religious Conversion': http://www.religiousfreedom.com/conference/Germany/rambo.htm (accessed December 2005).

frustration, the dissatisfaction and drudgery of human lives and how accepting Christ can transform it. Krishna Iyer includes humanitarian work as a legitimate way of propagating one's faith: 'Propagation is compassion with a creative dimension ... it may be by lecturing or by writing articles and books; it may be by washing lepers; it may be by giving love to the loveless and hope in life for the hopeless. Mahatma Gandhi also did the same.'[16]

Religious conversion seems also to be related to questions of authority and power. The Hindu apprehension is also that conversion into Christianity will jeopardise the internal security of India, fomenting rebellions against the Union and the states. This apprehension has been aggravated by the insurgency in some of the states of the North East, mainly among the ethnic group of the Nagas, most of whom are Christian. Swami Tattwamayananda, quotes the words of the well-known anthropologist Dr. Verrier Elwin (paradoxically son of an Anglican Bishop and former missionary in India): 'It (the tribal population India) will be turned into querulous, anti-national, aggressive community, with none of the old virtues and few of the new which will be a thorn in the side of the future Government of India.'[17] But such a phenomenon did not arise in the tribes of the Santhal region or in Nicobar. Hence, the conclusion must be that the dissensions and separatism in the North East were mainly due to ethnic disparities, not religious issues.

Another of the perceived problems with Christian conversion is that it brings about cultural change. As we have seen, it is alleged that Christians are subject to Westernisation on conversion. There is some truth in this, since Christian rituals are mainly based on the Western culture of their missionaries, though there are many moves in the Christian church in India to indigenise rituals, music, and church architecture. The effect on dress, food and etiquette of conversion is marginal, and it is difficult to distinguish an Indian Christian woman from a Hindu woman, for example.

The whole issue of culture in India is fraught with problems. The Sangh Parivar might like to feel that Indian culture is identical with Hindu culture. However, several points should be noted.

---

[16] Iyer, 'Human rights and religious conversion', p. 32.
[17] Quoted in Tattwamayananda, 'Religious conversion', p. 53.

First, Indian culture is very diverse. Secondly, the Muslim and Christian faiths in India have had inputs into the composite culture that is Indian culture. The saffronization of India that seems to be the objective of the Sangh Parivar may be an effort to change this, but in a pluralistic nation such as India this will be virtually impossible. Thirdly, many Hindus are themselves abandoning old Indian culture. It is in rural India that the hold of old Indian culture is strongest. In the urban context, the apparel, eating habits and the like are undergoing a sea change. This is not something that is fostered by Christian missionaries, but rather a spontaneous evolution of culture due to the rapid dissemination of cultural elements in the media such as television. The number of Hindus who listen to classical Indian music for instance has gone down considerably. Western pop music and the syncretic East-West Bollywood music are the most popular with the urban educated Hindus. Urban Hindus themselves wear salwar kameez (of Islamic provenance) and shirts and trousers rather than the sari or the kurta and pyjama. There is no evidence that Christian missionaries in India ever imposed a dress code or tried to change cultural practices except in church rituals. However, many of the Hindutva protagonists, like Ashok Chowgule, feel that Christian conversion has destroyed the convert's past history and culture.[18] That said, it is arguable that the Hindutva parties are pursuing a romantic notion of Hindu culture, which is more mythical than real.

In response to such concerns, however, many Christian leaders now feel that it is time for the Christian church to indigenise and leave the Western garb in which Christianity came to India. To this end they are now trying to promote use of the vernacular in worship, the use of Indian music and musical instruments in church, the use of Sanskritic terms such as *Om*, *Bhagavan* ('God') and *shanti* ('peace') in liturgy, the use of flowers and water and sacred oil lamps in ritual, and indigenous church architecture. However, this has also led to further opposition, in that some Hindu leaders of the Sangh Parivar are apprehensive about these changes and characterise them as an attempt to hoodwink Hindus and attract them to accept Christianity, much as De Nobili wore

---

[18] A. Chowgule, *Christianity in India: The Hindutva Perspective* (Mumbai: Hindu Vivek Kendra, 1999), pp. 17–25.

Brahmin dress, sported the *kuduma* (shaven head with tuft of hair) and the sacred thread to make Christianity appeal to Brahmins.[19]

Conversion of Sikhs to Christianity

Doctrinally speaking it is much easier for Sikhs than Hindus to convert to Christianity. The religion is eclectic and, in reality, the founder Guru Nanak (1496–1539) often emphasised the equality and even identity of all religions. He used to say, 'The mosque and the temple are the same, Hindu worship and Mussulman prayer are the same, the Puranas and the Qur'an are the same, the Hindu God and the Muhammadan God are the same'.[20] Guru Nanak was not exposed to Christianity, since there were hardly any Christians around in the Punjab during his time,[21] but it is highly probable that he would have postulated an identity of Sikhism and Christianity as he did in the Hinduism case, had he possessed knowledge of the Christian faith.

The Sikh understanding of God is also very close to the Judeo-Islamic Christian tradition. While God is considered free of personal attributes, he is worshipped as Saguna and is not the impersonal deity of Hindu monism. God is often called by the appellation *Nam* (lit. name) which has a strong resemblance to the Yahweh terminology of the Semitic tradition. Reincarnation is part of their belief, but apparently the related *Varnashrama dharma* (duties relating to caste, and stage of life) ideology of Hinduism is not there in Sikhism. Sikhs are averse to too much ritualism that recalls to mind the attitude of Protestant Christianity. Sikhism, like Christianity, is adverse to idolatry. Guru Arjan Dev said, 'The stone he calls his god, in the end, drowns him with itself ... Know that a boat of stone carries one not across.'[22] Meditation of God is enjoined on all Sikhs. The elements of Christian monasticism are apparent in Sikh religious practice. Theoretically Sikhism emphasises meditation on God above any other religious ritual. The importance of the Word of God, as in Christianity, is

---

[19] E.g. Chowgule, President of VHP Mumbai, in response to Dr. Gabriel, date: 29.1.1998: Hindu Christian Studies1@lists-acusd.edu.
[20] See www.sikhs.org/philos.htm (accessed December 2005).
[21] He did meet some Christians and Jews during his journeys to Arabia.
[22] See www.sikhs.org/philos.htm.

practiced most fully in Sikhism, where the reverence of the Granth (Scripture) is very prominent.

It should also be recalled that the Sikhs had a better rapport with the British colonial power, which was viewed as a Christian power in those days, than any other religious group of India. As a matter of fact, Sikh soldiers remained loyal to the British during the traumatic rebellion of 1857 and actually assisted the British in putting down what is now called the First Indian War of Independence.

Caste in Sikhism

Theoretically speaking, conversion to Christianity to escape caste-based prejudice and discrimination could not have been a motivating factor in Sikh communities. The teaching of Sikhism is strongly against the caste system. Nanak frequently went out of his way to denounce Brahminical pretensions and rejected the notion that salvation had anything to do with the hierarchy of castes, a feature of the Hindu notion of *varnashrama dharma*.[23] It should also be remembered that three out of the five Panj Pyaras were Dalits. However, Sikhism is not entirely devoid of casteism. This is not strange in the Indian milieu, where there are caste-like configurations in both Islam and Christianity, and caste-based prejudices and separatism exist in these faiths which theoretically are entirely opposed to the idea of caste. Vatsala Vedantam writes that there are even separate quarters for Dalit Sikhs in Gurudwaras.[24] Sikhs usually marry only within caste lines. It is also pointed out that the ten Gurus of Sikhism did not marry outside their Khatri caste. It is even strange that the ten Gurus of a religion that preaches against caste should all be from the same caste. It is said that the Jats who form the elite in Sikhism are on the whole endogamous and look down upon Sikhs of other castes. *Christianity Today* comments that, 'despite Sikhism's origins, discrimination against Dalits runs deep here. Dalit Sikhs often must worship in their own shrines, or

---

[23] See W.H. McLeod, *Exploring Sikhism* (New Delhi: Oxford University Press, 2000), p. 219.

[24] V. Vedantam, 'Still Untouchable: The Politics of Religious Conversion': www.religion-online.org/showarticle.asp?title=2661 (accessed December 2005).

gurdwaras. Marriages between low-caste and upper-caste Sikhs are prohibited. Upper-caste Sikhs generally avoid social interaction with Dalits.[25] Apparently, in spite of Sikhism's anti-caste principles, discrimination against Dalits is an undeniable feature of Sikh society. Dalit Sikhs are often constrained to worship in their own *gurudwaras*. Marriages between low-caste and upper-caste Sikhs are prohibited. Social interaction between upper-caste Sikhs and Dalit Sikhs are very limited.

Christian Proselytisation in the Punjab

According to *Christianity Today*, over the last several years, several thousand Sikhs, many of them Dalits, have left Sikhism for Christianity.[26] In April 2003, 200 Dalits converted in the town of Moga. Another forty-eight converted in Amritsar, the province's capital and home to Sikhism's revered Golden Temple. This Christian journal might have a bias in portraying the social ills of Sikhism, but there is no reason to disbelieve the above facts, which are relatively well-known.

There is little evidence that many Sikhs have converted to Christianity to escape caste-based discrimination, though one Sikh writer confesses that he is driven closer to Christianity by the inducement of Christian egalitarianism. What is evident is that there is considerable misgiving on the part of the Sikh leadership about Christian evangelism among Sikhs and the conversion of some Sikhs to Christianity. Apparently, Christian missionary bodies preaching redressal of social ills, supplemented with financial help, have gained acceptance among a section of the economically backward. The conversion of Mazhabis to Christianity in colonial Punjab has been well documented and was probably prompted by a desire for egalitarianism in the Christian community.[27] More recently, one young Sikh recalled the following:

---

[25] *Christianity Today* 47.7 (June 2003), p. 24.
[26] Ibid.
[27] See J.C.B. Webster, 'Dalits and Christianity in Colonial Punjab: Cultural Interactions', in J.M. Brown and R.E. Frykenburg (eds.), *Christians, Cultural Interactions, and Indian Religious Traditions* (London: Routledge, Curzon, 2002), pp. 92–118.

As a child I remember my father coming home drunk and shouting at us without any control. There was no food in the house and we were reduced to beggary. Once, some missionaries came home and taught us lessons for a better life. This made my father give up his bad habits and he started going to work. With the Lord's blessings things changed for the better. My father adopted Christianity and I followed suit.[28]

Harbajan Singh, who converted to Christianity in 1986 and is now pastor of a village church, witnessed that he was a drunkard and indulged in 'all kinds of bad things' until his conversion. He built the church with his own hands in 1991, meanwhile receiving death threats.[29] However, another villager attributes the conversions to inducements of cash and other material favours: 'When I asked the boys as to why they have converted to Christianity, they said they had been given cash and free education. In our village alone, 5 to 6 people have converted and, of course, their generations to come would also be Christians.'[30] However, in Raipur district twenty-two families which converted to Christianity represented to the district authorities that their conversion was genuine and induced by their perusal of the Bible, and there were no material allurements or any pressure upon them. Apparently, the authorities have taken the Sikh allegations seriously since the same report in the Time News Network informs that two priests and a nun were sentenced to imprisonment in the Raigarh court on charges of forcible conversion.

Opposition from the Sikh Leadership

The National Minorities Council (NCM) has stepped into the fray, alleging in a letter to the Catholic Bishop's Council of India that Christian missionary teams fully supported with medical teams have been going around villages in the Punjab, alluring Sikhs to the Christian faith. Tarlochan Singh, Chair of the NCM, exhorts Christians to stop this practice to prevent estrangement between two minorities of India, owing to their public denouncement of each other's faith and

---

[28] *Travel Times, India* (14 March 2003).
[29] *Christianity Today* (July 2003).
[30] *Travel Times, India* (14 March 2003).

attempting to gain numerical strength by conversion. This reveals that, as in the Hindu case, Sikhs, who are a majority in the Punjab, are also apprehensive of losing their demographic superiority through conversions to other faiths.

The situation is complex and it is difficult to make sense of these happenings, some of which seem to be somewhat contradictory. Conversion to Christianity may not be so much dependent on a need to escape caste-based discrimination as in the Hindu case, since casteism is not so strong in Sikhism as in Hinduism. Yet Christian missionaries are apparently successful in attracting many Sikhs away from the faith of their forefathers. As with the Hindus there is concern among Sikh leaders that they may lose the demographic dominance that they have enjoyed in Punjab. It should be remembered, of course, that it is along religious lines that Punjab had been divided into the India and Pakistan regions, and later into Sikh Punjab and Hindu Hariyana. So the existence of the Sikh state and the claims for autonomy rest on Sikh preponderance in the Punjab. Thus the erosion of their ranks by Christian conversion could be intimidating to the Sikh leadership. True conversion by Christians is not going to dent the Sikh population significantly. Nevertheless, in such issues the thinking is more emotional than rational, and much tension could be generated, however insubstantial the reasons might be.

Sadhu Sundar Singh

A significant example of conversion from Sikhism to Christianity is that of Sadhu Sundar Singh, whose conversion was not due to Christian evangelism, but rather to a vision of Christ. Sundar Singh, from a prominent family of Rampur, was deeply religious and on a quest to know God and religious truth. He must have been to some extent frustrated by the faith of his forefathers, since he decided to commit suicide if God did not make the truth known to him. It is said that while he was about to commit suicide by throwing himself before a train, a vision of Christ appeared to him and saved him from disaster. Sundar Singh's conversion has some parallels with that of Paul, since he had at times been antagonistic to Christians, no doubt prompted by the exhortations of his family, and he had publicly burned the Bible.

Sundar Singh declined to follow the traditional model of a Christian missionary, though he indeed became a very effective evangelist of the Christian faith and even died in the course of a missionary journey to the forbidden and remote nation of Tibet. Nor did he espouse the Brahminical or Sanskritized interpretation of Christianity in vogue then among many converts to Christianity from Hinduism. However, he was fully committed to indigenis-ation of the Christian faith and is said to have stated, 'The water of life should be served in an Indian cup.' He chose the model of a *sannyasin*, an ascetic or renouncer. As Powell states, 'for the rest of his short life he remained a "Christian Sadhu", adopting an ecstatic form of preaching to present Christianity to remote hill peoples, in a devotional idiom more akin to some indigenous expressions of religious fervour than to the sermons being preached in the missionary churches of the Punjab.'[31] He aban-doned all material possessions and lived a mendicant's life throughout his post-conversion span of life.

Conclusion

The problems arising from conversion of Hindus and Sikhs cannot be dismissed (as some Christians tend to do) as a political tactic by the Sangh Parivar and other protagonists of the Hindutva doc-trine. It goes much deeper than that. Moderate Hindus and Sikhs also have voiced their opposition to Christian evangelisation. Christians have to abjure aggressive tactics on conversion and especially casting aspersions on Sikhism and Hinduism. Such tactics only play into the hands of extremists. Hinduism is per-ceived as a tolerant religion, but of late many of the Hindutvavadins have cast similar aspersions on Christianity. This mutual recrimination does not benefit anyone. If Christians seem to have an obsession with proselytisation, the Sangh Parivar has a similar obsession with the saffronization (or Hinduization) of India. India is religiously pluralistic and the makers of the Indian Constitution rightly decided that the state should be secular in the

[31] A.A. Powell, 'Pillar of a New Faith', in R.E. Frykenberg (ed.), *Christians and Missionaries in India: Cross-Cultural Communication Since 1500* (Grand Rapids, MI: Eerdmans, 2003), p. 227.

sense of being religiously neutral and even-handed. That there are now attempts to undermine this decision could lead to widespread religious tensions in the subcontinent. If Hindu domination replaces Western domination in India it could lead to the fragmentation of India. Already there have been such demands, which are partly religious and partly ethnic in origin. Kashmir, the Punjab and Nagaland have all witnessed such secessionist tendencies. It is up to the rulers of India to avoid such developments. The focus has necessarily to be on human rights, freedom of speech and other rights enshrined in the constitution of India. However, proclamation of faith and propagation of religion has to be done with sensitivity and discretion.

In India, religions have coexisted for centuries. There have been many periods in Indian history when such coexistence has been marked by a harmonious symbiosis. The Indian spirit has largely been to accommodate dissent, differences of opinion and diversity, be they ethnic, linguistic, or religious. This diversity enriches India. The democratic principle is a great opportunity for Indians to make their nation into a great exemplar of pluralism and peaceful coexistence of religions, for instance. Under the British and the Mughals, Hinduism, Sikhism and Christianity have demonstrated that they could coexist harmoniously and present a concerted front against exploitation and colonial oppression. The success of Gandhi and the Independence movement rested largely on such cooperation. There is no reason why, in modern democratic India where there is such a vast body of enlightened individuals, this cannot continue to the glory and prosperity of India.